THE AU

Aubrey de Selincourt, a distinguished classicist, had a life-long interest in the sea and brought a special awareness to his role as editor of this volume. He was himself the author of three books on sailing and the sea, most notably *A Capful of Wind* and *Family Afloat*.

THE BOOK OF THE SEA

EDITED BY

Aubrey de Selincourt

CHATHAM PUBLISHING

LONDON

NOTE: All passages from foreign literature in this book,
except where the translator is mentioned,
have been translated by the editor.
The Roman numerals in the text refer to the
Notes at the end of the volume.

Copyright © Aubrey de Selincourt 1961

This edition published in Great Britain in 2002 by
Chatham Publishing,
99 High Street, Rochester,
Kent ME1 1LX

Distributed by
Gerald Duckworth & Co Ltd,
61 Frith Street,
London W1D 3JL

First published 1961 by Eyre & Spottiswoode

British Library Cataloguing in Publication Data
A catalogue record for this book is available
from the British Library

ISBN 1 86176 208 9

All rights reserved. No part of this publication may
be reproduced or transmitted in any form or by any
means, electronic or mechanical, including photocopying,
recording, or any information storage and retrieval system,
without either prior permission in writing from the
publisher or a licence permitting restricted copying.

Printed and bound in Great Britain by
Bookcraft (Bath) Ltd, Midsomer Norton, Avon

H.G.D.

PVERO MECVM AMICITIA IVNCTO

NEQVE IMMEMORI SENIS

HVNC LIBELLVM

GRATO ANIMO

DONAVI

Contents

Introduction

Introduction

To make some sort of anthology about ships and the sea is an easy task, almost as easy as to make some sort of an anthology about love, both subjects being answerable for the use or waste of many thousands of gallons of ink in all the literatures known to men. It is less easy, however, to make an anthology about the sea which shall be an honest one, 'speaking', to borrow an old poet's words, 'to those who know.'

I myself stand only on the outermost fringes of knowledge, having been a mere summer sailor, pottering about in one yacht or another along the Channel coast, and having only once in fifty years encountered, for my sins, that beautiful but treacherous sea in a really savage mood, when I was too much awed by the sheer magnificence of the spectacle to be much frightened and too deeply fascinated by the gallantry of my friend's little yacht not to believe that she would come through it in safety, as indeed she did.

My knowledge, in short, is just sufficient to give me a proper respect for the men who really did, and do, their business in great waters: for the old explorers, for the modern trawlermen, for the navies of the world, for the lifeboatmen, the coasters, the pilots and the tramps – yes, and for those inspired lunatics the present-day yachtsmen, who in their hundreds year after year, following the lead of such men as Voss, Slocum and McMullen, take their ten-tonners across the oceans or around the globe, and are seldom drowned.

Our attitude towards the sea has greatly changed in the past hundred, or hundred and fifty, years. We have become romantic about it, as about other great elemental forces in nature and in ourselves. We even pretend, some of us, that we love it, though no true seaman would ever admit such an absurdity. The ancient attitude to the sea was eminently practical. There the thing was, a familiar presence; it had to be crossed, sometimes, for one reason or another – worse luck; and though the end of the trip might bring pleasure or profit, the trip itself was disagreeable and dangerous, a necessary nuisance.

For us, I need hardly say, the literature of the sea like so many other sorts of literature, begins with Greece. The Greeks wrote constantly of the sea: indeed, they could hardly help it, living as they did in such intimate and unavoidable contact with it. On the Greek mainland with its deeply indented coastline one cannot get as far from the sea even as one can in England, while the rest of Greece, even more Greek in some respects than the mainland, is islands. The Greeks lived with the sea, and the brief temporal glory of Athens was founded upon her use of it. No wonder Greek literature has a flavour of salt. Sea-metaphors are as common in Greek poetry as they are in Shakespeare. The Greeks were good seamen, one imagines, within their restricted range – coastal navigation, mostly, and island-hopping; and they were certainly good shipwrights, if we can take vase-pictures as accurate representations of the kind of hull they used to design. Commenting on one of them Keble Chatterton wrote that it had so many good points that 'we wonder, not unnaturally, if we have advanced so much after all during the twenty-four hundred years since she was designed, for such a bow and such a stern would win applause in any port.' Much of their shipbuilding lore the Greeks learned from Egypt, and from the Phoenicians who were better deep-sea sailors than themselves, though unfortunately they have left no written records. We should be grateful indeed for the log of some old Phoenician captain, describing, perhaps, a landfall on the Cornish coast, or, better still, some account of the remarkable voyage made by Phoenician sailors in the seventh century before Christ around the African continent, when, sailing westward, they had, as Herodotus tells us, 'the midday sun on their right hand' – a detail which proves, for us, that they were in the southern hemisphere, though Herodotus himself, not knowing the geographical fact, took it merely as a tall story.

As is to be expected, then, with so amphibious a people, the Greeks wrote of the sea with a beautiful precision. They described what they saw, and what they knew. Had you, with your modern romantic notions, asked one of them if he loved the sea, he would have stared, or laughed; to be sure, they could *look* at the sea, on occasion, with pleasure, as Homer must have done to enable him to find certain memorable phrases – describing, for instance, the long waves rolling towards the beach, or the shudder on the water when it is darkened by a puff of wind, or the island of Scheria which 'lay like a shield on the misty deep'; or Aeschylus when he wrote of the 'laughter of sunlit water'; or Alcman's 'blossom' on lightly breaking waves: not to mention the splendid conventional adjectives which crop up continually in the *Odyssey* and the *Iliad* – the 'unharvested sea', the 'sea with many voices', the 'wine-dark sea', all of them epithets which slipped out, so to speak, without thought once they had been invented. One might add to the list the adjective *haliporphyros* which we translate, I suppose, as *sea-purple*, though that word conveys little. Only twice in my life have I seen the sea as I believe the Greek word describes it: once close in-shore off the island of Gozo, and again off the Cornish coast near Fowey. A blue sea and a green sea are both of them beautiful, and common; on the occasions of which I speak it was neither blue nor green; it had a dark brightness beyond either: it was almost violet.

But all this indicates in the Greeks an aesthetic pleasure only, and the writer's natural urge to find an image for what he sees. In the Greeks' relationship with the sea, as a presence and a power, there was, on the contrary, no pleasure at all. To use it was one of the conditions, and a hard one, of living; empire, commerce and daily rations (the Greeks ate an inordinate quantity of salt fish) depended upon it; but they had no illusions about its inimical character and the general unpleasantness, in addition to the constant danger, of seafaring. The resigned and sorrowful realism of the many epitaphs for drowned sailors, which occur in the Greek Anthology, would be sufficient evidence for this. But what the Greeks wrote of the sea was true: it is that quality of truth which gives their writing, as it gives to all writing, its value.

The Romans were never familiar with the sea as the Greeks were. Their destiny drove them to use it, but there was never a trace of salt in the Roman blood. When they wrote of nautical matters, they tended to be either over-brief and severely factual, like Caesar who devoted but half a page to the disconcerting effect of a spring tide accompanied by a south-westerly gale on the Kentish coast, and did not mention at all, so far as I remember, the numerous and great navigational hazards on the north and north-west coasts of France, though either he or his officers must have had repeated experience of them; or else they are silly, like Tacitus, who gravely recorded that some vessels sent north to explore the Scottish coast were forced to turn back because the water became too heavy and sticky to row in. Had some literary lady asked Tacitus why he said the water was sticky, he would not, one fears, have had the grace to reply, 'Ignorance, Madam, pure ignorance,' as Dr Johnson did when asked his reason for describing *pastern*, in his Dictionary, as the knee of a horse.

The Latin poets, in the main, were imitative and over-literary when they wrote of the sea; even Virgil makes an only moderately good job of the Trojan fleet's tempestuous approach to the north-African coast: his storm is a picture-storm, the details remembered, and not improved in the remembering, from Homer, rather than the real thing, not unlike the picture-scenes of the countryside in our own 18th-century poetry, before Coleridge and Wordsworth had taught the poets to use their own eyes. Now and again one chances upon a revelatory phrase, a direct and personal seeing, like Virgil's *tremulo lumine* of the movement of moonlight on water, or his description (included in this book) of the ships' keels cutting the reflections of the trees in the placid Tiber. But such things are rare. The beautiful poem of Catullus, of which I have printed a

xvi

version, is altogether exceptional in Latin literature – but then Catullus was exceptional in many ways. I am not aware of any other example in ancient literature, either Latin or Greek, of the very modern sentiment of personal affection for a boat. In general neither the Greeks nor the Romans, I fancy, ever used or owned a vessel of any kind for pleasure. Assuredly not for what you or I – grave citizens – would call pleasure, for certain Roman Emperors did, one reads, build absurd barges (like the one designed with a collapsible cabin-roof by the ingenious Nero, an account of which will be found on a later page of this book), and in these barges they would float, on stately occasions, across the Bay of Naples when the weather smiled; and Cicero, defending poor Caelius, sadly admits the charges of his enemies that the foolish young man was wont to debauch himself with visits to Baiae, loungings on the beach, beanfeasts, songs, symphonies – and *boats*. But such aquatic sportings, whether of a Nero or of a Caelius, hardly ring true to a modern ear.

When I speak of our changed modern attitude to the sea, of the romanticism and sentiment with which we have come to regard it, I would make it quite clear that I have not professional seamen in mind. I am thinking only of *us*, the outsiders, the watchers and dreamers, the men and women who have ringside seats for the show. Sailors have not changed; they are practical men, as they always were, and as they must be, if their hard and dangerous work is to be done. Sailors have much superstition, but little sentiment; for the sea they have no sentiment at all, what they have being reserved for the ships they sail in. These – the old bitches and bastards which make their life a misery and seem so often to do their best to drown them – they grumblingly and resentfully love. It is an odd but touching trait in human nature. Perhaps I should say 'was', not 'is', for maybe my own sentiment is leading me back into an era which is gone for ever. I could believe that some dirty British coaster might inspire affection of a sort in the men who handled her and her cargo of cheap tin trays; but it is hard to imagine a man (one of something like a thousand) *loving*, say, the *Queen Elizabeth* or the *United States*. Admiration, even touched with awe, of so superb a machine is natural and inevitable; but not love. Except, perhaps, from her Master. Love needs life to inspire it, and a sailing vessel is alive in a way that no ship with mechanical power can ever be.

But we outsiders, spectators of the great and continuing drama of man's commerce with the sea, look upon it very differently from our ancestors. We have come to read significances into it, which would have puzzled them. We see in it types and symbols of our own inner lives, of their frustrations and desires. The change began, I suppose, as a part of the whole intellectual and spiritual movement which, round about the beginning of last century, turned away from the old acceptances, to explore, under the impulse of a newly-discovered Mystery, certain dark areas of the mind and heart: to penetrate, as far as might be, what Keats called the dark passages leading out in every direction from the Chamber of Maiden Thought. The most notable mark of that age was the expression in its literature of a new relationship between man and nature: not that such a relationship can ever, in fact, *be* new; but it can be looked at in different lights, and spoken of with differing emphasis. The ancients peopled the natural world with Powers of all sorts, gods, demons or spirits, benevolent or hostile – usually hostile, until one got on the right side of them. Nature for them was an alien Life which had to be propitiated. Christianity chased the pagan spirits from mountain and sea, moor and stream; and when, with Chaucer, modern literature began – for I speak of literature, not of popular belief, which is a different matter – Nature, though still hostile to man was no longer haunted. It was a part of God's creation and not the chief part: at the worst it was a harsh challenge to men's courage and industry, at the best a sort of drop-scene, pleasant or unpleasant, to set off their multifarious activities. Chaucer, in his description of the Shipman, is interested only in that old scoundrel's acquired skills and highly questionable conduct; in his ship (apart from her name) and her sea-faring, and in the sea itself, he is interested not at all.

xviii

When the Roman poet Juvenal said that the subject of his poems was *whatever men do*, he described, not inadequately, the tendency of all European literature from its earliest beginnings up to that odd shift of emphasis which we call the Romantic Movement. For the Romantics were not content to describe what men do, simply as men: they wanted also to describe what they, as individuals, obscurely felt and dimly imagined. Unlike their immediate predecessors, who were mainly urban intellectuals, the writers of the early nineteenth century were often social misfits and rebels, solitary dreamers, country-dwellers; and they came to look on Nature not as alien and haunted, as the ancients did, not as a more or less separate, and secondary, part of creation, as their immediate predecessors did, but almost as an extension of themselves. Not only in Wordsworth, but in nearly all the chief writers of the period, the boundary between Nature and Man is felt to be fluid and uncertain. One life interpenetrates both. When Keats wrote an ode to autumn or the nightingale, he was writing of the movements of his own heart, to which he found counterparts in the season and in the bird.

Now it is precisely this shift of emphasis, most clearly seen at the start of the Romantic Movement, but in many ways still with us, which accounts for the wide difference between the old literature of the sea, and the new – that, namely, of the past hundred years or so. Take, for instance, the magnificent collection of *Voyages* compiled by Hakluyt. The ten volumes stand on my shelf, and I constantly browse in them; yet I can think of few passages in all those many pages suitable for inclusion in an anthology such as this. Why is this so? Because the accounts are dull? Far from it; they are of fascinating interest, but – and this is my point – there is little about either ships or the sea in them. They are accounts, in fact, not of voyages, but of the objects and results of voyages. The practical interest is everywhere paramount. Those workman-like and admirable stories, written for the most part by non-literary men, have, like Juvenal's verses, human endeavour, human hopes and disappointments, as their centre: never the sea. The detestable sea must indeed be crossed, but the less said about the crossing, the better. And as for the ships, we are told their names and tonnage, but of all that we, nowadays, would really care to know of them – their behaviour, their appearance (I don't mean their rig merely, or their build, which we know pretty well, but their individual beauties or defects) their *personalities* in short – there is never a word.

Those splendid seamen, our ancestors, do not seem, from the writings they have left us, to have been aware of their ships at all. They were mere means to ends; they were treated, though before the days of machinery, as cavalierly as one would treat a machine. This is contrary to modern sentiment.

Which was the first truly modern book about the sea I do not pretend to know. Perhaps it was *Moby Dick* – written just over a hundred years ago. That book was a portent, and had as much influence on all subsequent sea-literature as the *Lyrical Ballads*, fifty years earlier, had had upon poetry. There are good judges who do not care for *Moby Dick*, who are irked by a certain cloudy mysticism which hangs over it; they find it pretentious; if, they say, a man wants to write of whaling, it is better to do it like Frank Bullen, directly, without nonsense, than to clutter up the story with gropings after the Ineffable. Well – perhaps; but the point I wish to make is that those gropings, that cloudy mysticism, whether one approves or deprecates them, are of the essence of our modern, romantic attitude to the sea. Once men had been made aware of the light that never was on sea or land, of the

Something far more deeply interfused,
Whose dwelling is the light of setting suns
And the round ocean and the living air,

their relationship with all the elemental forces of nature – and of those forces the sea is the mightiest – was changed. They could never again see them with the same eyes.

And so, for Melville, the sea has become a Power: it is not dead matter but a living force, almost conscious. It is the hero of his book every bit as much as the White Whale is, or

Captain Ahab. The whale himself is an aspect of this elemental power, no less mysterious, no less destructive; both of them equally are the objects of Ahab's hate, both of them are projections – gigantic symbols, rather – of Ahab's obsessed imagination. When, therefore, Melville in *Moby Dick* described the sea, he was looking inward as well as outward; he knew the sea as well as any man has known it, and his descriptions are true – but they are not factual descriptions; they are evocations. He did for our understanding of the sea what Wordsworth,

'nurtured alike by beauty and by fear,'

did for landscape; he not only brought it alive with its own blind, enormous life, but linked it by subtle threads to movements obscure but powerful, in the human mind. And he did it with authority, because his book, like all genuine works of imagination, is securely founded upon fact.

Moby Dick, then, marks, I think, the beginning of modern sea-literature. It is the first major work about the sea itself – as distinct from works about adventures *on* the sea which is a quite different thing. Since it was written, sea-literature has pullulated, and most of it, in various ways, has followed the lines marked out by Melville. It is descriptive and interpretative; it dwells upon the varying aspects of the sea's face as lingeringly as upon the expressions in the eyes of a friend, or enemy; and when the theme is a voyage, the object of the voyage is of little importance beside the voyage itself and the unremitting struggle it involves between a man and the elements. How unintelligible to Shakespeare or to Chaucer, not to mention the Ancients, would be, for instance, Mr Masefield's poem *Dauber*, in which the ship's cargo, so far as I remember, is not even mentioned, and the object of young Dauber in going to sea was not the natural one of earning a living but an irresistible desire to know what the sea looked like, and to communicate his knowledge in paint – to know the sea, and the men who fought it, and the way of a ship upon it, things which landsmen are ignorant of and would be the better for understanding. The better? The ancients would have said the worse, and no doubt they had reason on their side. But in these matters we are not concerned with reason nowadays; there is something, it seems, in the modern consciousness which seeks its satisfaction in all solitary places – in deserts and jungles, amongst polar ice, on mountains and on the sea. These things are at the same time a challenge and a fulfilment.

There is nothing surprising about this. Human nature changes very little, and very slowly; what may seem a change is often only a necessary reaction to changed conditions. It is as natural for people in one age to try to escape from nature as it is, in another, to try to escape into it: it is all a question of redressing the balance. Older generations were close enough to the elements – indeed, too close for comfort – in the course of their ordinary lives, and so felt no need to deepen the acquaintance; it is only when, in different social and economic conditions, people begin, however unconsciously, to feel that their lives are cut off from their natural roots, that they become uneasy, and look about in strange places for a new source of refreshment and strength. One of those strange places has been the sea. 'The world is too much with us,' and one way of escaping from it, a way taken by, it seems, a growing number of men and women every year, is by going to sea: not, to be sure, as professional seamen, but as playboys – or yachtsmen. Nothing else can explain the astonishing fact that every year nowadays from every country with a strip of seaboard in both hemispheres men, and women too, set out in little sailing craft for ocean voyages under no external compulsion whatever, but simply for – of all things – *pleasure*. What a word to describe the physical miseries and mental harassments, the discomfort and exhaustion, the ever-present anxieties and fears, of such voyages! I talked once with one well-known voyager soon after his arrival in this country from crossing the Atlantic in a boat of almost indecent smallness, and he told me how, when he lay in bed and listened to the wind, he still, in his safe warm house, stiffened with fear and felt a touch of ice at the base of his spine; yet nothing would surprise me less than to learn that he was off again on another venture. There are many

xxii

odd things in the world, but none, as the Greek poet said, so odd as man. Let us be thankful that it is so.

These amateur voyages have produced a flood of literature, some of it good, much of it indifferent. Personally I can read it all with pleasure, making allowances for strong hands which are happier to handle a rope than a pen. A little of it I have included in this volume, but not much; mostly I have confined myself to the masters, though some of the passages I have put in will not, I hope, be too familiar to my readers. Above all, I have excluded everything which has not the ring of authenticity – and is not an honest recording of something done or seen. We Englishmen are supposed to know ships and the sea; but how few of us in fact do! Nothing comes more readily to an English pen than claptrap about nautical matters and a sad misuse of nautical terms and metaphors. Do we not remember the splendour of the appointments in Sir Brian Newcome's dining-room, where the table-cloth was 'broad as the main sheet of an ammiral'? or the statement of a learned Shakespearian critic that he and a fellow-worker were, in the elucidation of some problem, 'somewhat on the same tack'? or poor Allan Cunningham who, with his merry lads, setting sail with a following wind, left old England on the lee? or the remarkable passage in *The Mill on the Floss*, where Maggie rows with one oar only in the rushing stream, and takes to both again when she is in calmer water? There is no end to such things, even in good English literature; indeed I have often thought that the only non-specialist English writers who have taken the trouble never to make gaffs of this kind were Shakespeare and Dickens. Those two can always be trusted to talk sense on nautical matters. They share that distinction with the Greeks.

But this is not an anthology of nautical nonsense, however amusing it might be to make one. It is a collection only of the best I know. And that best is, fortunately, scattered about in great profusion. I say fortunately, for it is a fact that the best writing about ships and the sea has always been of a high literary quality. Of Melville I have already said something, and another example, of a very different kind, was his fellow-countryman Joshua Slocum, that wonderful little man (thin as a reef-point) who built *Spray* and in her circumnavigated the globe. Slocum was a professional seaman; he was not what is called a cultivated man, yet he wrote prose as nervous, as clear and as beautiful as any I know. He had style, and he proved once more that the secret of style is, first, to be master of one's subject, and then to know exactly what one wants to say about it, and to say it without fuss. That a man's reach should exceed his grasp may work well enough as a maxim in morality; but it won't do for literature. Least of all will it do for sea-literature, which more than any other sort is rendered nugatory by half-knowledge. 'Everywhere,' wrote Hilaire Belloc, 'the sea is a teacher of truth. I am not sure that the best thing I find in sailing is not this salt of reality.' The same salt must be in the books – stories, poems, workaday accounts, logs, whatever they may be – which deal with it.

The Face of the Sea

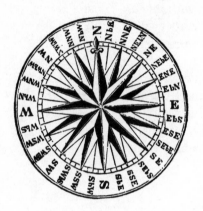

Beginning

. . . when the moon was born, there was no ocean. The gradually cooling earth was enveloped in heavy layers of cloud, which contained much of the water of the new planet. For a long time its surface was so hot that no moisture could fall without immediately being reconverted to steam. This dense, perpetually renewed cloud-covering must have been thick enough that no rays of sunlight could penetrate it. And so the rough outlines of the continents and the empty ocean basins were sculptured out of the surface of the earth in darkness, in a Stygian world of heated rock and swirling clouds and gloom.

As soon as the earth's crust cooled enough, the rains began to fall. Never have there been such rains since that time. They fell continuously, day and night, days passing into months, into years, into centuries. They poured into the waiting ocean basins, or, falling upon the continental masses, drained away to become sea.

That primeval ocean, growing in bulk as the rains slowly filled its basins, must have been only faintly salt. But the falling rains were the symbol of the dissolution of the continents. From the moment the rains began to fall, the lands began to be worn away and carried to the sea. It is an endless, inexorable process that has never stopped – the dissolving of the rocks, the leaching out of their contained minerals, the carrying of the rock fragments and dissolved minerals to the ocean. And over the aeons of time, the sea has grown ever more bitter with the salt of the continents.

RACHEL L. CARSON: *The Sea Around Us*

The Great Sea

The sea is the source of the waters, and the source of the winds. Without the great sea, not from the clouds could come the flowing rivers or the heaven's rain; but the great sea is the father of clouds, of rivers and of winds.

XENOPHANES

Spice Islands

We did not anchor at Penang until the fiftieth day out from the Cape. For six weeks we had been out of sight of land.

I shall never forget the charm of first scenting the spice islands and the tropical vegetation, long before land was in sight. These delicious flavours came off many miles to sea, and the scented airs were very pleasant after so long a voyage. I was up aloft, as usual, one morning at six o'clock. There was no land in sight, though I could smell it distinctly; and we must have been from 60 to 80 miles from the nearest coast of Acheen Head.

REAR ADML. V. A. MONTAGUE: *A Middy's Recollections*

The Milky Way

I was exultant over the prospect of once more entering the Strait of Magellan and beating through again into the Pacific, for it was more than rough on the outside coast of Tierra del Fuego. It was indeed a mountainous sea. When the sloop was in the fiercest squalls, with only the reefed fore-staysail set, even that small sail shook her from keelson to truck when it shivered by the leech. Had I harboured the shadow of a doubt for her safety, it would have been that she might spring a leak in the garboard at the heel of the mast; but she never called me once to the pump. Under pressure of the smallest sail I could set she made for the land like a race-horse, and steering her over the crests of the waves so that she might not trip was nice work. I stood at the helm now and made the most of it.

Night closed in before the sloop reached the land, leaving her feeling the way in pitchy darkness. I saw breakers ahead before long. At this I wore ship and stood offshore, but was immediately startled by the tremendous roaring of breakers again ahead and on the lee bow. This puzzled me, for there should have been no broken water where I supposed myself to be. I kept off a good bit, then wore round, but finding broken water also there, threw her head again offshore. In this way, among dangers, I spent the rest of the night. Hail and sleet in the fierce squalls cut my flesh till the blood trickled over my face; but what of that? It was daylight, and the sloop was in the midst of the Milky Way of the sea, which is north-west of Cape Horn, and it was the white breakers of a huge sea over sunken rocks which had threatened to engulf her through the night. It was Fury Island I had sighted and steered for, and what a panorama was before me now and all around! It was not the time to complain of a broken skin. What could I do but fill away among the breakers and find a channel between them, now that it was day? Since she had escaped the rocks through the night, surely she would find her way by daylight. This was the greatest sea adventure of my life. God knows how my vessel escaped.

The sloop at last reached inside of small islands that sheltered her in smooth water. Then I climbed the mast to survey the wild scene astern. The great naturalist Darwin looked over this seascape from the deck of the *Beagle*, and wrote in his journal, 'Any landsman seeing the Milky Way would have nightmare for a week.' He might have added 'or seaman' as well.

JOSHUA SLOCUM: *Sailing Alone Around the World*

The Deeps

But though, to landsmen in general, the native inhabitants of the seas have ever been regarded with emotions unspeakably unsocial and repelling; though we know the sea to be an everlasting terra incognita, so that Columbus sailed over numberless unknown worlds to discover his one superficial western one; though, by vast odds, the most terrific of all mortal disasters have immemorially and indiscriminately befallen tens and hundreds of thousands of those who have gone upon the waters; though but a moment's consideration will teach, that however baby man may brag of his science and skill, and however much, in a flattering future, that science and skill may augment; yet for ever and for ever, to the crack of doom, the sea will insult and murder him, and pulverize the stateliest, stiffest frigate he can make; nevertheless, by the continual repetition of these very impressions, man has lost that sense of the full awfulness of the sea which aboriginally belongs to it.

Consider the subtleness of the sea; how its most dreaded creatures glide under water, unapparent for the most part, and treacherously hidden beneath the loveliest tints of azure. Consider also the devilish brilliance and beauty of many of its most remorseless tribes, as the dainty embellished shape of many species of sharks. Consider, once more, the universal cannibalism of the sea, all whose creatures prey upon each other, carrying on eternal war since the world began.

Consider all this, and then turn to this green, gentle and most docile earth; consider them both, the sea and the land; and do you not find a strange analogy to something in yourself? For as this appalling ocean surrounds the verdant land, so in the soul of man there lies one insular Tahiti, full of peace and joy, but encompassed by all the horrors of the half-known life. God keep thee! Push not off from that isle; thou canst never return.

HERMAN MELVILLE: *Moby Dick*

First Sight of the Sea

Will it be thought a digression (it may spare some unwelcome comparisons) if I endeavour to account for the *dissatisfaction* which I have heard so many persons confess to have felt (as I did myself feel in part on this occasion) *at the sight of the sea for the first time*? I think the reason usually given (referring to the incapacity of actual objects for satisfying our preconceptions of them) scarcely goes deep enough into the question. Let the same person see a lion, an elephant, a mountain for the first time in his life, and he shall perhaps feel himself a little mortified. The things do not fill up that space which the idea of them seemed to take up in his mind. But they have still a correspondency to his first notion, and in time grow up to it, so as to produce a very similar impression: enlarging themselves (if I may say so) upon familiarity. But the sea remains a disappointment. Is it not, that in the *latter* we had expected to behold (absurdly, I grant, but, I am afraid, by the law of imagination unavoidably) not a definite object, as those wild beasts, or that mountain compassable by the eye, but *all the sea at once*, THE COMMENSURATE ANTAGONIST OF THE EARTH? I do not say we tell ourselves so much, but the craving of the mind is to be satisfied with nothing less.

I will suppose the case of a young person of fifteen (as I then was) knowing nothing of the sea but from description. He comes to it for the first time – all that he has been reading of it all his life, and *that* the most enthusiastic part of life, all that he has gathered from narratives of wandering seamen, what he has gained from true voyages and what he cherishes as credulously from romance and poetry, crowding their images and exacting strange tributes from expectation. He thinks of the great deep, and of those who go down unto it; of its receiving the mighty Plate, or the Orellana, into its bosom, without disturbance or sense of augmentation; of Biscay swells, and the mariner

> For many a day, and many a dreadful night,
> Incessant labouring round the stormy Cape;

7

of fatal rocks, and the 'still-vex'd Bermoothes'; of great whirlpools, and the water-spout; of sunken ships, and sumless treasures swallowed up in the unrestoring depths; of fishes and quaint monsters, to which all that is terrible on earth

> *Be but as buggs to frighten babes withal,*
> *Compared with the creatures in the sea's entrail;*

of naked savages, and Juan Fernandez; of pearls and shells; of coral beds, and of enchanted isles; of mermaids' grots.

I do not assert that in sober earnest he expects to be shown all these wonders at once, but he is under the tyranny of a mighty faculty, which haunts him with confused hints and shadows of all these; and when the actual object opens first upon him, seen (in tame weather too, most likely) from our unromantic coasts – a speck, a slip of sea-water, as it shows to him – what can it prove but a very unsatisfying and even diminutive entertainment? or if he has come to it from the mouth of a river, was it much more than the river widening? And even out of sight of land, what had he but a flat watery horizon about him, nothing comparable to the vast, o'er-curtaining sky, his familiar object, seen daily without dread or amazement? Who, in similar circumstances, has not been tempted to exclaim with Charoba, in the poem of Gebir,

> *Is this the mighty ocean? Is this* all?

CHARLES LAMB: *Last Essays of Elia*

The Pacific

When gliding by the Bashee isles we emerged at last upon the great South Sea; were it not for other things, I could have greeted my dear Pacific with uncounted thanks, for now the long supplication of my youth was answered; that serene ocean rolled eastwards from me a thousand leagues of blue.

8

There is one knows not what sweet mystery about this sea, whose gently awful stirrings seem to speak of some hidden soul beneath; like those fabled undulations of the Ephesian god over the buried Evangelist St John. And meet it is, that over these sea-pastures, wide-rolling watery prairies and Potters' Fields of all four continents, the waves should rise and fall, and ebb and flow unceasingly; for here millions of mixed shades and shadows, drowned dreams, somnambulisms, reveries; all that we call lives and souls, lie dreaming, dreaming still; tossing like slumberers in their beds; the ever-rolling waves but made so by their restlessness.

To any meditative Magian rover, this serene Pacific, once beheld, must ever after be the sea of his adoption. It rolls the midmost waters of the world, the Indian ocean and Atlantic being but its arms. The same waves wash the moles of the new-built Californian towns, but yesterday planted by the recentest race of men, and lave the faded but still gorgeous skirts of Asiatic lands, older than Abraham; while all between float milky-ways of coral isles, and low-lying, endless, unknown Archipelagoes, and impenetrable Japans.

HERMAN MELVILLE: *Moby Dick*

Two Voices

(i)   . . . the island valley of Avilion,
Where falls not hail, or rain, or any snow,
Nor ever wind blows loudly; but it lies
Deep-meadow'd, happy, fair with orchard lawns
And bowery hollows crown'd with summer sea.

ALFRED LORD TENNYSON: *The Passing of Arthur*

(ii)   On the beach of a northern sea
Which tempests shake eternally—

As once the wretch there laid to sleep—
Lies a solitary heap,
One white skull and seven dry bones
On the margin of the stones,
Where a few grey rushes stand,
Boundaries of the sea and land:
Nor is heard one voice of wail
But the sea-mews', as they sail
O'er the billows of the gale. . . .

P. B. SHELLEY: Lines Written Among the Euganean Hills

Farewell

As the *Leopoldine* drew away, Margaret, as if drawn by a magnet, followed her along the cliffs.

Soon the land came to an end, and the girl had to stop. She sat down at the foot of a great stone cross, which stood there, at the cliff's edge, amongst reeds and stones. The cliff was high, and the sea spread out before her seemed to slope upward toward the far horizon, so that the vessel, as she drew off-shore, appeared as she diminished to be ascending the inclined plane of the vast semicircle of sea. A slow, heavy swell was running, the effect, may be, of a formidable blow elsewhere, beyond the horizon, though within the visible field of vision all was still quiet.

Margaret continued to gaze, determined to imprint upon her memory every detail of the vessel, the precise outline of its sails and hull, to be able to know it again, even in the distance, when, one day, she should come back to this same spot in expectation of its return.

Ceaselessly, regularly, the great marching swells rolled in from the west, breaking one after another in ineffective strength on the same rocks, tumbling with unvarying monotony to run flooding up the same stretches of beach, until, in some odd way, their muted but restless movement in the serene air under the tranquil sky, seemed to suggest that the ocean-bed had been filled too full and needed to pour its surplus water on to the land.

Meanwhile the vessel was growing smaller with distance, and harder and harder to distinguish. Doubtless she had the tide fair, for there was little wind that evening, yet she was drawing swiftly away from the land. Already she was no more than a grey smudge – a speck, almost – and soon she would reach the far edge of the circle of vision, and enter the immeasurable beyond where darkness was even now beginning to fall.

PIERRE LOTI: *Pêcheur d'Islande*

The Spirit of Man

An abyss as bitter as the sea.

CHARLES BAUDELAIRE

Solitudes

(i)

. . . one serene and moonlight night, when all the waves rolled by like scrolls of silver, and, by their soft, suffusing seethings, made what seemed a silvery silence, not a solitude.

HERMAN MELVILLE: *Moby Dick*

(ii)

In the serene weather of the tropics it is exceedingly pleasant at the masthead; nay, to a dreamy and meditative man, it is delightful. There you stand, a hundred feet above the silent decks, striding along the deep, as if the masts were gigantic stilts, while beneath you and between your legs, as it were, swim the hugest monsters of the sea, even as ships once sailed between the boots of the famous Colossus at old Rhodes. There you stand, lost in the infinite series of the sea, with nothing ruffled but the waves. The tranced ship indolently rolls; the drowsy trade-winds blow; everything resolves you into languor. For the most part, in this tropic whaling life, a sublime uneventfulness invests you; you hear no news, read no gazettes; extras with startling accounts of commonplaces never delude you into unnecessary excitements; you hear of no domestic afflictions, bankrupt securities, fall of stocks; are never troubled with the thought of what you shall have for dinner – for all your meals for three years and more are snugly stowed in casks, and your bill of fare is immutable.

HERMAN MELVILLE: *Ibid.*

Port After Stormy Seas

The worn-out Trojans, seeking land where'er
The nearest coast invites, for Libya steer.
There is a Bay whose deep retirement hides
The place where Nature's self a Port provides,
Framed by a friendly island's jutting sides,
Bulwark from which the billows of the Main
Recoil upon themselves, spending their force in vain.
Vast rocks are here; and, safe beneath the brows
Of two heaven-threatening cliffs, the Floods repose.
Glancing aloft in bright theatric show
Woods wave, and gloomily impend below;
Right opposite this pomp of sylvan shade
Wild crags and lowering rocks a cave have made;
Within, sweet waters gush; and all bestrown
Is the cool floor with seats of living stone;

12

Cell of the Nymphs, no chains, no anchors here
Bind the tired vessels, floating without fear;
Led by Aeneas, in this shelter meet
Seven ships, the scanty relics of his Fleet;
The Crews, athirst with longings for the land,
Here disembark, and range the wish'd-for strand.

VERGIL: *Aeneid*, tr. by William Wordsworth. (i)

The Lost Mate

Yes, when the stars glistened
All night long, on the prong of a moss-scalloped stake,
Down, almost amid the slapping waves,
Sat the lone singer, wonderful, causing tears.

He called on his mate;
He poured forth the meanings which I, of all men, know.
Yes, my brother, I know;
The rest might not – but I have treasured every note;
For once, and more than once, dimly, down to the beach
        gliding,
Silent, avoiding the moonbeams, blending myself with the
        shadows,
Recalling now the obscure shapes, the echoes, the sounds
        and sights after their sorts,
The white arms out in the breakers tirelessly tossing,
I, with bare feet, a child, the wind wafting my hair,
Listened long and long.

Listened to keep, to sing – now translating the notes,
Following you, my brother.

Soothe! Soothe! Soothe!
Close on its wave soothes the wave behind,

And again another behind, embracing and lapping, every
    one close, –
But my love soothes not me, not me.

Low hangs the moon – it rose late;
O it is lagging – O I think it is heavy with love, with love.

O madly the sea pushes, pushes upon the land,
With love – with love.
O night! do I not see my love fluttering out there among
    the breakers?
What is that little black thing I see there in the white?
O past! O life! O songs of joy!
In the air – in the woods – over fields;
Loved! loved! loved! loved! loved!
But my love no more, no more with me.
We two together no more.

WALT WHITMAN: *A Word out of the Sea*

The Whale Boats

At such times, under an abated sun; afloat all day upon smooth,
slow heaving swells; seated in his boat, light as a birch canoe;
and so sociably mixing with the soft waves themselves, that
like hearth-stone cats they purr against the gunwale; these are
the times of dreamy quietude, when beholding the tranquil
beauty and brilliancy of the ocean's skin, one forgets the tiger
heart that pants beneath it; and would not willingly remember,
that this velvet paw but conceals a remorseless fang.

These are the times, when in his whale-boat the rover softly
feels a certain filial, confident, land-like feeling towards the
sea; that he regards it as so much flowery earth, and the distant
ship revealing only the tops of her masts seems struggling
forward, not through high rolling waves, but through the tall
grass of a rolling prairie: as when the western emigrants'

horses only show their erected ears, while their hidden bodies widely wade through the amazing verdure.

The long-drawn virgin vales; the mild blue hill-sides; as over these there steals the hush, the hum; you almost swear that play-wearied children lie sleeping in these solitudes, in some glad May-time, when the flowers of the woods are plucked. And all this mixes with your most mystic mood; so that fact and fancy, half-way meeting, interpenetrate and form one seamless whole.

HERMAN MELVILLE: *Moby Dick*

The Waters

The world below the brine,
Forests at the bottom of the sea – the branches and leaves,
Sea-lettuce, vast lichens, strange flowers and seeds – the
    thick tangle, the openings, and the pink turf,
Different colours, pale grey and green, purple, white and
    gold – the play of light through the water,
Dumb swimmers there among the rocks – coral, gluten,
    grass, rushes – and the aliment of the swimmers,
Sluggish existences grazing there, suspended, or slowly
    crawling close to the bottom:
The sperm-whale at the surface, blowing air and spray, or
    disporting with his flukes,
The leaden-eyed shark, the walrus, the turtle, the hairy
    sea-leopard, and the sting-ray.
Passions there, wars, pursuits, tribes – sight in those
    ocean-depths – breathing that thick breathing air, as
    so many do.
The change thence to the sight here, and to the subtle air
    breathed by beings like us, who walk this sphere:
The change onward from ours to that of beings who walk
    other spheres.

WALT WHITMAN: *Leaves of Grass*

She was called *Forgetfulness:* a powerful little caieque built to
the shallow-bosomed shape which the fisherfolk call 'Racers'
because they are judged speedier than the normal deep-hulled
models. The sea-raiding people had put a tank-engine in her
which gave her about twelve knots. You felt the power at
once as she fanned away from the stone quay and out into the
harbour, edging towards the black buoys which, the captain
said, marked mine-fields. Huddled in our coats we watched
the black uninviting headland of rock paying out past us like
a rapidly diminishing rope, drawing us nearer to the proper
sea. Across the waters, from the direction of Turkey, the light
had broken through in one place; a drop of red had leaked
between the interstices of sea and sky, and was running round
the rim of the horizon like the knife that slips along the rim of
the oyster to let the light in with it. The red mingled with the
black and turned it purple; the meniscus of the sea copied the
tone: strengthened it: turned it green, and an edge of the sun
shone for a second across the waste of waters and islands,
hideous, like a head with one eye. Then the darkness again
and the steady throb of the engines. The boy was posted at the
prow. He strained through the mist and guided the helmsman
with shouts and gestures.

'So we'll get to Patmos after all,' said E., unpacking the
sandwiches and the little bottle of cognac.

Patmos, I thought, was more an idea than a place, more a
symbol than an Island.

Yet to the boy crouching at the prow, his eyes fixed upon
the mist-darkened territory ahead, it had no doubt become a
name like any other, marking only a brief, stony point in an
oft-repeated routine, distinguished at the most by a special
tavern where the wine was resinous or a house where the
conversation seemed the better for a beautiful elder daughter.
From time to time as he peered, he saw the shapes of islands
come up on us like battleships, and with a brief wild cry, as of

some trapped sea-bird, shook his arm to right or left, guiding us to the safety of the deeper channel. A few yards away the wet fangs of rock would emerge and slide back into their unearthly vagueness, and the note of the propeller alter its tensity. Once the mist drew back for an instant and we saw, tinkling upon a scrubby headland, a swarm of sheep like gold bugs, loitering among arbutus, while on a rock commanding the prospect stood a motionless hooded figure like a janitor. Their bells were softly dumbed out in the mist, losing volume but not their richness.

The sun had somehow swindled us and climbed into heaven without once shining directly upon the water. Through a cloud-surface with a thick yellow nap like a carpet it allowed its beams to diffuse themselves over everything with a dense coppery hue, turning the water to lead beneath us. It increased our range of sight, however, and with it our speed. From where he sat at the tiller the captain made a chopping motion with his hand to indicate, in Greek fashion, the fact that we were making better time. The boy came aft and sat for a while to make conversation. Points of water glistened in his beard and hair. 'Patmos,' he said, 'you will like it. All foreigners like it. They have good fruit and water.' Then raising himself the better to cup his hands about a box of English matches as he lit a cigarette, he added, with a touch of medieval wonder: 'And there is a telephone. The Abbot speaks to it every day.'

'Have you ever used it?' I asked him.

'I? What for?'

The sense of blindness had now given place to a sense of headache. The atmosphere had become warmer, but the clouds still lay between us and the sun, which burned with a bilious humid intensity upon the sea. The last of the islands that lined the corridor between Leros and Patmos like ancestral totems, was kicking in our wake. Presently we should see our objective through the trembling curtain of the mist. . . .

Our attention was caught by a cry from the boy who had returned to the prow. Away to the northward the mist had shifted and beyond it, gleaming in a single pencil of sunlight

17

was a white cape – lifted like the wing of an albatross upon the very place where sky and sea met. For an instant this snowy apparition paused, and then the beam moved slowly along the mass to pick out a turret, a battlement, the cupola of a chapel. 'The monastery,' said the captain. 'Patmos.'

LAWRENCE DURRELL: *Reflections on a Marine Venus*

Sea Sorrow

Rough wind that moanest loud,
   Grief too sad for song;
Wild wind, when sullen cloud
   Knells all the night long;
Sad storm, whose tears are vain,
Bare woods, whose branches strain,
Deep caves and dreary main,
   Wail for the world's wrong.

P. B. SHELLEY

An Arctic Explorer's Vision

The world that shall be! Again and again this thought comes back to my mind. I gaze far on through the ages. . . .

Slowly and imperceptibly the heat of the sun declines, and the temperature of the earth sinks by equally slow degrees. Thousands, hundreds of thousands, millions of years pass away, glacial epochs come and go; but the heat still grows ever less; little by little these drifting masses of ice extend far and wide, ever towards more southern shores, and no-one notices it, but at last all the seas of the earth become one unbroken mass of ice. Life has vanished from its surface, and is to be found in the ocean depths alone.

But the temperature continues to fall, the ice grows thicker and ever thicker; life's domain vanishes. Millions of years roll on, and the ice reaches the bottom. The last trace of life has disappeared; the earth is covered with snow. All that we lived for is no longer; the fruit of all our toil and sufferings has been blotted out millions and millions of years ago, buried beneath a fall of snow. A stiffened, lifeless mass of ice this earth rolls on in her path through eternity. Like a faintly glowing disc, the sun crosses the sky; the moon shines no more, and is scarcely visible. Yet still, perhaps, the northern lights flicker over the desert, icy plain, and still the stars twinkle in silence, peacefully as of yore. Some have burnt out, but new ones usurp their place; and round them revolve new spheres, teeming with new life, new sufferings without any aim. Such is the infinite cycle of eternity; such are nature's everlasting rhythms.

FRIDTJOF NANSEN: *Farthest North*

Whisperings

(i)   It keeps eternal whispering around
Measureless shores, and with its mighty swell
Gluts twice ten thousand caverns, till the spell
Of Hecate leaves them their old shadowy sound.
Often 'tis in such gentle temper found
That scarcely will the very smallest shell
Be moved for days from where it sometime fell,
When last the winds of Heaven were unbound.
     O ye! Who have your eye-balls vex'd and tired,
     Feast them upon the wideness of the Sea;
     O ye! Whose ears are dinned with uproar rude,
     Or fed too much with cloying melody, –
     Sit ye near some old cavern's mouth, and brood
     Until ye start, as if the sea-nymphs quired!

JOHN KEATS

(ii)   . . . as when ocean
Heaves calmly its broad swelling smoothness o'er
Its rocky marge, and balances once more
The patient weeds; that now unshent by foam
Feel all about their undulating home.

JOHN KEATS: *Sleep and Poetry*

Ice Pressure

When one pictures to oneself these enormous ice-masses, drifting in a certain direction, suddenly meeting hindrances – for example, ice-masses drifting from the opposite direction, owing to a change of wind in some more or less distant quarter – it is easy to understand the tremendous pressure that must result.

Such an ice-conflict is undeniably a stupendous spectacle. One feels oneself to be in the presence of Titanic forces, and it is easy to understand how timid souls may be overawed and feel as if nothing could stand before it. For when the packing begins in earnest, it seems as though there could be no spot on the earth's surface left unshaken. First you hear a sound like the thundering rumble of an earthquake far away on the great waste; then you hear it in several places, always coming nearer and nearer. The silent ice-world re-echoes with thunders; nature's giants are awakening to the battle. The ice cracks on every side of you, and begins to pile itself up; and all of a sudden you, too, find yourself in the midst of the struggle. There are howlings and thunderings round you; you feel the ice trembling, and hear it rumbling under your feet; there is no peace anywhere. In the semi-darkness you can see it piling and tossing itself up into high ridges nearer and nearer you – floes 10, 12, 15 feet thick, broken, and flung on the top of each other as if they were featherweights. They are quite near you now, and you jump away to save your life. But the ice splits in front of you, a black gulf opens, and water streams up. You turn in another direction, but there through the dark you can just see a new ridge of moving ice-blocks coming towards you. You try another direction, but there it is the same. All round there is thundering and roaring, as of some enormous water-fall, with explosions like cannon salvoes. Still nearer you it comes. The floe you are standing on gets smaller and smaller; water pours over it; there can be no escape except by scrambling over the rolling ice-blocks to get to the other side of the pack. But now the disturbance begins to calm down. The noise passes on, and is lost by degrees in the distance.

FRIDTJOF NANSEN: *Farthest North*

The Ship

I march across great waters like a queen,
I whom so many wisdoms helped to make:
Over the uncruddled billows of seas green
I blanch the bubbled highway of my wake.
By me my wandering tenants clasp the hands
And know the thoughts of men in other lands.

JOHN MASEFIELD: *The Ship*

A Moment's Gift

. . . The night alone near water when I heard
All the sea's spirit spoken by a bird.

JOHN MASEFIELD: *Biography*

Water Spout

As I sat below at the table plotting my noon position, I suddenly had a feeling that something was wrong. A glance through the companionway quickly changed my uneasiness to alarm, for there, directly behind and coming rapidly up to us, still in the first throes of birth, hung the largest waterspout we had ever seen. Its long black tentacle, suspended from the lowering tumultuous mother-cloud, writhed and groped half-way to the sea, like the arm of a Gargantuan octopus seeking a grip upon an enemy. Our eyes clung to it fascinated as it reached down and down, sometimes retreating but always growing again. There became audible the distant roaring or sighing sound that first warns of approach to a waterfall when travelling down stream in a canoe. Underneath, at the surface of the sea, the sympathetic disturbance suddenly became more intense as the incipient whirl revolved faster and faster, throwing off bits of foam and loose water. A distinct bulge in the surface appeared, as if sucked up by the parched column above, and rose higher every second. The spray and foam now began to be snatched upward, and before our eyes was formed a vapoury connection with the descending tube, linking cloud and sea. The connection established, more and more loose water shot whirling aloft, and the disturbed area at the base grew larger and more violent as it received the too heavy particles thrown away from the column by centrifugal force. The noise and tumult grew as the hissing of the column, the cry of the wind, and the crashing of the waters blended to form a fearsome roar. Augmented by more and more water the lower half suddenly reached maturity and groped out to clasp hands with the upper, and the sea and sky were united by a spinning weaving pillar of water.

The spout, moving slowly, reared itself higher and closer to our stern. Close enough now to be in the area of disturbed wind, our squaresail began to strain at its sheets and we gathered speed momentarily and seemed to be holding our own with the black twisting column, contact with which would have been disaster.

There has long been a somewhat superstitious belief among seamen that the firing of guns at a spout will break it up, and there have been cases where this has possibly proved efficacious. It is somewhat logical that the concussion of a heavy shot might break up the spout, but it is certainly almost impossible to expect a small gun to have any effect. Before I had finished loading my gun a sudden change occurred within the spout. The writhing increased and a weakening appeared half-way between cloud and sea, and this part became more and more tenuous until there was a gap that grew larger as the lower half bored its way back into the sea and the upper part withdrew slowly to the boiling lower surface of the cloud.

The black curtain was now directly overhead, and we were struck by a short-lived wind and rain squall of great intensity. We had been running under squaresail alone, and had held on to it in an effort to escape the spout. Now there was no time to get it off, and we tore through the water faster and faster, until the bow was high out of its proper element and the stern nearly under. *Svaap* travelled for a short time faster than I thought would have been possible, and water fell in such quantities that it was impossible to breathe without protecting the face. We held her before it and careered madly along for perhaps five minutes, expecting the sail to pull out of the bolt-ropes at any second. But everything held, and the wind shifted from east to north as it always did after squalls. Gradually it subsided and at last worked back to east again and we jogged slowly along on our course as if nothing had happened.

WILLIAM ALBERT ROBINSON: *Deep Water and Shoal*

End of the Voyage

Cheerly they rang her in, those beating bells,
The new-come beauty stately from the sea,
Whitening the blue heave of the drowsy swells,
Treading the bubbles down. With three times three
They cheered her moving beauty in, and she
Came to her berth so noble, so superb;
Swayed like a queen, and answered to the curb.

Then in the sunset's flush they went aloft,
And unbent sails in that most lovely hour
When the light gentles and the wind is soft,
And beauty in the heart breaks like a flower.
Working aloft they saw the mountain tower,
Snow to the peak; they heard the launchmen shout;
And bright along the bay the lights came out.

And then the night fell dark, and all night long
The pointed mountain pointed at the stars,
Frozen, alert, austere; the eagle's song
Screamed from her desolate screes and splintered scars.
On her intense crags where the air is sparse
The stars looked down; their many golden eyes
Watched her and burned, burned out, and came to rise.

JOHN MASEFIELD: *Dauber*

Waves

The sea presented a superb spectacle. With your eye at water
level you suffer a good deal of inconvenience, but the view-
point is much finer than from the lofty bridge of a steamship.
In the trough of the waves you are dominated by a colourless
sea entirely overspread by a sort of white powder which is

driven by the wind across the heaving surface. From the crests you see an ocean of foam; from time to time the top of a huge wave topples over and bursts into an unforgettable cloud of spray, shot with pink in the early light. Facing the wind it is difficult to open your eyes.

Still more striking are the extraordinary patches of indescribable green, 'electric green' as I always call it, which appears on the slopes of the larger waves, those which break or at least try to break before they are decapitated by the fury of the wind. This is an 'effect' which marine painters find almost impossible to reproduce, as it is essentially luminous; not that there are many who have really seen it. Sea water, permeated as it is with active phosphorescent organic life, from which its colour is derived (for sea water is coloured, as you may see by pouring some into a big wineglass), glows through and through with an inward light. On the flanks of the wave oily tracts gleam lividly, mixed with patches of whipped foam.

MARIN-MARIE: *Wind Aloft, Wind Alow*

The River

All other waters have their time of peace,
Calm, or the turn of tide, or summer drought;
But on these bars the tumults never cease,
In violent death this river passes out.

Brimming she goes, a bloody-coloured rush
Hurrying her heaped disorder, rank on rank,
Bubbleless speed so still that in the hush
One hears the mined earth dropping from the bank,

Slipping in little falls whose tingeings drown,
Sunk by the waves for ever pressing on,
Till with a stripping crash the tree goes down,
Its washing branches flounder and are gone.

Then, roaring out aloud, her water spreads,
Making a desolation where her waves
Shriek and give battle, tossing up their heads,
Tearing the shifting sandbanks into graves,

Changing the raddled ruin of her course
So swiftly, that the pilgrim on the shore
Hears the loud whirlpool laughing like a horse
Where the scurfed sand was parched an hour before.

And always underneath that heaving tide
The changing bottom runs, or piles, or quakes,
Flinging immense heaps up to wallow wide,
Sucking the surface into whirls like snakes.

If anything should touch that shifting sand,
All the blind bottom sucks it till it sinks;
It takes the clipper ere she comes to land,
It takes the thirsting tiger as he drinks.

And on the river pours – it never tires;
Blind, hungry, screaming, day and night the same
Purposeless hurry of a million ires,
Mad as the wind, as merciless as flame.

JOHN MASEFIELD: *The River*

Squall

. . . at last Jim looked astern where the other pointed with maniacal insistence. He saw a silent black squall which had eaten up already one third of the sky. You know how these squalls come up there about that time of the year. First you see a darkening of the horizon – no more; then a cloud rises, opaque like a wall. A straight edge of vapour lined with sickly whitish gleams flies up from the south-west, swallowing the stars in whole constellations; its shadow flies over the waters, and confounds sea and sky in one abyss of obscurity. And all is still. No thunder, no wind, no sound; not a flicker of lightning. Then in the tenebrous immensity a livid arch appears; a swell or two like undulations of the very darkness run past, and, suddenly, wind and rain strike together with a peculiar impetuosity as if they had burst through something solid.

JOSEPH CONRAD: *Lord Jim*

You would sail the sea? Then remember that the sea is wide.

PHOCYLIDES

Unfathomable sea, whose waves are years. . . .
Treacherous in calm, and terrible in storm,
 Who shall put forth on thee,
 Unfathomable Sea?

P. B. SHELLEY

A Freak Wave

We were lying on our bunks below trying to decide on our course of action. The wind seemed, if anything, to have increased and had backed a little to the south-west. The seas now tumbled more heavily and heaped up in stupendous confusion. When we looked out of the little portholes, we saw only the blue sky above or a foaming valley stretching away below us, as we pitched for a moment across the backbone of some huge monster of a sea. But there was nothing we could do, so we turned back to continue a shouted conversation above the noise.

Suddenly, in a weird hush, we heard a slight warning hiss high above the boat. The cabin darkened.

The sequence of events during the next few moments will for ever remain unknown to us. We remember only a fantastic roar and a deafening, stunning bang.

Charles was hurled out of his bunk on the port side into the cabin roof opposite, together with the radio and a mass of loose clothing, cans, and bedding.

Everything went dark as night, and water seemed to fill the cabin. We remember thinking only, 'This must be the end,' when we found ourselves in a heap in the starboard berth.

A second later, with a loud sucking noise and another tremendous bang, we saw light again. We watched the water fall down from the cabin roof drenching everything. We heard it swilling about heavily from side to side. The little boat had righted and resumed the old familiar dance on the *surface* of the sea.

Slowly we sorted ourselves out and in stupefied amazement, shaking violently with shock, scrambled out into the open cockpit. We imagined everything, mast, sails and gear would certainly be gone, and we could hardly believe our eyes when we saw everything dripping, but in place.

It is not easy to reconstruct exactly what happened. This is what we think: In an ocean gale there are always individual seas bigger and less stable than their fellows. They are sometimes called freak waves, built up to huge dimensions by some peculiar combination of wind and sea. They are the ones that get 'out of step' and pile up high above the confusion until with a tumult of breaking foam they burst. Woe betide any luckless victim in their path. The *Nova Espero* was the victim this time. . . . To cause the darkening in the cabin before we were actually struck, the top must have formed an arch over us, thus shutting out the light. A moment later, swept along under the curl of the breaker, we were turned almost over. That we were flung into the cabin roof bears out our belief that we were capsized to such an extent that the masthead was carried down beneath us to within a few degrees of vertical.

There she must have paused until the weight of the keel restored equilibrium, and she suddenly snapped back the way she went over. Probably if she had rolled completely over and came up the other way we would have found less water inside when we bobbed up afterwards, as the only opening where water could enter the cabin was the partly opened hatchway. If there had been a smoothly continued roll over, there would have been no pause, when upside down, to allow the water to enter as it did.

The *Nova Espero* has narrowly escaped destruction several times in her short life, but how she survived this punishment and came through unscathed we cannot imagine.

STANLEY SMITH AND CHARLES VIOLET:
The Wind Calls the Tune (ii)

Arctic Night

The temperature is between 38° and 40° below zero, but when there is added to this a biting wind with a velocity of from 9 to 16 feet per second, it must be allowed that it is rather cool in the shade.

FRIDTJOF NANSEN: *Farthest North*

The Swimmer

In yonder bay I bathed,
This sunny morning: swam my best, then hung, half swathed
With chill, and half with warmth, i' the channel's midmost
     deep.
You know how one – not treads, but stands in water? Keep
Body and limbs below, hold head back, uplift chin,

And, for the rest, leave care! If brow, eyes, mouth should win
Their freedom – excellent! If they must brook the surge,
No matter though they sink, let but the nose emerge.
So, all of me in brine lay soaking: did I care
One jot? I kept alive by man's due breath of air
I' the nostrils, high and dry. At times o'er these would run
The ripple, even wash the wavelet – morning's sun
Tempted advance, no doubt: and always flash of froth,
Fish-outbreak, bubbling by, would find me nothing loth
To rise and look around; then all was overswept
With dark and death at once. But trust the old adept!
Back went again the head, a merest motion made,
Fin-fashion, either hand, and nostril soon conveyed
Assurance light and life were still in reach as erst:
Always the last and – wait and watch – sometimes the first.
Try to ascend breast-high? Wave arms wide free of tether?
Be in the air and leave the water altogether?
Under went all again, till I resigned myself
To only breathe the air, that's footed by an elf,
And only swim the water, that's native to a fish.
But there is no denying that, ere I curbed my wish,
And schooled my restive arms, salt entered mouth and eyes
Often enough – sun, sky and air so tantalize!
Still, the adept swims, this accorded, that denied;
Can always breathe, sometimes see and be satisfied!

ROBERT BROWNING: *Fifine at the Fair* (iii)

The Wind Getting Up

A westerly current sweeps at all seasons of the year round the
Cape of Good Hope, and sometimes proves troublesome
enough to outward-bound ships. This stream is evidently
caused by the trade-wind in the southern parts of the Indian
ocean. For three days we were bamboozled with light south-

easterly airs and calms, but on the 8th of July, which is the depth of winter in that hemisphere, there came on a spanking snuffler from the north-west, before which we spun two hundred and forty miles, clean off the reel, in twenty-four hours.

Nothing is more delightful than the commencement of such a fair wind. The sea is then smooth, and the ship seems literally to fly along; the masts and yards bend forwards, as if they would drop over the bows, while the studding-sail booms crack and twist, and, unless great care be taken, some-time break across; but still, so long as the surface of the sea is plane it is astonishing what a vast expanse of canvas may be spread to the rising gale. By-and-bye, however, it becomes prudent to take in the royals, flying-jib, and top gallant studding-sails. The boatswain takes a look at the gripes and other fastenings of the boats and booms; the carpenter instinctively examines the port-lashings, and draws up the pump-boxes to look at the leathers; while the gunner sees that all the breechings and tackles of the guns are well secured before the ship begins to roll. The different minor heads of departments, also, to use their own phrase, smell the gale coming on, and each in his respective walk gets things ready to meet it. The captain's and gun-room steward beg the carpenter's mate to drive down a few more cleats and staples, and, having got a cod-line or two from the boatswain's yeoman, or a hank of marline stuff, they commence double lashing all the tables and chairs. The mariners' muskets are more securely packed in the arm-chest. The rolling tackles are got ready for the lower yards, and the master, accompanied by the gunner's mate, inspects the lanyards of the lower rigging. All these, and twenty other precautions are taken in a manner so slow and deliberate that they would hardly catch the observation of a passenger. It might also seem as if the different parties were afraid to let out the secret of their own lurking apprehension, but yet were resolved not to be caught unprepared.

CAPT. BASIL HALL, R.N., F.R.S.
The Lieutenant and the Commander

Landmarks

Nobly, nobly Cape Saint Vincent to the north-west died away;
Sunset ran, one glorious blood-red, reeking into Cadiz Bay;
Bluish 'mid the burning water, full in face Trafalgar lay;
In the dimmest North-east distance dawned Gibraltar grand
    and gray.
'Here and here did England help me: how can I help England?'
    – say,
Whoso turns as I, this evening, turn to God to praise and pray,
While Jove's planet rises yonder, silent over Africa.

ROBERT BROWNING: *Home Thoughts from the Sea* (iv)

Mullet

The dunes are a place of high winds and driven sand, of salt spray and sun. Now the wind is from the north. In the hollows of the dunes the beach grasses lean in the wind and with their pointed tips write endless circles in the sand. From the barrier beach the wind is picking up the loose sand and carrying it seaward in a haze of white. From a distance the air above the banks looks murky, as though a light mist is rising from the ground.

The fishermen on the banks do not see the sand haze; they feel its sting in eyes and face; they feel it as it sifts into their hair and through their clothing. They take out their handkerchiefs and tie them across their faces, and they pull long-visored caps low on their heads. A wind from the north means sand in your face and rough seas under your boat keel, but it means mullet, too.

The sun is hot as it beats down on the men standing on the beach. Some of the women and children are there too, to help the men with the ropes. The children are bare-footed, wading

32

in the pools left in the scoured-out depressions of the beach, ribbed with sand waves.

The tide has turned, and now one of the boats is shot out between the breakers to be ready for the fish when they come. It's not easy, launching a boat in this surf. The men leap to their places like parts of a machine. The boat rights itself, wallows into the green swells. Just outside the surf line the men wait at the oars. The captain stands in the bow, arms folded, leg muscles flexing to the rise and fall of the boat, his eyes on the water, looking toward the inlet.

Somewhere in that green water there are fish – hundreds of fish – thousands of fish. Soon they will come within reach of the nets. The north wind's blowing, and the mullet are running before it out of the sound, running down along the coast, as mullet have done for thousands upon thousands of years.

Half a dozen gulls are mewing above the water. That means the mullet are coming. The gulls don't want the mullet; they want the minnows that are milling about in alarm as the larger fish move through the shallows. The mullet are coming down just outside the breakers, travelling about as fast as a man could walk on the beach. The lookout has marked the school. He walks toward the boat, keeping opposite the fish, signalling their course to the crew by waving his arms.

The men brace their feet against the thwarts of the boat and strain to the oars, pulling the boat in a wide semi-circle to the shore. The net of heavy twine spills silently and steadily into the water over the stern and cork floats bob in the water in the wake of the boat. Ropes from one end of the net are held by half a dozen men on shore.

There are mullet in the water all around the boat. They cut the surface with their back fins; they leap and fall. The men lean harder to the oars, pulling for the shore to close the net before the school can escape. Once in the last line of surf and in water not more than waist deep, the men jump into the water. The boat is seized by willing hands and is dragged out on the beach.

The shallow water in which the mullet are swimming is a pale translucent green, murky with the loose sand which the waves are stirring up. The mullet are excited by their return to the sea with its bitter salt waters. Under the powerful drive of instinct they move together in the first lap of a journey that will take them far from the coastal shallows into the blue haze of the sea's beginnings.

A shadow looms on the green, sun-filled water in the path of the mullet. From a dim, grey curtain the shadow resolves itself into a web of slender, criss-cross bars. The first of the mullet strike the net, back water with their fins, hesitate. Other fish are crowding up from behind, nosing at the net. As the first waves of panic pass from fish to fish they dash shoreward, seeking a way of escape. The ropes held by fishermen on the shore have been drawn in so that the netting wall extends into water too shallow for a fish to swim. They run seaward, but meet the circle of the net that is growing smaller, foot by foot, as the men on shore and in water up to their knees brace themselves in the sliding sand and pull on the ropes – pull against the weight of water, against the strength of the fish.

As the net is closed and gradually drawn in to shore, the press of fish in the seine becomes greater. Milling in frantic efforts to find a way of escape, the mullet drive with all their combined strength of thousands of pounds against the seaward arc of the net. Their weight and the outward thrust of their bodies lift the net clear of the bottom, and the mullet scrape bellies on the sand as they slip under the net and race into deep water. The fishermen, sensitive to every movement of the net, feel the lift and know they are losing fish. They strain the harder, till muscles crack and backs ache. Half a dozen men plunge out into water chin-deep, fighting the surf to tread the lead line and hold the net on the bottom. But the outer circle of cork floats is still half a dozen boat lengths away.

Of a sudden the whole school surges upward. In a turmoil of flying spray and splashing water mullet by the hundred leap over the cork line. They pelt against the fishermen, who turn their backs to the fish raining about them. The men strive desperately to lift the cork line above the water so that the fish will fall back into the circle when they strike the net.

Two piles of slack netting are growing on the beach; the heads of many small fishes no longer than a man's hand caught in the meshes. Now the ropes attached to the lead lines are drawn in faster and the net takes on the shape of a huge, elongated bag, bulging with fish. As the bag is drawn at last into the shallow fringe of the surf the air crackles with a sound like the clapping of hands as a thousand head of mullet, with all the fury of their last strength, flap on the wet sand.

The fishermen work quickly to take the mullet from the net and toss them into the waiting boats. By a dexterous shake of the net, they toss on the beach the small fish that are gilled in the seine. There are young sea-trout and pompano, mullet of the last year's spawning, young ceros and sheepshead and sea bass.

Soon the bodies of the young fish – too small to sell, too small to eat – litter the beach above the water line, the life oozing from them for want of means to cross a few yards of dry sand and return to the sea. Some of the small bodies the sea would take away later; others it would lay up carefully beyond reach of the tides among the litter of sticks and sea-weeds, of shells and sea-oats stubble. Thus the sea unfailingly provides for the hunters of the tide lines.

After the fishermen had made two more hauls and then, as the tide neared the full, had gone away with laden boats, a flocks of gulls came in from the outer shoals, white against the greying sea, and feasted on the fish. As the gulls bickered among themselves over the food, two smaller birds in sleek, black plumage walked warily among them, dragging fish up on the higher beach to devour them. They were fish crows, who took their living from the edge of the water, where they found dead crabs and shrimps and other sea refuse. After sundown the ghost crabs would come in legions out of their holes to swarm over the tide litter, clearing away the last traces of the fish. Already the sand-hoppers had gathered and were busy at their work of reclaiming to life in their own beings the materials of the fishes' bodies. For in the sea nothing is lost. One dies, another lives, as the precious elements of life are passed on and on in endless chains.

All through the night, as the lights in the fishing village went out one by one and fishermen gathered around their stoves because of the chill north wind, mullet were passing unmolested through the inlet and running westward and southward along the coast, through black water on which the wave crests were like giant fishes' wakes, silver in the light of the moon.

RACHEL L. CARSON: *Under the Sea-Wind*

> . . . but I saw
> Too far into the sea, where every maw
> The greater on the less feeds evermore –
> But I saw too distinct into the core
> Of an eternal fierce destruction,
> And so from happiness I far was gone.

JOHN KEATS: *Letter to Reynolds*

The net of Ruin – AESCHYLUS

Fish

In a cool curving world he lies
And ripples with dark ecstasies.
The kind luxurious lapse and steal
Shapes all his universe to feel
And know and be; the clinging stream
Closes his memory, glooms his dream,
Who lips the roots o' the shore, and glides
Superb on unreturning tides.

Those silent waters weave for him
A fluctuant mutable world and dim,
Where wavering masses bulge and gape
Mysterious, and shape to shape
Dies momently through whorl and hollow,
And form and line and solid follow
Solid and line and form to dream
Fantastic down the eternal stream;
An obscure world, a shifting world,
Bulbous, or pulled to thin, or curled,
Or serpentine, or driving arrows,
Or serene slidings, or March narrows.
There slipping wave and shore are one,
And weed and mud. No ray of sun
But glow to glow fades down the deep
(As dream to unknown dream in sleep);
Shaken translucency illumes
The hyaline of drifting glooms;
The strange soft-handed depth subdues
Drowned colour there, but black to hues,
As death to living, decomposes –
Red darkness of the heart of roses,
Blue brilliant from dead starless skies,
And gold that lies behind the eyes,
The unknown unnameable sightless white
That is the essential flame of night,
Lustreless purple, hooded green,
The myriad hues that lie between
Darkness and darkness. . . .

RUPERT BROOKE: *The Fish*

The earth is full of thy riches; so is this great and wide sea,
wherein are things creeping innumerable, both small and
great beasts. There go the ships; and there is that leviathan,
whom thou hast made to play therein.

PSALM 104

37

You Cannot Forget the Sea

Do you see that haystack? It stands well there
On the west cliff, against the western sky,
Bird-haunted, washed in colour, dawn to evening,
Harvest of all this summer's upland fields –
Below it, far below, the eye remembers
The wild cliff falling sheer, the wild plain
Strewn with gigantic boulders that once fell
In some huge ruin and rush of earth
When none were here, and now is cattle pasture,
And hawthorne groves, and little shaggy meadows
Yellow with cowslips; but never tamed by time;
And then the sea: you cannot forget the sea.
Westward you hear it break on Rocken End;
– Go down, and it will stun your ears with sound –
There drove the wrecks, before they built the
      lighthouse;
Beneath those sullen rocks and muttering shingle
Are ground in sand a thousand sailors' bones
And ribs of noble ships; but once in June –
Once long ago in June we went to the cliff's edge
Beside the corn to wait for the full moon.
It was dark before the moon came; we lay still,
Not seeing each other's faces, and we heard the sea;
Louder than that high field of whispering corn,
Louder only than that; kind, like the breath
Of the heart you sleep on . . .
                    You cannot forget the sea;
Below that haystack: eight hundred feet below.

IRENE RUTHERFORD MCLEOD

Sea Beasts

Most ugly shapes and horrible aspects,
     Such as Dame Nature selfe mote feare to see,
     Or shame, that ever should so fowle defects
     From her most cunning hand escaped bee;
     All dreadfull pourtraicts of deformitee:
     Spring-headed Hydraes, and sea-shouldring Whales,
     Great whirlpooles, which all fishes make to flee,
     Bright Scolopendraes, arm'd with silver scales,
Mighty Monoceros, with immeasured tayles.

The dreadfull Fish, that hath deserv'd the name
     Of Death, and like him lookes in dreadfull hew,
     The griesly Wasserman, that makes his game
     The flying ships with swiftnesse to pursew,
     The horrible Sea-satyre, that doth shew
     His fearfull face in time of greatest storme,
     Huge Ziffius, whom Mariners eschew
     No lesse then rockes (as travellers informe)
And greedy Rosmarines with visages deforme.

All these, and thousand thousands many more,
     And more deformed Monsters thousand fold,
     With dreadfull noise and hollow rombling rore
     Came rushing in the fomy waves enrold,
     Which seem'd to fly for feare, them to behold:
     Ne wonder, if these did the knight appall;
     For all that here on earth we dreadfull hold
     Be but as bugs to fearen babes withall,
Compared to the creatures in the seas entrall.

EDMUND SPENSER: *The Faerie Queene*

Once by the Pacific

The shattered water made a misty din.
Great waves looked over others coming in,
And thought of doing something to the shore
That water never did to land before.
The clouds were low and hairy in the skies,
Like locks blown forward in the gleam of eyes.
You could not tell, and yet it looked as if
The shore was lucky in being backed by cliff,
The cliff in being backed by continent;
It looked as if a night of dark intent
Was coming, and not only a night, an age.
Someone had better be prepared for rage.
There would be more than ocean-water broken
Before God's last *Put out the Light* was spoken.

ROBERT FROST

Sunrise

Much has been said of the sunrise at sea; but it will not compare
with the sunrise on shore. It wants the accompaniments of the
songs of birds, the awakening hum of men, and the glancing
of the first beams upon trees, hills, spires and house-tops, to
give it life and spirit. But though the actual rise of the sun at
sea is not so beautiful, yet nothing will compare with the early
breaking of day upon the wide ocean.

There is something in the first grey streaks stretching along
the eastern horizon and throwing an indistinct light upon the
face of the deep, which combines with the boundlessness and
unknown depth of the sea around you, and gives one a feeling
of loneliness, of dread, and of melancholy foreboding, which
nothing else in nature can give. This gradually passes away

as the light grows brighter, and when the sun comes up, the ordinary, monotonous sea day begins.

R. H. DANA: *Two Years Before the Mast*

Sunset

So when the Sun in bed,
Curtain'd with cloudy red,
   Pillows his chin upon an Orient wave. . . .

JOHN MILTON: *On the Morning of Christ's Nativity*

Tristram Bathes in the Cornish Sea

. . . with a cry of love that rang
As from a trumpet golden-mouthed, he sprang,
As toward a mother's where his head might rest
Her child rejoicing, toward the strong sea's breast
That none may gird nor measure; and his heart
Sent forth a shout that bade his lips not part,
But triumphed in him silent: no man's voice,
No song, no sound of clarions that rejoice,
Can set that glory forth which fills with fire
The body and soul that have their whole desire
Silent, and freer than birds or dreams are free
Take all their will of all the encountering sea.
And toward the foam he bent and forward smote,
Laughing, and launched his body like a boat
Full to the sea-breach, and against the tide
Struck strongly forth, with amorous arms made wide
To take the bright breast of the wave to his,
And on his lips the sharp sweet minute's kiss

Given of the wave's lip for a breath's space curled
And pure as at the daydawn of the world.
And round him all the bright rough shuddering sea
Kindled, as though the world were even as he,
Heart-stung with exultation of desire:
And all the life that moved him seemed to aspire,
As all the sea's life, toward the sun: and still
Delight within him waxed with quickening will
More smooth and strong and perfect as a flame
That springs and spreads, till each glad limb became
A note of rapture in the tune of life,
Live music wild and keen as sleep and strife:
Till the sweet change that bids the sense grow sure
Of deeper depth and purity more pure
Wrapped him and lapped him round with clearer cold,
And all the rippling green grew royal gold
Between him and the far sun's rising rim.

A. C. SWINBURNE: *Tristram of Lyonesse* (v)

Sappho

    but me –
Men shall not see bright fire nor hear the sea,
Nor mix their hearts with music, nor behold
Cast forth of heaven, with feet of awful gold
And plumeless wings that make the bright air blind
Lightning, with thunder for a hound behind
Hunting through fields unfurrowed and unsown,
But in the light and laughter, in the moan
And music, and in grasp of lip and hand
And shudder of water that makes felt on land
The immeasurable tremor of all the sea,
Memories shall mix and metaphors of me.

A. C. SWINBURNE: *Sappho*

42

Bells by the Sea

Oft on a Plat of rising ground
I hear the far-off Curfeu sound
Over som wide-water'd shoar,
Swinging slow with sullen roar . . .

JOHN MILTON: *Il Penseroso*

Watch the Barometer

Fair laughs the morn, and soft the zephyr blows,
While proudly riding o'er the azure realm
In gallant trim the gilded vessel goes;
   Youth on the prow, and Pleasure at the helm;
Regardless of the sweeping whirlwind's sway,
That, hush'd in grim repose, expects his evening prey.

THOMAS GRAY: *The Curse upon Edward*

Desolation

Mark where the pressing wind shoots javelin-like
Its skeleton shadow on the broad-back'd wave:
Here is a fitting spot to dig Love's grave;
Here where the ponderous breakers plunge and strike,
And dart their hissing tongues high up the sand:
In hearing of the ocean, and in sight
Of those ribb'd wind-streaks running into white. . . .

GEORGE MEREDITH: *Modern Love*

Foam-Flecks

The bright thin grey foam-blossom, glad and hoar,
That flings its flower along the flowerless shore
On sand or shingle.

A. C. SWINBURNE: *Tristram of Lyonesse*

Sea Creatures

And God created the great Whales, and each
Soul living, each that crept, which plenteously
The waters generated by thir kindes,
And every Bird of wing after his kinde;
And saw that it was good, and bless'd them, saying:
Be fruitful, multiply, and in the Seas
And Lakes and running Streams the waters fill;
Forthwith the Sounds and Seas, each Creek and Bay
With Frie innumerable swarme, and Shoales
Of Fish that with their Finns and shining Scales
Glide under the green Wave, in Sculles that oft
Bank the mid sea: part single or with mate
Graze the Sea weed thir pasture, and through Groves
Of Coral stray, or sporting with quick glance
Show to the Sun thir wav'd coats dropt with gold,
Or in thir pearlie shells at ease, attend
Moist nutriment, or under Rocks thir food
In joined Armour watch; on smooth the Seale
And bended Dolphins play; part huge of bulk
Wallowing unweildie, enormous in thir Gate
Tempest the Ocean; there Leviathan
Hugest of living creatures, on the Deep
Stretcht like a Promontorie sleeps or swims,

And seems a moving land, and at his Gilles
Draws in, and at his Trunck spouts out a Sea.

JOHN MILTON: *Paradise Lost*

The South-Wester

Only at gathered eve knew we
The marvels of the day: for then
Mount upon mountain out of sea
Arose, and to our spacious ken
Trebled sublime Olympus round
In towering amphitheatre.
Colossal on enormous mound,
Majestic gods we saw confer.
They wafted the Dream-messenger
From off the loftiest, the crowned:
The Lady of the hues of foam
In sun-rays: who, close under dome,
A figure on the foot's descent,
Irradiate to vapour went,
As one whose mission was resigned;
Dispieced, undraped, dissolved to threads,
Melting, she passed into the mind,
Where immortal with mortal weds.

GEORGE MEREDITH: *The South-Wester*

Winter Sea

Into the snow she sweeps,
Hurling the haven behind,
The *Deutschland*, on Sunday; and so the sky keeps,
For the infinite air is unkind,

45

And the sea flint-flake, black-backed in the regular blow,
Sitting Eastnortheast, in cursed quarter, the wind;
  Wiry and white-fiery and whirlwind-swivelled snow
Spins to the widow-making unchilding unfathering
    deeps.

G. M. HOPKINS: The Wreck of the Deutschland

. . . I saw dun-coloured waves leaving trailing hoods of white
breaking on the beach. Before going I took a last look at the
breakers, wanting to make out how the comb is morselled so
fine into string and tassel, as I have lately noticed it to be.
I saw big smooth flinty waves, carved and scuppled in shallow
grooves, much swelling when the wind freshened, burst on the
rocky spurs of the cliff at the little cove and break into bushes
of foam. In an enclosure of rocks the peaks of the water romped
and wandered and a light crown of tufty scum standing high
on the surface kept slowly turning round: chips of it blew off
and gadded about without weight in the air.

At eight we sailed for Liverpool in wind and rain. . . . I did
not look much at the sea: the crests I saw ravelled up by the
wind into the air in arching whips and straps of glassy spray
and higher broken into clouds of white and blown away.
Under the curl shone a bright juice of beautiful green. The
foam exploding and smouldering under water makes a chryso-
prase green.

G. M. HOPKINS: Journal

Moon Bathers

Falls from her heaven the Moon, and stars sink burning
Into the sea where blackness rims the sea,
Silently quenched. Faint light that the waves hold
Is only light remaining; yet still gleam

The sands where those now-sleeping young moon
    bathers
Came dripping out of the sea and from their arms
Shook flakes of light, dancing on the foamy edge
Of quiet waves. They were all things of light
Tossed from the sea to dance under the moon –
Her nuns, dancing within her dying round,
Clear limbs and breasts silvered with moon and waves
And quick with windlike mood and body's joy,
Withdrawn from alien vows, by wave and wind
Lightly absolved and lightly all forgetting.
    An hour ago they left. Remains the gleam
Of their late motion on the salt sea-meadow,
As loveliest hues linger when the sun's gone
And float in the heavens and die in reedy pools –
So slowly, who shall say when light is gone?

JOHN FREEMAN: *Moon Bathers*

The Old Ships

I have seen old ships sail like swans asleep
Beyond the village which men still call Tyre,
With leaden age o'ercargoed, dipping deep
For Famagusta and the hidden sun
That rings black Cyprus with a lake of fire;
And all those ships were certainly so old
Who knows how oft with squat and noisy gun,
Questing brown slaves or Syrian oranges,
The pirate Genoese
Hell-raked them till they rolled
Blood, water, fruit and corpses up the hold.
But now through friendly seas they softly run,
Painted the mid-sea blue or shore-sea green,
Still patterned with the vine and grapes in gold.

But I have seen,
Pointing her shapely shadows from the dawn,
An image tumbled on a rose-swept bay,
A drowsy ship of some yet older day;
And, wonder's breath indrawn,
Thought I – who knows – who knows – but in that
    same
(Fished up beyond Aeaea, patched up new
– Stern painted brighter blue –)
That talkative, bald-headed seaman came
(Twelve patient comrades sweating at the oar)
From Troy's doom-crimson shore,
And with great lies about his wooden horse
Set the crew laughing, and forgot his course.

It was so old a ship – who knows, who knows?
– And yet so beautiful, I watched in vain
To see the mast burst open with a rose,
And the whole deck put on its leaves again.

J. E. FLECKER: *The Old Ships*

Quiet Waters

(i)   Through many a fair sea-circle, day by day,
    Scarce rocking, her full-busted figure-head
    Stared o'er the ripple feathering from her bows.

ALFRED LORD TENNYSON: *Enoch Arden*

(ii)   . . . such a tide as moving seems asleep,
      Too full for sound or foam,
    When that which drew from out the boundless deep
      Turns again home.

ALFRED LORD TENNYSON: *Crossing the Bar*

Off Shoreham

. . . the ebb was rushing out of that river, and there was no making port, though we were just outside.

There were others in the same plight under the warm summer sky of that evening: a London barge, a Norwegian ship with timber, and a little snorting steamer, which let go her anchor with a rush somewhat further out just at the moment when we also dropped anchor in that very shallow water, in not five fathoms deep. A great full moon rose up out of the east, out of the seas of England, and the night was warm. There was a sort of holiness about the air. I was even glad that we had thus to lie outside under such a calm and softly radiant sky, with its few stars paling before their queen.

HILAIRE BELLOC: *The Cruise of the Nona*

Spray Rainbow

The rainbow of the salt sand wave.

JOHN KEATS: *Ode on Melancholy* (vi)

The Young Neptune

Have ye beheld the young God of the Seas,
My dispossessor? Have ye seen his face?
Have ye beheld his chariot, foam'd along
By noble winged creatures he hath made?
I saw him on the calmed waters scud
With such a glow of beauty in his eyes,
That it enforc'd me to bid sad farewell
To all my empire. . . .

JOHN KEATS: *Hyperion*

49

St Alban's Race

Some years ago I was running down this coast with many companions – too many for so small a craft. All was with us: an excellent wind, bright sun, and a clear air. I warned my companions about this mischievous patch (which is also haunted), and I said we would go right outside and cheat it. So we put the bow a point or two off the course we were making, so as to get right out into the open and leave the exasperation by St Alban inshore in the place to which his bad temper belongs. But not a bit of it. Even as we were looking landward, and laughing to see the tumble of water between us and the cliff, which tumble we thought thus to have escaped, even as we thought we had passed it, *the thing ran at us.*

It came on in a long line of white, just like a lot of dogs running up to play. It was abominably conscious and alive. It had said: 'Here is a boat which thinks that, because it has gone outside, it can escape me,' so it galloped up in a rush, and swarmed all around us, and we were in for an hour of it before we got to the regular water beyond.

I know a man who so dislikes this patch of curse upon the sea that he boasts of passing it as of a feat, though, in truth, there is no feat in it at all, but only an annoyance. So much did he pride himself upon the passage of it once that, on coming into harbour, and being asked to write something in the visiting book of the inn, he put down his name, and the date, and this poem:

I made my passage through St Alban's race
And came to anchor in this bloody place.

The person who owned the inn was very angry on seeing this poem, and asked that it might be rubbed out. This man of whom I speak very humbly did, and substituted for the offensive couplet a long, long poem in the heroic style, all in rhyming decasyllabic couplets, and iambic at that, which poem is to be read there to this day.

You gentlemen of England – if gentlemen I may still call you – who travel about in mechanical ships as big as a street of houses, know nothing of these things.

HILAIRE BELLOC: The Cruise of the Nona

Tides

. . . there is no end to the mystery of the tides. Why is there a tide at Venice? It is not much of a thing, but it is there. And, for that matter, there is *a* tide in the lake of Geneva. Here, again, the learned come barging in and tell us all about it. Closed basins (they say) like the Adriatic, even quite small ones like the Lake of Geneva, have their little tides after the fashion of water swung in a basin. The explanation is given in some simile like this: 'If you shake a basin slightly, the water will begin to swing with a regular movement back and forth. So it will. But who shakes the Lake of Geneva? Or who catches the Adriatic at either end, and gives it a regular balance up and down, exactly so often, every so many hours?

All this questioning sounds like the Book of Job; but, note you, that I, for my part, am with Job, and against the scientists. For Job, or God, or whoever it was who set the catechism, put the questions and was careful to avoid the answers, and for my part I will do the same, not only in the matter of the tides, but for the whole basketful of things on which the scientists have been pontificating with increasing uppishness for the last 200 years, until at last they have led us to the morass wherein we are sinking. When they pontificate on tides it does no great harm, for the sailorman cares nothing for their theories, but goes by real knowledge, and I by my sworn authority, the Admiralty texts, the like of which for excellence the world has not: 'High water, full and change, six hours, thirteen minutes after Dover. The stream is barely perceptible in the first two hours of the flood, but runs very strongly in the third, and through three-quarters of the fourth hour; after which it slackens. There is no perceptible stream in the last two hours of the flood.' Or again: 'On rounding the Devil's Point the tide is lost.' There is no theorising, no mumbo-jumbo. The thing itself, reality, is stated; and it is true. There is not even a passing wonderment as to where the tide goes to when it is lost. The *Channel Pilot* tells you the truth. You stick blindly to its text and you are saved.

There are many parts of the sea where the tide goes round like a clock, and no-one can tell you why. Instead of the stream setting first east, let us say, with the flood and then west with the ebb, it goes all round the compass. It sets northwest with the beginning of the flood, then north, then northeast, then east, and so on. Looking all round about itself like a performing dog, and slowly and ceaselessly revolving. It behaves not like an eddy, but like spokes. It is perfectly incomprehensible.

There is also this about the tides, which we all know to be true, and which we can see at work any day, but which I defy any man to rationalize: when the tide runs up a narrow river – or, indeed, any river – it will be still running up, say, ten miles from the mouth, when it is running *down* again, say, five miles from the mouth. What happens in between? Slack water, of course. But *how* is there slack water? How can the running *down* be going on at one point, and, immediately beyond, the running *up*, without a division? How can the water go on running up from a reservoir below which it is running down? It does, and it is all God's providence, and I accept it as I do teeth, or any other oddity. But I will not pretend to explain it.

The sea teaches one the vastness and the number of things, and, therefore, the necessary presence of incalculable elements, perpetually defeating all our calculations. The sea, which teaches all wisdom, certainly does not teach any man to despise human reason. I suppose there was never yet any Kantian fool or worser pragmatist who would not have been cured of his folly by half a week of moderate weather off the Onion. No-one at sea can forego the human reason or doubt that things are things, or that true ideas are true. But the sea does teach one that the human reason, working from a number of known premises, must always be on its guard, lest the conclusion be upset in practice by the irruption of other premises, unknown or not considered. In plain words, the sea makes a man practical; and the practical man is, I suppose, as much the contrary of the pragmatist as the sociable man is the contrary of the socialist, or the peaceable man the contrary of the pacifist.

HILAIRE BELLOC: *Ibid.*

Sea Voices

. . . the sea is all about us;
The sea is the land's edge also, the granite
Into which it reaches, the beaches where it tosses
Its hints of earlier and other creation:
The starfish, the horseshoe crab, the whale's backbone;
The pools where it offers to our curiosity
The more delicate algae and the sea anemone.
It tosses up our losses, the torn seine,
The shattered lobster-pot, the broken oar
And the gear of foreign dead men. The sea has many
    voices,
Many gods and many voices.
           The salt is on the briar rose,
The fog is in the fir trees.
           The sea howl
And the sea yelp, are different voices
Often together heard: the whine in the rigging,
The menace and caress of wave that breaks on water,
The distant rote in the granite teeth,
And the wailing warning from the approaching headland
Are all sea voices, and the heaving groaner

Rounded homewards, and the seagull:
And under the oppression of the silent fog
The tolling bell
Measures not our time, rung by the unhurried
Ground swell, a time
Older than the time of chronometers, older
Than time counted by anxious worried women
Lying awake, calculating the future,
Trying to unweave, unwind, unravel
And piece together the past and the future,
Between midnight and dawn, when the past is all
    deception,
The future futureless, before the morning watch
When time stops and time is never ending;
And the ground swell, that is and was from the beginning,
Clangs
The bell.

                T. S. ELIOT: *The Dry Salvages*

Dover Beach

The sea is calm to-night.
The tide is full, the moon lies fair
Upon the straits; on the French coast the light
Gleams and is gone; the cliffs of England stand
Glimmering and vast, out in the tranquil bay.
Come to the window, sweet is the night air!
Only, from the long line of spray
Where the sea meets the moon-blanch'd land,
Listen! you hear the grating roar
Of pebbles which the waves draw back, and fling,
At their return, up the high strand,
Begin, and cease, and then again begin,
With tremulous cadence slow, and bring
The eternal note of sadness in.

Sophocles long ago
Heard it on the Aegean, and it brought
Into his mind the turbid ebb and flow
Of human misery; we
Find also in the sound a thought,
Hearing it by this distant northern sea.
  The sea of faith
Was once, too, at the full, and round earth's shore
Lay like the folds of a bright girdle furl'd.
But now I only hear
Its melancholy, long, withdrawing roar,
Retreating to the breath
Of the night-wind down the vast edges drear
And naked shingles of the world.

MATTHEW ARNOLD: *Dover Beach*

The Enemy

As to the sea, it has no human attributes whatever, though it will absorb anything the poet will give it. It is as alien as the stars, which are bright over lovers, but were just as friendly to Scott's little party when the blizzard stopped. We may feel what we like when we witness, from a ship off Sumatra, a tropical sunset. But the spectacle of the billows of the unlighted Western ocean, in a winter twilight, is enough to make a man feel that he ought to have a religion, yet that is only a confession of man's wondering and questioning mind. There is more pertaining to man in a kitchen midden than in the spacious ocean when it most attracts us. Man, fronting the sea, the sea which is, inexplicably, both hostile and friendly to him because it knows nothing of his existence and his noble aims, is saddened, and is driven to meet its impersonal indifference with fine phrases, that his sense of his worth and his dignity

may be rehabilitated. He knows that it is absurd to pretend to
any love for the sea.

H. M. TOMLINSON: *Gifts of Fortune*

Ocean's Nursling

Underneath Day's azure eyes
Ocean's nursling, Venice lies,
A peopled labyrinth of walls,
Amphitrite's destined halls,
Which her hoary sire now paves
With his blue and beaming waves.
Lo! the sun upsprings behind,
Broad, red, radiant, half-reclined
On the level quivering line
Of the waters crystalline;
And before that chasm of light,
As within a furnace bright,
Column, tower, and dome, and spire
Shine like obelisks of fire,
Pointing with inconstant motion
From the altar of dark ocean
To the sapphire-tinted skies.

P. B. SHELLEY: *Lines Written Among the Euganean Hills*

Winter Calm

. . . the sharp stars pierce Winter's crystal air
And gaze upon themselves within the sea.

P. B. SHELLEY: *Prometheus Unbound*

The Chesil Bank

There is no harbour on the curved sweep of this bank of shingle for many miles in either direction. The line of the beach in the north curves so imperceptibly that to the eye it looks straight; towards the southern end it sweeps round like the blade of a sickle, and is as sharp in the run. The five-fathom mark is close inshore, so the first line of breakers is direct upon the shingle. The usual weather, of course, is westerly, nearly always south of west. And in that direction I suppose the next land would be the Bahamas, but I have only local maps, and can lay no exact course to what landfall is in the eye of the wind. Anyhow, there is so much ocean between us and the next land that the waves come in, with any seaward breeze, in regular and massed attacks. They growl as they charge. In summer weather like this it is a cheerful noise, for they are only playing roughly. Then they break and make the shingle fly, with a roar, and a myriad little stones, as a wave draws back, follow it with thin cries.

Both the sea and the coast look bare and barren. Terns in couples patrol up and down, and so close to me that I can see their black caps. Occasionally one will dive – two seconds under water – and it comes up with something which glitters for an instant. On the ridge of the shingle bank a little vegetation is recumbent, forming close mats and cushions, with sere stalks that quiver in the wind as though apprehensive of their footing. The sea appears even more infertile than the desert of stones. You feel that you and your book, and the terns which now and then find something which glitters, are all the intruding life there is. But some distance away there are a few boats drawn up high and dry; they make good shelters to leeward of sun and wind, and they have a strong but pleasing smell. And at odd times, usually towards evening, a crew of six men will come along to get out one of the boats. She is launched down the slope on wooden rollers, in short runs. Half the crew go in her, and one of them throws a seine net

steadily over-side. The other fellows take charge of the shore
end of the seine. The boat goes round a considerable bight,
and then lands the other end of the net. If you imagine that
hauling that net and its floats, when any tide is running, is
nothing but fun, the men will not object if you put on your
weight. . . . The feet crunch and slip steadily, while the floats
of the net seem to bob no nearer the shore. The weight comes
with a rush just about when you feel it is better to read books
than to handle seine nets. There is a heaving and a slapping on
the stones. To most of us, of course, fish is fish. There is only
fish. Yet one haul of the net is almost sure to bring in forms
that are fishes certainly, but which demand to be named.
They are so challenging that they stick in the memory, and must
be exorcised with names, as we resolve, by putting names to
them, all the mysteries that trouble us.

H. M. TOMLINSON: *Gifts of Fortune*

A Desolate Shore

I rode one evening with Count Maddalo
Upon the bank of land which breaks the flow
Of Adria towards Venice: a bare strand
Of hillocks, heaped from ever-shifting sand,
Matted with thistles and amphibious weeds
Such as from earth's embrace the salt ooze breeds,
Is this; an uninhabited sea-side,
Which the lone fisher, when his nets are dried,
Abandons; and no other object breaks
The waste, but one dwarf tree and some few stakes
Broken and unrepaired, and the tide makes
A narrow space of level sand thereon,
Where 'twas our wont to ride while day went down.
This ride was my delight. I love all waste
And solitary places; where we taste

The pleasure of believing what we see
Is boundless, as we wish our souls to be.
And such was this wide ocean, and this shore
More barren than its billows; and yet more
Than all, with a remembered friend I love
To ride as then I rode; – for the winds drove
The living spray along the sunny air
Into our faces; the blue heavens were bare,
Stripped to their depths by the awakening north;
And, from the waves, sound like delight broke forth
Harmonising with solitude, and sent
Into our hearts aerial merriment.
So, as we rode, we talked. . . .

P. B. SHELLEY: *Julian and Maddalo*

On a Picture of Peele Castle in a Storm
Painted by Sir George Beaumont

I was thy neighbour once, thou rugged pile!
Four summer weeks I dwelt in sight of thee,
I saw thee every day, and all the while
Thy Form was sleeping on a glassy sea.

So pure the sky, so quiet was the air!
So like, so very like, was day to day!
Whene'er I looked, thy Image still was there,
It trembled, but it never passed away.

How perfect was the calm! it seemed no sleep;
No mood, which season takes away, or brings;
I could have fancied that the mighty Deep
Was even the gentlest of all gentle things.

59

Ah! then, if mine had been the painter's hand,
To express what then I saw, and add the gleam,
The light that never was, on sea or land,
The consecration, and the poet's dream,

I would have planted thee, thou hoary Pile
Amid a world how different from this!
Beside a sea that could not cease to smile,
On tranquil land, beneath a sky of bliss. . . .

So once it would have been – 'tis so no more;
I have submitted to a new control:
A power is gone, which nothing can restore;
A deep distress hath humanised my soul.

Not for a moment could I now behold
A smiling sea, and be what I have been;
The feeling of my loss will ne'er be old;
This, which I know, I speak with mind serene.

Then, Beaumont, Friend! who would have been
            the Friend,
If he had lived, of Him whom I deplore,
This work of thine I blame not, but commend:
This sea in anger, and that dismal shore.

O 'tis a passionate work! – yet wise and well,
Well chosen is the spirit that is here;
That Hulk which labours in the deadly swell,
This rueful sky, this pageantry of fear.

Farewell, farewell, the heart that lives alone,
Housed in a dream, at distance from the Kind!
Such happiness, wherever it be known,
Is to be pitied, for 'tis surely blind.

But welcome fortitude, and patient cheer,
And frequent sights of what is to be borne!
Such sights, or worse, as are before me here –
Not without hope we suffer and we mourn.

WILLIAM WORDSWORTH (vii)

Bermudas

Where the remote Bermudas ride
In the ocean's bosom unespied,
From a small boat that rowed along
The listening winds received this song:

'What shall we do but sing His praise,
That led us through the watery maze,
Unto an isle so long unknown,
And yet far kinder than our own?
Where He the huge sea-monsters wracks,
That lift the deep upon their backs,
He lands us on a grassy stage,
Safe from the storms, and prelate's rage;
He gave us this eternal spring
Which here enamels everything,
And sends the fowls to us in care
On daily visits through the air;
He hangs in shades the orange bright
Like golden lamps in a green night,
And does in the pomegranates close
Jewels more rich than Ormus shows;
He makes the figs our mouths to meet,
And throws the melons at our feet;
But apples plants of such a price
No tree could ever bear them twice;
With cedars chosen by His hand,
From Lebanon He stores the land,

And makes the hollow seas, that roar,
Proclaim the ambergris on shore;
He cast (of which we rather boast)
The Gospel's pearl upon our coast,
And in these rocks for us did frame
A temple where to sound his name.
Oh! let our voice His praise exalt,
Till it arrive at Heaven's vault,
Which thence (perhaps) rebounding may
Echo beyond the Mexique Bay.'

Thus sang they, in the English boat,
An holy and a cheerful note;
And all the way, to guide their chime,
With falling oars they kept the time.

ANDREW MARVELL

Shakespeare's Cliff

How fearful
And dizzy 'tis to cast one's eyes so low!
The crows and choughs that wing the midway air
Show scarce so gross as beetles; half way down
Hangs one that gathers samphire, dreadful trade!
Methinks he seems no bigger than his head;
The fishermen, that walk upon the beach,
Appear like mice, and yond tall anchoring bark
Diminished to her cock; her cock, a buoy
Almost too small for sight. The murmuring surge
That on the unnumbered idle pebbles chafes
Cannot be heard so high. I'll look no more;
Lest my brain turn, and the deficient sight
Topple down headlong.

WILLIAM SHAKESPEARE: *King Lear* (viii)

Image of Eternity

Thou glorious mirror, where the Almighty form
Glasses itself in tempests; in all time,
Calm or convulsed – in breeze, or gale, or storm,
Icing the pole, or in the torrid clime
Dark-heaving; – boundless, endless and sublime –
The image of Eternity – the throne
Of the Invisible; even from out thy slime
The monsters of the deep are made; each zone
Obeys thee; thou goest forth, dread, fathomless, alone.

LORD BYRON: *Childe Harold's Pilgrimage*

On his Poem, The Faerie Queene

Like as a ship, that through the Ocean wyde
   Directs her course unto one certaine coast,
   Is met of many a counter winde and tyde,
   With which her winged speed is let and crost,
   And she herself in stormie surges tost;
   Yet making many a borde, and many a bay,
   Still winneth way, ne hath her compasse lost:
   Right so it fares with me in this long way,
Whose course is often stayd, yet never is astray.

EDMUND SPENSER: *The Faerie Queene*

The Aldeburgh Oyster-Dredger

(i)   Nor angler we on our wide stream descry,
          But one poor dredger where his oysters lie:
          He, cold and wet, and driving with the tide,
          Beats his weak arms against his tarry side,
          Then drains the remnant of diluted gin

To aid the warmth that languishes within;
Renewing oft his poor attempts to beat
His tingling fingers into gathering heat.

The Suffolk Sea

(ii)   Be it the summer noon: a sandy space
The ebbing tide has left upon its place;
Then just the hot and stony beach above
Light twinkling streams in bright confusion move –
(For heated thus the warmer air ascends,
And with the cooler in its fall contends) –
Then the broad bosom of the ocean keeps
An equal motion; swelling as it sleeps,
Then slowly sinking; curling to the strand,
Faint, lazy waves o'er creep the ridgy sand,
Or tap the tarry boat with gentle blow,
And back return in silence, smooth and slow.
Ships in the calm seem anchored; for they glide
On the still sea, urged solely by the tide. . . .
    View now the winter storm! above, one cloud,
Black and unbroken, all the skies o'ershroud;
The unwieldy porpoise through the day before
Had roll'd in view of boding men on shore,
And sometimes hid, and sometimes show'd, his form,
Dark as the cloud and furious as the storm.
    All where the eye delights yet dreads to roam,
The breaking billows cast the flying foam
Upon the billows rising – all the deep
Is restless change; the waves so swell'd and steep,
Breaking and sinking, and the sunken swells,
Nor one, one moment, in its station dwells:
But nearer land you may the billows trace
As if contending in their watery chase;
May watch the mightiest till the shoal they reach,

Then break and hurry to their utmost stretch;
Curl'd as they come, they strike with furious force,
And then re-flowing take their grating course,
Raking the rounded flints, which ages past
Roll'd by their rage, and shall to ages last.
High o'er the restless deep, above the reach
Of gunner's hope, vast flights of wild-duck stretch;
Far as the eye can glance on either side
In a broad space and level line they glide;
All in their wedge-like figures from the north,
Day after day, flight after flight, go forth.
In-shore their passage tribes of seagulls urge,
And drop for prey within the sweeping surge;
Oft in the rough opposing blast they fly
Far back, then turn, and all their force apply,
While to the storm they give their weak complaining
    cry.
Darkness begins to reign; the louder wind
Appals the weak and awes the firmer mind;
But frights not him, whom evening and the spray
In part conceal – yon Prowler on his way:
Lo! he has something seen; he runs apace,
As if he fear'd companion in the chase;
He sees his prize, and now he turns again,
Slowly and sorrowing – 'Was your search in vain?'
Gruffly he answers, ''Tis a sorry sight!
A seaman's body – there'll be more to-night.'

GEORGE CRABBE: The Borough

Never More, Sailor

Never more, sailor,
Shalt thou be
Tossed on the wind-ridden
Restless sea.

Its tides may labour;
All the world
Shake 'neath that weight
Of waters hurled:
But its whole shock
Can only stir
Thy dust to a quiet
Even quieter.
Thou mock'st at land
Who now art come
To such a small
And shallow home;
Yet bore the sea
Full many a care
For bones that once
A sailor's were.
And though the grave's
Deep soundlessness
Thy once sea-deafened
Ear distress,
No robin ever
On the deep
Hopped with his song
To haunt thy sleep.

WALTER DE LA MARE: *Never More, Sailor*

Sun and Wind

(i)   O divine sky, O swift-winged breezes,
        O laughter of innumerable waves. . . .

AESCHYLUS: *Prometheus Bound*

(ii)　　　　　. . . the Sunny beames do glaunce and glide
　　　　　　　Upon the trembling wave.

EDMUND SPENSER: *The Faerie Queene*

Breeze on Calm Water

The first sign of the approach of a breeze across calm water is
a curious thing to watch. Homer observed it three thousand
years ago, and wrote of the shudder on the dark seas when the
wind was on them. Whether there is wind or not one can
always watch the approach of a stronger puff by the darkening
of the water to windward, and indeed in open boat sailing to
do so diligently is an important part of the helmsman's task.
But in a flat calm, as it was at the moment of which I am writing,
the coming of the first air presents a somewhat different
appearance.

I did not at first see the shudder on the sea of which Homer
wrote (I expect he was thinking of those stronger puffs on
already wind-ruffled water); but far away to the left and ahead
of us the smooth, shimmering, opaline surface of the swell
was cut and broken by a straight, dark line, the edge of which
looked almost as solid as land. For some minutes it did not
seem to move or to come any nearer to us; but soon there was
another darkening of the water, this time close on our left
hand, and appearing from its proximity to us not as a line, but
as a patch of irregular shape, clearly defined, the rest of the sea
around it being still as smooth as oil. Still our sails hung limp
and slatted as we rolled, though the wind was so near – until
suddenly it was upon us, and in an instant the whole sea, as
far as eye could reach, was stirred into life again, dark and
dancing under this new awakening breath. Our sails were all
taken aback; for the wind was from a different quarter, and
had chopped round to the south-west. We trimmed the sheets,
and Bob took the tiller, which no longer aimlessly and resent-

67

fully kicked and jerked, but kept a steady pressure against the hand. *Tessa* heeled, the weather rigging creaked as it took the strain, and once again the water under our lee went whispering by, and astern of us was whitened. It was like awakening from a dream.

AUBREY DE SELINCOURT: *A Capful of Wind*

Mediterranean Moonlight

This quicksilver no gnome has drunk: within
The walnut bowl it lies, veined and thin,
In colour like the wake of light that stains
The Tuscan deep, when from the moist moon rains
The inmost shower of its white fire – the breeze
Is still – blue Heaven smiles over the pale seas.

P. B. SHELLEY: *Letter to Maria Gisborne*

West Wind

Thou who didst waken from his summer dreams
The blue Mediterranean, where he lay
Lulled by the coil of his crystalline streams,

Beside a pumice-isle in Baiae's bay,
And saw in sleep old palaces and towers
Quivering within the wave's intenser day,

All overgrown with azure moss, and flowers
So sweet, the sense faints picturing them! Thou
For whose path the Atlantic's level powers

Cleave themselves into chasms, while far below
The sea-blooms and the oozy woods which wear
The sapless foliage of the ocean, know

Thy voice and suddenly grow grey with fear,
And tremble and despoil themselves. . . .

P. B. SHELLEY: Ode to the West Wind

Portland Bill

Like thousands of others I have stood on the flat rock at the
extreme end of the Bill, only a foot or two above the level of
the sea, and looked not without wonder at the small waves
lapping its base in all the gentleness of summer, and the tide
sliding past without ripple or murmur. In the shimmering heat
and windless air it looked a place for summer-sleepy nereids:
why, I could have dived off that rock and swum in that
innocent-looking sea as safely as if I had been in my own
Puckaster Cove in the Isle of Wight. Yet it was odd to see it
so, in such weather, at such a time and as a visitor from the
land. It upset my relationship with the place and gave it the
queer topsy-turveydom of a dream. I no longer seemed to
know it.

My real knowledge of Portland, like that of all men who
sail their boats up and down the Channel, is of a place to shun.
If there is any wind, I like to pass it six – or ten – miles to
the southward, or out of sight; for the sea in the neighbourhood
of Portland is by far the most dangerous area for small vessels
on the Channel shore.

The notorious race, the most turbulent on the South Coast,
is to be found about half a mile off the Bill, a little to the
Eastward on the flood tide, a little to the Westward on the
ebb. It extends seaward sometimes for two miles, sometimes
for as much as four, and disturbed water and irregular seas

are often to be met much further off than that. Various causes contribute to this evil thing. The narrowing of the Channel between the two opposed promontories of Portland and the Cotentin on the French coast accelerates the normal tidal stream; secondly, the under-sea continuation of the Portland rock in a south-south-westerly direction obstructs the flow. Nearly all rocky headlands have a submarine extension of greater or lesser magnitude – like the Bridge reef, for example, off the Needles; but that at Portland is much more pronounced than elsewhere. A glance at the chart will show that the soundings off the Bill suddenly decrease in an east-west line from twelve and fifteen and seventeen fathoms to seven, six and five, and as suddenly increase again. This means in effect that there is on the sea bottom a steep wall of rock some thirty, or possibly in some places, even sixty feet high, over which the tide must pour. Now when it is realised that the tide sweeps past at six knots and more at springs, it is not surprising that the disturbance on the surface, even in calm weather, is tremendous. Thirdly, the inshore tidal stream, following the curve of the coast, runs very hard directly to the southward along the whole length of the peninsula, then, passing the Bill, shoots seaward and meets the rush of the main stream at right angles, thus adding a powerful contributory cause to the confusion.

The result of these three things – the swiftness of the main tidal stream, its sudden and violent upward deflection by the underwater wall of rock, and its junction at right angles with the secondary stream – is a disturbance of the water which even during neap tides and in calm weather is dangerous to small boats, and during spring tides in rough weather very dangerous indeed even to steamships of a thousand tons. As I have pointed out before, mere waves are not in themselves dangerous at all, even to the smallest boats; one could ride in a bath-tub over a thirty-foot wave with the utmost comfort and convenience – provided that the wave did not break. In a heavy sea when the waves do break, there is, to be sure, great danger, but it can be faced by a well-found small vessel, if proper precautions are taken, because the waves, whether they break or not, march in a more of less orderly procession. But in a severe tide-race this is not so; here the waves are not orderly – they run amok. The sea is like a pot on the boil. A crested wave will run at you from any direction. Waves fold one upon another; they shoot up in perpendicular ridges which collide and burst, or leap into pinnacles which collapse upon themselves in a smother of foam. Any but a large craft in such conditions must be swamped or dismasted, or at the least so severely strained as to be past repair. That, of course, is Portland race at its worst: at spring tides and in hard weather. But even at its mildest it is a fearsome place. Claude Worth, one of the most distinguished of recent yachtsmen, sailed through it deliberately on one occasion – in fine weather, at neap tides, in a yacht of thirty tons. Never, he wrote, would he repeat the experiment. Admiral Muir in his book *Messing about in Boats* records a passage through the race in a vessel of similar size. One incident in the vivid description of his experience I particularly remember: a wave ran at him broad on the beam, flung the vessel over, broke into the mainsail and poured itself *over the gaff.* The yacht was got safely into Portland, and one of the coastguards, who had seen her in the broken water, remarked to the Admiral that it was lucky for him the race was so quiet that day, or he would never have come through alive.

I need hardly say that I have never seen Portland race at its worst; few have; but like many another yachtsman I have seen it often enough at close quarters in fine weather. For there is, at certain periods of the tide, a narrow belt, not more than a quarter of a mile wide, of quiet water between the race and the Bill through which, with due precaution, one can pass in safety and watch, not without a certain shortening of the breath, the horrid turmoil so close at hand.

AUBREY DE SELINCOURT: *The Channel Shore*

Two Glimpses

(i)   Asleep are the mountain peaks and chasms,
           Asleep the promontories and the hill-streams,
           All creeping things the back earth nourishes,
           The wild creatures of the mountains, the bees,
           And the monsters in the depths of the dark sea.
           Asleep are the tribes of long-winged birds. . . .

(ii)

Tell them – the girls with honey-sweet voices that speak of
love – that I am old, and my limbs no longer bear me up.
Would I were a gull, flying careless with the halcyons over the
blossom of the wave, the sea-purple bird of spring.

ALCMAN (about 650 B.C.)

Philoctetes' Farewell to Lemnos

My rock-hewn dwelling, sharer
Of my waking and watching through the nights;
Nymphs of meadow and stream,
Thunder of surf irresistible
Whose spume on many a day
Of southerly gales has drenched my head
However I might cower for shelter;
Hermes' hill, which ever and again
Echoed my cries when the storms beat upon me;
I leave you now. And you, fresh runnels
Of Apollo's stream, take the farewell
I never thought to bid you.
Farewell, my sea-girt island,
And send me fair winds for my sailing
Thither, where I must go.

SOPHOCLES: *Philoctetes*

To Sleep

Canst thou upon the high and giddy mast
Seal up the shipboy's eyes and rock his brains
In cradle of the rude, imperious surge. . . .

WILLIAM SHAKESPEARE: Henry IV. 2

Sunbows

Friend, were life no more than this is, well would yet the living
  fare.
All aflower and all afire and all flung heavenward, who shall
  say
Such a flash of life were worthless? This is worth a world of
  care –
Light that leaps and runs and revels through the springing
  flames of spray.

A. C. SWINBURNE: The Sunbows

The Rowboat

So forth they rowed, and that Ferryman
With his stiff oares did brush the sea so strong,
That the hoare waters from his frigot ran,
And the light bubbles daunced all along.

EDMUND SPENSER: The Faerie Queene

73

A Swimmer

I saw him beat the surges under him
And ride upon their backs; he trod the water,
Whose enmity he flung aside, and breasted
The surge most swoln that met him; his bold head
'Bove the contentious waves he kept, and oared
Himself with his good arms in lusty stroke
To th' shore, that o'er his wave-worn basis bowed,
As stooping to relieve him.

WILLIAM SHAKESPEARE: *The Tempest*

In the Salt Marshes

Tall the plumage of the rush-flower tosses,
    Sharp and soft in many a curve and line
Gleam and glow the sea-coloured marsh-mosses,
    Salt and splendid from the circling brine.
Streak on streak of glimmering sea-shine crosses
    All the land sea-saturate as with wine.

A. C. SWINBURNE: *In the Salt Marshes*

Breakers

(i)   With that the rolling sea resounding soft,
    In his big bass them fitly answered,
    And on the rocke the waves, breaking aloft,
    A solemne Meane unto them measured.

EDMUND SPENSER: *The Faerie Queene*

(ii)   . . . Roared as when the roaring breakers boom
            and blanch on the precipices. . . .

ALFRED LORD TENNYSON: *Boadicea*

The Quicksands of Unthriftihood

They passing by, a goodly Ship did see,
  Laden from far with precious merchandise,
  And bravely furnished, as ship might bee,
  Which through great disaventure or mesprize
  Her selfe had runne into that hazardize;
  Whose mariners and merchants with much toyle
  Labour'd in vaine to have recur'd their prize,
  And the rich wares to save from pitteous spoyle;
But neither toyle nor travell might her backe recoyle.

EDMUND SPENSER: *The Faerie Queene*

Fair Weather

Milk Sea

It was a lovely night, with scarcely any wind, the stars trying to make up for the absence of the moon by shining with intense brightness. The water had been more phosphorescent than usual, so that every little fish left a track of light behind him, greatly disproportionate to his size. As the night wore on, the sea grew brighter and brighter, until by midnight we appeared to be sailing on an ocean of lambent flames. Every little wave that broke against the ship's side sent up a shower of diamond-like spray, wonderfully beautiful to see, while a passing school of porpoises fairly set the sea blazing as they leapt and gambolled in its glowing waters. Looking up from sea to sky, the latter seemed quite black instead of blue, and the lustre of the stars was diminished till they only looked like points of polished steel, having quite lost for a time their radiant sparkle. In that shining flood the blackness of the ship stood out in startling contrast, and when we looked over the side our faces were strangely lit up by the brilliant glow.

For several hours this beautiful appearance persisted; fading away at last as gradually as it came. No satisfactory explanation of this curious phenomenon has ever been given, nor does it appear to portend any change of weather. It cannot be called a rare occurrence, although I have only seen it thrice myself – once in the bay of Cavite in the Philippine Islands; once in the Pacific, near the Solomon Islands; and on this occasion of which I now write. But no-one who has ever witnessed it could forget so wonderful a sight.

FRANK T. BULLEN: *The Cruise of the Cachalot*

Coral at Nukualofa

Naturally the coral does not grow so luxuriantly as in the open ocean, but one can see it safely at one's leisure as one drifts over it in a small boat on the glassy water.

That is an amazing sensation, and it is hard to realise that one is not suspended over a steep sandy cliff, crowned with a thicket of furze bushes. It is almost impossible to believe that these are not vegetable growths; I shall call them without apology by the names of the plants they resemble, it being understood always that everything is coral, and, moreover, in the way of colour would eclipse our most fiery autumn hill-side.

At the bottom of the steep slope of sand, where the blue of deep water changes to green, are tall clumps of broom; they are growing on fragments of solid rock which have fallen down from the overhanging verge of the cliff, and in the still water throw out their long, straight, slender spikes, dotted with crimson flowers, to a far greater distance than those nearer the surface. As the ground rises rapidly under us the growths become more bushy and stand closer together, and the brilliancy of their colours is no longer modified by the medium, now colourless, through which they are seen. Then all at once the cliff is hidden by the fringe of what might be furze, but each branch is tipped with blue instead of with gold. How far the solid rock is below us we cannot tell; nothing can be seen through the dense tangle. Here the tops of the plants are neatly levelled off; that patch of bright green, like a big club-moss, shows stalks all of the same length; the creeping juniper sends no errant twigs above the line of low water. But here and there are depressions in the close-cropped bank, where grow the pale leaves of a monstrous bog-violet, a saucer-shaped fungus, brown and purple, or the white hemispheres of mushrooms.

But not a tithe of the colour that delights us is in the coral or in anything of jelly, sessile or crawling. Brighter than any butterfly, flashing more changeably than any humming-bird, are the little burnished fishes that hover over and dart between the branches; some of gold, some of copper, some of emerald banded with deepest ultramarine, and some of the most marvellous blue that exists in the world, and all with iridescent lights and waves of other colours playing over them as they swim. One can hardly allot a definite tint to anything about a living coral reef; the dullest browns and purples, which seem most prevalent, with a changing ray of the sun are shot with green and violet.

CONOR O BRIEN: Across Three Oceans

In the Bay of Lerici

I sat and saw the vessels glide
Over the ocean bright and wide,
Like spirit-winged chariots sent
O'er some serenest element
For ministrations strange and far;
As if to some Elysian star
They sailed for drink to medicine
Such sweet and bitter pain as mine.
And the wind that winged their flight
From the land came fresh and light;
And the scent of winged flowers
And the coolness of the hours
Of dew, and sweet warmth left by day,
Were scattered o'er the twinkling bay.
And the fisher, with his lamp
And spear, about the low rocks damp
Crept, and struck the fish which came
To worship the delusive flame.

P. B. SHELLEY: The Bay of Lerici

Caverns

Sand-strewn caverns, cool and deep
Where the winds are all asleep;
Where the spent lights quiver and gleam,
Where the salt weed sways in the stream. . . .

MATTHEW ARNOLD: The Forsaken Merman

On Calais Beach

It is a beauteous evening, calm and free;
   The holy time is quiet as a nun
Breathless with adoration; the broad sun
Is sinking down in its tranquillity;
The gentleness of heaven is on the sea:
   Listen! the mighty Being is awake,
   And doth with his eternal motion make
A sound like thunder – everlastingly.

WILLIAM WORDSWORTH

The Sea of Being

Hence in a season of calm weather
   Though inland far we be,
Our souls have sight of that immortal sea
   Which brought us hither,
   Can in a moment travel thither,
And see the children sport upon the shore,
And hear the mighty waters rolling evermore.

WILLIAM WORDSWORTH: Ode: Intimations of Immortality

Aeneas on the Tiber

So their friends cried 'God speed you,' and the voyage
    began,
The painted ships gliding away through the shallow stream.
The water wondered to see them, and the woods wondered
At a sight so new, the coloured hulls, the warriors' shields
Far flashing on the river.   Day and night they strained
At the oars, up reach after reach of the winding stream,
Shadowed by trees of varying kind, whose image green
In the unruffled water was cut by the hurrying keels.

VERGIL: the *Aeneid*

The Ayr was calm, and on the level brine
Sleek Panope and all her sisters play'd.

JOHN MILTON: *Lycidas*

The moving waters at their priest-like task
Of pure ablution round earth's human shores.

JOHN KEATS: from the sonnet *Bright Star*

Fine Morning

There came a morning of such cerulean perfection, the sea a
deep wrinkled blue and the sky cloudless but for a few pale
shadows on the horizon, that it was bliss to be alive and breathing it. We were astern of the Convoy, and because the leading
escort vessels were nearly hull-down, we had a pretty illusion
of seeing the convexity of the world, and the ships of the
convoy – painted a light grey, all in trim parallel lines, their
smoke neatly brushed behind their right shoulders – looked as
though they were steaming over the edge of it.

83

While we were admiring this handsome sight, there came a curious noise from somewhere above the bridge, and the men working there, painting and scrubbing, looked up in surprise. Alone, aloft, in simple happiness, the look-out in the crow's-nest was singing. There was rude laughter, and some-one shouted, 'Shut your mouth and keep your eyes open! You're looking for destroyers, aren't you?'

ERIC LINKLATER: *The Art of Adventure*

Moonlight

(i)   Still as a slave before his lord
       The Ocean hath no blast,
His great bright eye most silently
       Up to the moon is cast.

(ii)   The harbour bay was clear as glass,
       So smoothly it was strewn!
And on the bay the moonlight lay,
       And the shadow of the moon.

    The rock shone bright, the kirk no less
       That stands above the rock;
The moonlight steeped in silentness
       The steady weathercock.

S. T. COLERIDGE: *The Ancient Mariner*

(iii)   Splendet tremulo sub lumine pontus.

VERGIL: the *Aeneid*

The Nib-Driver Becalmed

The sea that bounds South England has as many moods as any sea in the world, and one of its moods is that of calm vision like St Monica by the window at prayer.

When the Sea of South England is in this mood, it is very hard upon sailing men; especially if they have no horrible motor on board. For in this mood there is no wind upon the sea; all lies asleep.

The sea was in such a mood two or three years ago, when this writing fellow, Mr Jonah, sat in his little boat cursing the saintly calm of the great waters. It was hot; it was about five o'clock in the afternoon; and save for the drift of the tide he had not made as many miles since noon as he had passed hours. Now and then a little cat's paw would just dimple the silky water and then die out again. The big lugsail which was her only canvas (for such breath as there was came aft, and it was no use setting the jib) hung like despair in the soul of evil men grown old. To the North, in the haze, and fairly close by, was England; that famous island. But in the way of a port or shelter, or place to leave the boat till the next free day (and writers never have much spare time for sailing), there was none for many miles.

He had hoped to get into a river mouth of his acquaintance before evening: that hope he must now abandon. It was necessary for him to return to his disgusting labours with the pen, and he was anxious what he should do. With him was a younger companion; and when it was clear that things were hopeless, when the blazing sun had set in a sea of glass, and the long evening had begun, the unfortunate pedlar of prose and verse and rhetoric and tosh saw that there was nothing for it but to take to the oars. Before doing this he looked along the haze of the land through his binoculars and spotted a Coastguard Station. There he thought he would leave the craft for the night. His boat (it was the second and smaller of his fleet) was not too big to be hauled up above high-water mark, and there seemed no prospect of bad weather. He could return to push her off again in a few days.

They bent to the oars, and before darkness had quite fallen the keel had gently slid upon fine sand, and these two men, the nib driver and his younger companion, waded ashore with the warping rope, and on the end of it they bent a little kedge to hold her, for the tide had turned and the flood had begun.

HILAIRE BELLOC: Short Talks With the Dead (ix)

The Enchanted Isle

A ship is floating in the harbour now,
A wind is hovering o'er the mountain's brow;
There is a path on the sea's azure floor –
No keel has ever ploughed that path before;
The halcyons brood around the foamless isles;
The treacherous Ocean has forsworn its wiles;
The merry mariners are bold and free:
Say, my heart's sister, wilt thou sail with me?
Our bark is as an albatross, whose nest
Is a far Eden of the purple east;
And we between her wings will sit, while Night,
And Day, and Storm, and Calm pursue their flight,
Our ministers, along the boundless sea,
Treading each others' heels, unheededly.
It is an isle under Ionian skies,
Beautiful as a wreck of Paradise,
And, for the harbours are not safe and good,
This land would have remained a solitude
But for some pastoral people native there,
Who from the Elysian, clear, and golden air
Draw the last spirit of the age of gold –
Simple and spirited, innocent and bold.
The blue Aegean girds this chosen home,

With ever-changing sound and light and foam
Kissing the sifted sands, and caverns hoar;
And all the winds wandering along the shore
Undulate with the undulating tide:
There are thick woods where sylvan forms abide;
And many a fountain, rivulet and pond,
As clear as elemental diamond
Or serene morning air.

P. B. SHELLEY: Epipsychidion

Foul Weather

Orion's Passage from Dartmouth to the Solent

The barometer, after being stationary for an hour, persisted in rising again after nightfall, though the weather, when I went below to tea at 8 p.m., looked horribly bad. The moon, seen through a greasy cloud, was sufficient warning by itself. At 8.30 Slade called out that he should be glad if I would go on deck, as it was becoming serious. I knew it by the roar and the motion, but wishing to make sure of a meal while it was possible, I delayed for another half hour; by which time the barometer had discovered its mistake and had taken a sudden turn downwards, and the gale had set in.

Though it seemed a very hazardous proceeding to bring the vessel to the wind under such a press of sail, we were obliged to watch for an opportunity and do it, being too short-handed to reef before the wind. 9.45 p.m. bore up again on the course with three reefs down, then shifted third jib for storm and stowed the former, wringing wet and stiff as pasteboard, on the cabin floor. 10 p.m. passed a barque lying-to. 10.30 p.m. lowered throat and trussed mainsail.

The wind shifting for a time to S.S.W. sent up a troublesome cross sea, that washed the deck pretty freely, extinguishing the binnacle lantern three times before the precaution was taken of protecting it with canvas. At the same time the great sea was so threatening on the quarter that we had to run off dead before it every few minutes, and make an average by luffing to windward when it was safe to do so. The running to leeward became at length such a frequent necessity, that if persevered in, there was a chance of being embayed near Portland. Consequently shortly after midnight, as it was very dark and thick with rain, and the gale was then very heavy, we watched for a chance and hove-to, with foresail to windward, not daring to run any longer.

The Portland Lights, bearing E. about 11 miles, were visible from the top of the sea. The play of the boom was so violent that the weather topping-lift parted immediately after coming to the wind. As the parting of the other would probably have caused great damage, it was necessary to take the mainsail off her without delay. We had been wishing it off her before, but were afraid to tackle a job of such difficulty until compelled to do it. Having lashed a cork fender to the lee rail, we got the boom down upon it inch by inch, and secured it with tackles and powerful lashings, then lowered and gathered in the sail. It was a long and heavy work for three hands in such a tremendous sea. When the mainsail was down the foresail was let draw, and she sailed herself to the southward with the helm lashed two points to leeward.

Notwithstanding the lee helm, which very frequently brought her up all shaking, I allowed two knots an hour gained to the southward. This was correct, as at 4 a.m. the Portland Lights bore N.E. At this time, being well to the southward of Portland and anxious to go ahead and get out of it, we managed to set the trysail, reefed, and put her on the course again – which, as before, was very irregular, every sea requiring to be watched, as well as it was possible to do so in the dark.

Judging from the last sight of the Portland Lights that they would be in one about 6 a.m. distant 9 miles, I altered the course at that hour to east and re-set the log. 8 a.m. log marked 15 knots. The land from St Alban's to the Durlston was visible, the latter bearing N.N.E. about 6 miles. Altered course to E. by N. The sea was enormous – at times grand, and at times very terrible, looking as if it would break over the mast-head. However, none came on board worth mentioning, except one small head, that didn't look where he was going, swamped me at the helm both inside and out, and broke down the canvas over the steerage. It was just a warning to rig the pump and to strengthen the steerage cover with battens underneath.

For hours I had been most uncomfortably nervous about the passage of the Needles Channel, which is a gradually shoaling bar of considerable extent connecting the Shingles Shoal and the Bridge Reef, and I thought about sailing round the Island to avoid the difficulty. This wretched feeling of anxiety died away considerably as the morning advanced, and I saw how safely we were borne on by some of the most alarming breakers. Several times, in the deep water, huge seas broke in our wake, and came rushing on in a mountain of foam. To those unacquainted with the power of the vessel destruction would have seemed inevitable, but owing to her powerful quarters and short elliptical stern, she rose steadily and regularly, and the seas passed harmlessly under her, excepting the little head before mentioned, which was heaped up high and thin by collision with our own wave, and was driven on deck by the wind.

Shortly after 8 a.m. the sky was tolerably clear, and the wind less violent; but the clouds, thick with rain, were banking up heavily again in the S.W. For a while there seemed reason to hope we should outstrip them and make the Bar before they dispensed their favours, but they came on at such a rattling pace that we were overtaken in less than an hour, and the gale raged more furiously than ever, driving clouds of spoon-drift before it, and forcing us through the water at 9 knots, with only the little reefed trysail drawing.

The steering was so hard that my left hand and arm were benumbed. I could use them as a log, feeling pressure at the shoulder, but could not feel the tiller. My mate was a first-class seaman, but his sight was not sharp enough to dodge the sea by night, nor to anticipate its course at any time; and the man who understands the vessel best, especially a small vessel, must be at the helm when a mistake or a little carelessness may cause all to be overwhelmed in a moment.

It was of such vital importance to cross in the best water that, as the dreaded time drew near, I would have given a good deal for a reassuring glimpse of the chart; but I recollected passing close to the buoy two years before, and fortunately

remembered the appearance of the Needles and Alum Bay
sufficiently well to run through the Channel on that mark, viz.
the N.W. side of the rocks and the long white cliff just coming
into view out of a right line.

9 a.m. passed close to the Nun-buoy of the S.W. Shingles
without seeing it. Though the man and the lad were keeping an
anxious look-out, it was not sighted until we were past, and on
the top of the next great sea beyond. It was not wanted, however, to show that we were in the Channel – the appearance of
the sea proved that, it being the only spot free from dangerous
breakers. While remarking this, we were picked up like a feather
and carried over the inner edge of the Bar into deeper water by
three or four enormous waves that towered up in walls of
water just short of breaking. After this the sea lost its dangerous
character.

The general scene, viewed from just outside the Bar, was
awfully grand and imposing. . . . From the Needles to a quarter
of a mile S.W., and thence across to Sun Corner, a space including all Scratchell Bay, was a confused mass of breakers, a
cauldron of raging surf from which arose a cloud of spray to
the height of about 150 feet, shrouding the weather side and
the upper part of the Needles Point and Rocks in a thick haze.
Thence, assuming the form of a well-defined stratum of cloud,
the spray travelled at a great rate up Alum Bay until it came to
the coloured cliff, a mile distant, over which it curved grace-
fully on to the land above. . . . .

I am too great a novice to accept safety as a matter of course.
The reaction upon my feelings after crossing the Bar was
greater than I care to express, or desire to experience again
if there be equal cause for it, however agreeable a successful
result may be. One feeling of unmixed satisfaction I had in the
knowledge that my vessel was equal to such an occasion.

R. T. MCMULLEN: *Down Channel* (x)

94

A Running Ship

And now the Storm-blast came, and he
Was tyrannous and strong:
He struck with his o'ertaking wings
And chased us south along.

With sloping masts and dipping prow,
As who pursued with yell and blow
Still treads the shadow of his foe
And forward bends his head,
The ship drove fast, loud roar'd the blast,
And Southward aye we fled.

S. T. COLERIDGE: *The Ancient Mariner*

Tern in the Great Gale of 1896

Tuesday, Sept 22. Brought up in south-west corner of Torbay, off a little sandy beach. Bower and forty fathoms chain. Blowing hard, so tied up third reef in case of a shift of wind.

Wednesday, Sept 23. Wind and rain in night, but slept securely knowing that I was prepared. Wind W., breezing up again harder than yesterday. Must be back by Monday, and cannot leave the ship anywhere, as I shall not be able to fetch her; so shall start this afternoon, so as to get to Needles in daylight tomorrow.

By the afternoon it was blowing a gale, W., and I felt like staying where I was until the weather improved, but time is short. So I read a few pages of 'Sirius' and hardened my heart.

Lit binnacle lamps and tied canvas round. Lit riding light and put it in well. Started with three reefs in mainsail, single reef in staysail, and spitfire jib, at about 6 p.m. Wind W., blowing hard, with rain. Determined to get well to southward while

I could, as if I found the sea very bad I might have to run her off before it very often. (This turned out to be fortunate.) Course S.E., therefore. As I drew away from the land I found the sea very heavy and as much wind as I wanted for my three reefs. Binnacle lamps went out, but I had the Start light and an occasional look at compass to guide me, as riding-light burned all right. About an hour after dark wind increased so much that she would not have any more, so watched my chance and hove her to on starboard tack and hauled down my fourth reef – very heavy work. Wind inclined to back. Stood away on course again, very often dead before it, but getting to southward when I could. Rain. No lights visible.

Thursday Sept 24. She dished up several small seas with her long low counter, but soon after midnight sea was so heavy and irregular that she was almost out of hand. While I was waiting for a chance to heave her to, a great sea came over the taffrail, completely burying the vessel. I was nearly taken overboard, and the cockpit was filled to the coamings. She broached-to, and I expected that the next sea would finish her. But luckily it only partly broke on board, and then there was a smooth during which I got in the slack of the mainsheet and all fast before she began to pay off again. Headsails were already aback, so I lashed helm a-lee, and she lay fairly quiet. Pumped ship. Had brandy, bread and a chop, and felt the better for it. About 3.30 a.m. crawled along deck and furled staysail. The steering and pumping had kept me warm, but now, sitting in the well – of course soaked to the skin – the cold wind seemed to blow clean through me.

Just as the first streaks of dawn began to appear, wind backed S.W., and blew harder than ever, and she would not lie any more, at one moment all shaking, next fell off and lay over, until I thought sometimes that the mast would go. Sea-anchor and warp were all ready, so led warp through hawsepipe, bent on drogue, and put it over. Tried to take in jib, but it flogged itself to rags as soon as I started the halyard. Let go throat halyard and got throat down, so that gaff was nearly up-and-down the mast. Got boom amidships. Slacked peak halyards, and sail flogged horribly. Paid out drogue warp as she gathered sternway, slacked topping-lifts and got boom on deck and mainsheet fast. Then gradually got sail off without accident. Slowly paid out the whole forty fathoms of warp.

After she was once fairly astream of her drogue she shipped no more heavy water. She stood first on one end, then on the other, but climbed each sea safely. The wind tore off the tops of the seas, and the spray came in sheets, everything white as far as one could see. Daylight; no land visible. At about 11 a.m. wind suddenly veered to W., and blew – I don't want to pile on superlatives, but I have been in a pampero off the Plate, and a heavy gale of wind in the South Pacific, and I have never known the wind so strong or the seas so steep and so near breaking. A large barque, the *Rose Ellen* of Wilmington, passed quite close, running up Channel under bare poles. Managed to change my clothes and to feed. About 2 p.m. wind moderated a little. By 6 p.m. blowing only a moderate gale, but still too much wind and sea for one to make sail single-handed.

Tried to fix riding-light to runner, but finally gave it up as it would not keep alight. About 9.30 p.m. lay down on cabin floor and slept until midnight.

Friday Sept 25. Less wind and sea now, but judged it best to ride to my drogue a few hours longer. Several times from the top of the sea caught sight of Portland lights bearing about N.N.E., distant perhaps ten miles. Glad to know approximately my position. At dawn blowing a hard breeze only, and less sea. Shook out close reef, hoisted treble-reefed mainsail, got drogue on board, hoisted reefed staysail, and away. Very difficult getting drogue aboard, as in hurry of getting it over I had omitted to bend tripping line. Nothing in sight. Course E ½ S., which I guessed would clear St Catherine's, as I did not fancy the Needles with the sea that was running.

After three or four hours sailing it suddenly cleared and showed me the Isle of Wight from the Needles to St Catherine's. Passed about two miles south of St Catherine's. Brought up in St Helen's Roads at about 3.30 p.m.

97

Very cold; lit coke stove. Had tea – pints of it – but could not eat. Turned in at about 6.30 and slept the clock round.

*   *   *

No-one who was interested in maritime affairs in 1896 is likely to forget this gale, and the enormous destruction which it wrought among shipping on our south and west coasts. I remember a whole page of *The Times* filled with accounts of wrecks and loss of life at sea. Large numbers of fishing vessels and coasters, and literally hundreds of lives were lost. Several of the Havre fishermen, in running for shelter, were lost with all hands in the broken water of the Estuary.

CLAUDE WORTH: Yacht Cruising (xi)

Squally Weather

These fierce flaws are beyond my knowledge. From all directions the seas run at us, and amongst the hurly-burly the black ship drives. How it blows! The water in the bilge is over the mast-step; not a sail but you can see daylight through it, and some are blown to rags. Each wave is worse than the last, and there'll be real trouble soon. The seams are opening – jump to it, now, and stop them if you can, and let's run for shelter. Come, lads, no shirking; you're on your mettle, all of you. Remember you've been in trouble before – so play the man now!

ALCAEUS (600 B.C.)

Bad-Weather Signs

Look, Glaucus, the sea is getting up already, and a pillar of cloud is standing on the heights of Gyrea – sure sign of a storm.

ARCHILOCHUS (650 B.C.)

98

He busied himself with his logbook, swaying easily to the
motion of the boat; and I for my part tried to write up my
diary, but I could not fix my attention. Every loose article
in the boat became audibly restless. Cans clinked, cupboards
rattled, lockers uttered hollow groans. Small things sidled
out of dark hiding-places, and danced grotesque drunken
figures on the floor, like goblins in a haunted glade. The mast
whined dolorously at every heel, and the centre-board hic-
coughed and choked. Overhead another horde of demons
seemed to have been let loose. The deck and mast were con-
ductors which magnified every sound and made the tap-tap
of every rope's end resemble the blows of a hammer, and the
slapping of the halliards against the mast the rattle of a Maxim
gun. The whole tumult beat time to a rhythmical chorus which
became maddening.

'We might turn in now,' said Davies; 'it's half past ten.'

'What, sleep through this!' I exclaimed. 'I can't stand this,
I must *do* something. Can't we go for another walk?'

I spoke in bitter, half-delirious jest.

'Of course we can,' said Davies, 'if you don't mind a bit of a
tumble in the dinghy.'

I reconsidered my rash suggestion, but it was too late now
to turn back, and some desperate expedient was necessary. I
found myself on deck, gripping a backstay and looking giddily
down and then up at the dinghy, as it bobbed like a cork in
the trough of the sea alongside, while Davies settled the
sculls and rowlocks.

'Jump,' he shouted, and before I could gather my wits and
clutch the sides we were adrift in the night, reeling from hollow to hollow of the steep curling waves. Davies nursed our
walnut-shell tenderly over their crests, edging her slantwise
across their course. He used very little exertion, relying on the
tide to carry us to our goal. Suddenly the motion ceased. A
dark slope loomed up out of the night, and the dinghy rested
softly in a shallow eddy.

'The West Hohenhörn,' said Davies. We jumped out and sank into soft mud, hauled up the dinghy a foot or two, then mounted the bank and were on hard wet sand. The wind leapt on us and choked our voices.

'Let's find my channel,' bawled Davies. 'This way. Keep Neuerk light right astern of you.'

We set off with a long stooping stride in the teeth of the wind, and straight towards the roar of the breakers on the farther side of the sand. A line of Matthew Arnold's: 'The naked shingles of the World,' was running in my head. 'Seven miles from land,' I thought, 'scuttling like sea-birds on a transient islet of sand, encircled by rushing tides and hammered by ocean, at midnight in a rising gale – cut off even from our one dubious refuge.' It was the time, if ever, to conquer weakness. A mad gaiety surged through me as I drank the wind and pressed forward. It seemed but a minute or two and Davies clutched me.

'Look out!' he shouted. 'It's my channel.'

The ground sloped down, and a rushing river glimmered before us. We struck off at a tangent and followed its course to the north, stumbling in muddy rifts, slipping on seaweed, beginning to be blinded by a fine salt spray and deafened by the thunder of the ocean surf. The river broadened, whitened, roughened, gathered itself for the shock, was shattered and dissolved in milky gloom. We wheeled away to the right, and splashed into yeasty froth. I turned my back to the wind, scooped the brine out of eyes, faced back and saw that our path was barred by a welter of surf. Davies's voice was in my ear and his arm was pointing seaward.

'This – is – about where – I bumped first – worse then – nor'-west wind – this – is – nothing. Let's – go – right – round.'

We galloped away with the wind behind us, skirting the line of surf. I lost all account of time and direction. Another sea barred our road, became another river as we slanted along its shore. Again we were in the teeth of that intoxicating wind. Then a point of light was swaying and flickering away to the left, and now we were checking and circling. I stumbled against something sharp – the dinghy's gunwale. So we had completed the circuit of our fugitive domain, that dream-island – nightmare island as I always remember it.

'You must scull too,' said Davies. 'It's blowing hard now. Keep her nose *up* a little — all you know!'

We lurched along, my scull sometimes buried to the thwart, sometimes striking at the bubbles of a wave top. Davies, in the bows, said 'Pull!' or 'Steady!' at intervals. I heard the scud smacking against his oilskin back. Then a wan, yellow light glanced over the waves. 'Easy! Let her come!' and the bowsprit of the *Dulcibella*, swollen to spectral proportions, was stabbing the darkness above me. 'Back a bit! Two good strokes. Ship your scull. Now jump!' I clawed at the tossing hull and landed in a heap. Davies followed with the painter, and the dingy swept astern.

'She's riding beautifully now,' said he, when he had secured the painter. 'There'll be no rolling on the flood, and it's nearly low water.'

I don't think I should have cared, however much she had rolled. I was finally cured of funk.

It was well that I was, for to be pitched out of your bunk on to wet oil-cloth is a disheartening beginning to a day. This happened about eight o'clock. The yacht was pitching violently, and I crawled on all fours into the cabin, where Davies was setting out breakfast on the floor.

'I let you sleep on,' he said; 'we can't do anything till the water falls. We should never get the anchor up in this sea. Come and have a look round. It's clearing now,' he went on, when we were crouching low on deck, gripping cleats for safety. 'Wind's veered to nor'-west. It's been blowing a full gale, and the sea is at its worst now – near high water. You'll never see it worse than this.'

I was prepared for what I saw – the stormy sea for leagues around, and a chaos of breakers where our dream-island had stood – and took it quietly, even with a sort of elation. The *Dulcibella* faced the storm as doggedly as ever, plunging her bowsprit into the sea and flinging green water over her bows. A wave of confidence and affection for her welled through me. I had been used to resent the weight and bulk of her unwieldly anchor and cable, but I saw their use now; varnish, paint, spotless decks, and snowy sails were foppish absurdities of a hateful past.

ERSKINE CHILDERS: The Riddle of the Sands

The Calm

Stormes chafe, and soon weare out themselves, or us;
In calmes, Heaven laughs to see us languish thus.
As steady as I can wish that my thoughts were,
Smooth as thy mistresse glasse, or what shines there,
The sea is now. And, as the Iles which wee
Seeke, when wee can move, our ships rooted bee.
As water did in stormes, now pitch runs out:
As lead, when a fir'd Church becomes one spout.
And all our beauty, all our trimme, decayes,
Like courts removing, or like ended playes.
The fighting place now seamens ragges supply;
And all the tackling is a frippery.
No use of lanthornes; and in one place lay
Feathers and dust, to day and yesterday.
Earth's hollownesses, which the world's lungs are,
Have no more winde than the upper valt of aire.
We can nor lost friend nor sought foes recover,
But meteorlike, save that we move not, hover.
Onely the Calenture together drawes
Deare friends, which meet dead in great fishes jawes:
And on the hatches as on Altars lyes
Each one, his owne Priest, and owne Sacrifice. . . .
He that at sea prays for more winde, as well
Under the poles may begge cold, heat in hell.
What are wee then? How little more alas

Is man now, than before he was? he was
Nothing; for us, wee are for nothing fit;
Chance, or ourselves still disproportion it.
Wee have no power, no will, no sense – I lye,
I should not then thus feele this miserie.

JOHN DONNE

The Storm

Then like two mighty Kings, which dwelling farre
Asunder, meet against a third to warre,
The South and West winds joyn'd, and, as they blew,
Waves like a rowling trench before them threw.
Sooner than you read this line, did the gale,
Like shot, not fear'd till felt, our sailes assaille;
And what at first was call'd a gust, the same
Hath now a stormes, anon a tempests, name.
Jonas, I pitty thee, and curse those men,
Who when the storm rag'd most, did wake thee then;
Sleepe is paines easiest salve, and doth fulfill
All offices of death, except to kill.
But when I wak'd, I saw that I saw not;
Ay, and the Sunne, which should teach mee had forgot
East, West, Day, Night, and I could onely say,
If the world had lasted, now it had been day.
Thousands our noyses were, yet wee 'mongst all
Could none by his right name, but thunder call:
Lightning was all our light, and it rain'd more
Than if the Sunne had drunk the sea before.
Some coffin'd in their cabbins lye, equally
Griev'd that they are not dead, and yet must dye;
And as sin-burden'd soules from graves will creepe,
At the last day, some forth their cabbins peepe:
And tremblingly aske what newes, and doe heare so,
Like jealous husbands, what they would not know.

Some sitting on the hatches, would seeme there
With hideous gazing to feare away feare.
Then note they the ships sicknesses, the Mast
Shak'd with this ague, and the Hold and Wast
With a salt dropsie clog'd, and all our tacklings
Snapping, like too-high-stretched treble strings.
And from our totter'd sailes, ragges drop downe so,
As from one hang'd in chaines a yeare ago.
Pumping hath tir'd our men, and what's the gaine?
Seas into seas throwne, we suck in againe;
Hearing hath deaf'd our saylers; and if they
Knew how to heare, there's none knows what to say.
Compar'd to these storms, death is but a qualme,
Hell somewhat lightsome, and the Bermuda calme.
All things are one, and that one none can be,
Since all formes, uniforme deformity
Doth cover, so that wee, except God say
Another *Fiat*, shall have no more day.

JOHN DONNE

Embayed

The ship continued to hold her course good, and we were
within half a mile of the point, and fully expected to weather
it, when again the wet and heavy sails flapped in the wind,
and the ship broke off two points as before. The officers and
seamen were aghast, for the ship's head was right on to the
breakers. 'Luff now, all you can, quarter-master,' cried the
captain. 'Send the men aft directly. My lads, there is no time
for words – I am going to *club-haul* the ship, for there is no
room to wear. The only chance you have of safety is to be cool,
watch my eye, and execute my orders with precision. Away to
your stations for tacking ship. Hands by the best bower anchor.
Mr Wilson, attend below with the carpenter and his mates,

ready to cut away the cable at the moment that I give the order. Silence, there, fore and aft. Quarter-master, keep her full again for stays. Mind you ease the helm down when I tell you.'

About a minute passed before the captain gave any further orders. The ship had closed – to within a quarter of a mile of the beach, and the waves curled and topped around us, bearing us down upon the shore, which presented one continued surface of foam, extending to within half a cable's length of our position. The captain waved his hand in silence to the quarter-master at the wheel, and the helm was put down. The ship turned slowly to the wind, pitching and chopping as the sails were spilling. When she had lost her way; the captain gave the order, 'Let go the anchor. We will haul all at once, Mr Falcon,' said the captain. Not a word was spoken, the men went to the fore brace, which had not been manned; most of them knew, although I did not, that if the ship's head did not go round the other way, we should be on shore, and among the breakers, in half a minute. I thought at the time that the captain had said that he would haul all the yards at once; there appeared to be doubt or dissent on the countenance of Mr Falcon; and I was afterwards told that he had not agreed with the captain, but he was too good an officer, and knew that there was no time for discussion, to make any remark; and the event proved that the captain was right. At last the ship was head to wind, and the captain gave the signal. The yards flew round with such a creaking noise, that I thought the masts had gone over the side, and the next moment the wind had caught the sails, and the ship, which for a moment or two had been on an even keel, careened over to her gunnel with its force. The captain, who stood upon the weather-hammock rails, holding by the main rigging, ordered the helm amidships, looked full at the sails and then at the cable, which grew broad upon the weather bow, and held the ship from nearing the shore. At last he cried, 'Cut away the cable!' A few strokes of the axes were heard, and then the cable flew out of the hawse-hole in a blaze of fire, from the violence of the friction, and disappeared under a huge wave, which struck us on the chess-tree, and deluged us with water fore and aft. But we were now on the other tack, and the ship regained her way and we had evidently increased our distance from the land.

'My lads,' said the captain to the ship's company, 'you have behaved well, and I thank you; but I must tell you honestly that we have more difficulties to get through. We have to weather a point of the bay on this tack. Mr Falcon, splice the main-brace, and call the watch. How's her head, quarter-master?'

'S.W. by S. Southerly, Sir.'

'Very well, let her go through the water.' And the captain, beckoning to the master to follow him, went down into the cabin. . . .

Before twelve o'clock, the rocky point which we so much dreaded was in sight, broad on the lee bow, and if the low sandy coast appeared terrible, how much more did this, even at a distance: the black masses of rock, covered with foam, which each minute dashed up in the air, higher than our lower mast-heads. The captain eyed it for some minutes in silence, as if in calculation.

'Mr Falcon,' he said at last, 'we must put the mainsail on her.'

'She can never bear it, Sir.'

'She *must* bear it,' was the reply. 'Send the men aft to the main sheet. See that careful men attend the buntlines.'

The mainsail was set, and the effect of it upon the ship was tremendous. She careened over so that her lee channels were under water, and when pressed by a sea, the lee side of the quarter-deck and gangway were afloat. She now reminded me of a goaded and fiery horse, mad with the stimulus applied; not rising as before, but forcing herself through whole seas, and dividing the waves, which poured in one continual torrent from the forecastle down upon the decks below. Four men were secured to the wheel – the sailors were obliged to cling, to prevent being washed away – the ropes were thrown in confusion to leeward, the shot rolled out of the lockers, and every eye was fixed aloft, watching the masts, which were expected every moment to go over the side. A heavy sea struck us on the broadside, and it was some moments before the ship appeared to recover herself; she reeled, trembled, and stopped her way, as if it had stupefied her. The first lieutenant looked at the captain, as if to say, 'This will not do.' 'It is our only chance,' answered the captain to the appeal. That the ship went faster through the water, and held a better wind, was certain; but just before we arrived at the point, the gale increased in force. 'If anything starts, we are lost, Sir,' observed the first lieutenant again.

'I am perfectly aware of it,' replied the captain in a calm tone; 'but, as I said before, and you must now be aware, it is our only chance. The consequence of any carelessness or neglect in the fitting and securing of the rigging, will be felt now; and this danger, if we escape it, ought to remind us how much we have to answer for if we neglect our duty. The lives of a whole ship's company may be sacrificed by the neglect or incompetence of an officer when in harbour. I will pay you the compliment, Falcon, to say that I feel convinced that the masts of the ship are as secure as knowledge and attention can make them.'

The first lieutenant thanked the captain for his good opinion, and hoped it would not be the last compliment he would pay him.

'I hope not too; but a few minutes will decide the point.'

The ship was now within two cables' length of the rocky point; some few of the men I observed to clasp their hands, but most of them were silently taking off their jackets and kicking off their shoes, that they might not lose a chance to escape, provided the ship struck.

''Twill be touch and go indeed, Falcon,' observed the captain (for I had clung to the belaying-pins, close to them for the last half-hour that the mainsail had been set). 'Come aft; you and I must take the helm. We shall want *nerve* there, and only there, now.'

The captain and first lieutenant went aft, and took the fore-spokes of the wheel, and O'Brien, at a sign made by the captain, laid hold of the spokes behind him. An old quarter-master kept his station at the fourth. The roaring of the seas on the rocks, with the howling of the wind, were dreadful; but the sight was more dreadful than the noise. For a few moments I shut my eyes, but anxiety forced me to open them again. As near as I could judge, we were not twenty yards from the rocks, at the time that the ship passed abreast of them. We were in the midst of the foam, which boiled around us; and as the ship was driven nearer to them, and careened with the wave, I thought that our mainyard-arm would have touched the rock; and at this moment a gust of wind came on, which laid the ship on her beam-ends, and checked her progress through the water, while the accumulated noise was deafening. A few moments more the ship dragged on, another wave dashed over her and spent itself upon the rocks, while the spray was dashed back from them and returned upon the decks. The main rock was within ten yards of her counter, when another gust of wind laid us on our beam-ends, the foresail and mainsail split, and were blown clean out of the bolt-ropes – the ship righted, trembling fore and aft. I looked astern: the rocks were to windward on our quarter, and we were safe.

CAPTAIN MARRYAT: *Peter Simple*

The Breakwater at Bude

Do I remember very long ago
Standing beside the breakwater at Bude:
A fierce gale and Atlantic tide in flood
Threw waves like avalanches over it;
And on the rock at the far end did sit
A single man, and by me on the shore
Were watching him a hundred eyes and more:
He waited for his opportunity
And made a dash between two waves to flee

Across the mole; but as he reached half-way
A breaker roaring, towering for its prey,
Swept down and hurled him over in the sea.
Upon the calmer side he seemed to be,
And struck out swimming strongly; but alas
A hidden backwash on that side there was
That like a mill-race sucked him from the shore;
And as with beating hearts we looked, before
Our eyes, a few yards off, the man went down,
And boatless, ropeless, dumb, we watched him drown
And caught across the storm one fearful cry,
Ere he threw up his arms and sank to die.
That cry brings back to me across long years
Our helplessness, our frenzy, and our tears.

R. C. K. ENSOR

Cape Horn

Having a fine wind, we were soon up with and passed the
latitude of the Cape, and having stood far enough to the
southward to give it a good berth, we began to stand to the
eastward, with a good prospect of being round, and steering to
the northward on the other side, in a very few days. But ill
luck seemed to have lighted upon us. Not four hours had we
been standing on in this course before it fell dead calm, and
in half an hour it clouded up, a few straggling blasts with spits
of snow and sleet, came from the eastward, and in an hour more
we lay hove to under a close-reefed main topsail, drifting
bodily off to leeward before the fiercest storm that we had yet
felt, blowing dead ahead from the eastward. It seemed as
though the genius of the place had been roused at finding that
we had nearly slipped through his fingers, and had come down
upon us with tenfold fury. The sailors said that every blast,
as it shook the shrouds and whistled through the rigging, said
to the old ship, 'No, you don't! no, you don't!'

For eight days we lay drifting about in this manner. Some-times – generally towards noon – it fell calm, once or twice a round copper ball showed itself for a few moments in the place where the sun ought to have been, and a puff or two came from the westward, giving some hope that a fair wind had come at last. During the first two days we made sail for these puffs, shaking the reefs out of the topsails and boarding the tacks of the courses, but finding that it only made work for us when the gale set in again, it was soon given up, and we lay-to under our close reefs. We had less snow and hail than when we were farther to the westward; but we had abundance of what is worse to a sailor in cold weather – drenching rain. Snow is blinding, and very bad when coming upon a coast; but, for genuine discomfort, give me rain in freezing weather. A snowstorm is exciting, and it does not wet through the clothes (which is important to a sailor), but a constant rain there is no escaping from. It wets to the skin and makes all protection vain. We had long ago run through all our dry clothes, and as sailors have no other way of drying them except by the sun, we had nothing to do but to put on those which were the least wet. At the end of each watch, when we came below, we took off our clothes and wrung them out, two taking hold of a pair of trousers – one at each end – and jackets in the same way. Stockings, mittens, and all were wrung out also, and then hung up to drain and chafe dry against the bulk-heads. Then, feeling over our clothes, we picked out those which were the least wet, and put them on, so as to be ready for a call, and turned in, covered ourselves up with blankets, and slept until three knocks on the scuttle, and the dismal sound of 'All starbowlines ahoy! Eight bells there below! Do you hear the news?' drawled out from on deck and the sulky answer of 'Ay, ay!' from below, sent us up again.

On deck all was as dark as a pocket, and either a dead calm with the rain pouring steadily down, or more generally a violent gale dead ahead, with rain pelting horizontally, and occasional variations of hail and sleet, decks afloat with water swashing from side to side, and constantly wet feet – for boots could not be wrung out like drawers, and no composition could stand the constant soaking. In fact, wet and cold feet are inevitable in such weather, and are not the least of those little items which go to make up the grand total of the discomforts of a winter passage round the Cape. Few words were spoken between the watches as they shifted; the wheel was relieved, the mate took his place on the quarterdeck, the lookouts in the bows, and each man had his narrow space to walk fore and aft in, or rather to swing himself forward and back in, from one belaying pin to another − for the decks were too slippery with ice and water to allow of much walking. To make a walk, which is absolutely necessary to pass away the time, one of us hit upon the expedient of sanding the deck, and afterwards, whenever the rain was not so violent as to wash it off, the weather-side of the quarter-deck, and a part of the waist and forecastle, were sprinkled with the sand which we had on board for holy-stoning; and thus we made a good promenade, where we walked fore and aft, two and two, hour after hour, in our long, dull and comfortless watches. The bells seemed to be an hour or two apart, instead of half an hour, and an age to elapse before the welcome sound of eight bells. The sole object was to make the time pass on. Any change was sought for which would break the monotony of the time, and even the two hours trick at the wheel, which came round to each of us in turn every other watch, was looked upon as a relief. Even the never-failing resource of long yarns, which eke out many a watch, seemed to have failed us now; for we had been so long together that we had heard each others' stories told over and over again, till we had them by heart; each one knew the whole history of each of the others, and we were fairly and literally talked out. Singing and joking we were in no humour for, and, in fact, any sound of mirth or laughter would have struck strangely upon our ears, and would not have been tolerated any more than whistling or a wind instrument. The last resort, that of speculating upon the future, seemed now to fail us, for our discouraging situation, and the danger we were really in (as we expected every day to find ourselves drifted back among the ice), 'clapped a stopper' upon all that. From saying, '*when* we get home,' we began insensibly to alter it to '*if* we get home'; and at last the subject was dropped by a tacit consent.

R. H. DANA: *Two Years Before the Mast*

Ariel Imitates St Elmo's Fire

ARI.   I boarded the king's ship; now on the beak,
Now in the waist, the deck, in every cabin,
I flamed amazement: sometimes I'd divide
And burn in many places, on the topmast,
The yards and bowsprit, would I flame distinctly,
Then meet and join. Jove's lightnings, the precursors
O' the dreadful thunderclaps, more momentary
And sight-outrunning were not; the fire and cracks
Of sulphurous roaring the most mighty Neptune
Seemed to besiege and make his bold waves tremble,
Yea, his dread trident shake.

PROS. My brave spirit!
Who was so firm, so constant, that this coil
Would not infect his reason?

ARI.   Not a soul
But felt a fever of the mad and play'd
Some tricks of desperation. All but mariners
Plunged in the foaming brine and quit the vessel,
Then all a-fire with me. The king's son, Ferdinand,
With hair up-staring, then like reeds, not hair,
Was the first man that leapt; cried, 'Hell is empty,
And all the devils are here.'

WILLIAM SHAKESPEARE: *The Tempest*

Off Finisterre

I embarked in the Thames on board the M— steamer. We had a most unpleasant passage to Falmouth. The ship was crowded with passengers; most of them were poor consumptive individuals, and other invalids fleeing from the cold blasts of England's winter to the sunny shores of Portugal and Madeira. In a more uncomfortable vessel, especially steamship, it has never been my fate to make a voyage. The berths were small and insupportably close, and of these wretched holes mine was amongst the worst, the rest having been bespoken before I arrived on board; so that, to avoid the suffocation which seemed to threaten me should I enter it, I lay upon the floor of one of the cabins throughout the voyage. We remained at Falmouth twenty-four hours, taking in coal and repairing the engine, which had sustained considerable damage.

On Monday the 7th we again started, and made for the Bay of Biscay. The sea was high and the wind strong and contrary, nevertheless, on the morning of the fourth day we were in sight of the rocky coast to the north of Cape Finisterre. I must here observe that this was the first voyage that the captain who commanded the vessel had ever made on board of her, and that he knew little or nothing of the coast towards which we were bearing. He was a person picked up in a hurry, the former captain having resigned his command on the ground that the ship was not seaworthy and that the engines were frequently unserviceable. I was not acquainted with these circumstances at the time, or perhaps I should have felt more alarmed than I did, when I saw the vessel approaching nearer and nearer the shore, till at last we were only a few hundred yards distant. As it was, however, I felt very much surprised, for having passed it twice before, both times in steam vessels, and having seen with what care the captains endeavoured to maintain a wide offing, I could not conceive the reason of our being now so near this dangerous region. The wind was blowing hard towards the shore, if that can be called a shore which consists of steep, abrupt precipices, on which the surf was breaking with the noise of thunder, tossing up clouds of spray and foam to the height of a cathedral. We coasted slowly along, rounding several tall forelands, some of them piled up by the hand of nature in the most fantastic shapes. About nightfall Cape Finisterre was not far ahead – a bluff, brown granite mountain, whose frowning head may be seen far away by those who traverse the ocean. The stream which poured round its breast was terrific, and though our engines plied with all their force, we made little or no way.

By about eight o'clock at night the wind had increased to a hurricane, the thunder rolled frightfully, and the only light we had to guide us on our way was the red forked lightning which burst at times from the bosom of the big black clouds which lowered over our heads. We were exerting ourselves to the utmost to weather the Cape, which we could descry by the lightning on our lee, its brow being frequently brilliantly lighted up by the flashes which quivered around it, when suddenly, with a great crash, the engine broke, and the paddles, on which depended our lives, ceased to play.

I will not attempt to depict the scene of horror and confusion which ensued; it may be imagined, but never described. The captain, to give him his due, displayed the utmost coolness and intrepidity. He and the whole crew made the greatest exertions to repair the engine, and when they found their labour in vain, endeavoured, by hoisting the sails and by practising all possible manoeuvres, to preserve the ship from impending destruction. But all was of no avail, we were hard on a lee-shore, to which the howling tempest was impelling us. About this time I was standing near the helm, and I asked the steersman if there was any hope of saving the vessel or our lives. He replied, 'Sir, it is a bad affair. No boat could live for a minute in this sea, and in less than an hour the ship will have her broadside on Finisterre, where the strongest man-of-war ever built must go to shivers instantly. None of us will see the morning.' The captain, likewise, informed the other passengers in the cabin to the same effect, telling them to prepare themselves, and having done so, he ordered the door to be fastened, and none to be permitted to come on deck. I, however, kept my station, though almost drowned with water, immense waves continually breaking over our windward side and flooding the ship. The water-casks broke from their lashings, and one of them struck me down and crushed the foot of the unfortunate man at the helm, whose place was instantly taken by the captain. We were now close to the rocks, when a horrid convulsion of the elements took place. The lightning enveloped us as with a mantle, the thunders were louder than the roar of a million cannon, the dregs of the ocean seemed to be cast up, and in the midst of all this turmoil the wind, without the slightest intimation, *veered right about* and pushed us from the horrible coast faster than it had previously driven us towards it.

The oldest sailors on board acknowledged that they had never witnessed so providential an escape. I said from the bottom of my heart, 'Our Father, hallowed be thy name.'

The next day we were near foundering, for the sea was exceedingly high, and our vessel, which was not intended for sailing, laboured terribly and leaked much. The pumps were continually working. She likewise took fire, but the flames were extinguished. In the evening the steam-engine was partially repaired, and we reached Lisbon on the 13th, where in a few days we completed our repairs.

GEORGE BORROW: *The Bible in Spain* (xii)

Xerxes at Sea

There is another account, different from the preceding, according to which Xerxes, on his retreat from Athens, travelled by land only as far as Eion on the Strymon; here he turned the army over to Hydarnes for the march to the Hellespont, and himself crossed to Asia in a Phoenician ship.

During the passage they were caught by a strong wind, blowing from the mouth of the Strymon, accompanied by a heavy sea; in the worsening weather the ship, loaded as she was with a crowd of Persians who were travelling home with the King and packed the deck, was in considerable danger, and Xerxes in sudden fright called out to the ship's master to ask if there was any way of getting out of it alive. 'None whatever, my Lord,' the man replied, 'unless we can rid ourselves of this crowd on deck.' Upon this Xerxes is supposed to have said: 'Gentlemen, now is the moment for each one of you to prove his concern for the King; for my safety, it seems, is in your hands. . . .'

The Persian noblemen bowed low, and then, without more ado, jumped overboard; and the ship, lightened of her load, came safely to her port on the Asian coast. The moment Xerxes had gone ashore he presented the master with a gold crown as a reward for saving the King's life, and then, to punish him for causing the death of a number of Persians, cut off his head.

Personally, I do not find this second account of Xerxes' return at all convincing – especially as regards what happened to the Persians. If the ship's master had really said to Xerxes what he is supposed to have said, surely not one in ten thousand would doubt that Xerxes would have made the people on deck go below – after all, they were Persian noblemen – and would then have flung overboard an equivalent number of rowers, who were mere Phoenicians.

HERODOTUS: *Histories*

Cyclone

But now a change was evidently imminent. Of course, we forward had no access to the barometer; not that we should have understood its indications had we seen it, but we all knew that something was going to be radically wrong with the weather. For instead of the lovely blue of the sky we had been so long accustomed to by day and night, a nasty, greasy shade had come over the heavens, which, reflected in the sea, made that look dirty and stale also. That well-known appearance of the waves before a storm was also very marked, which consists of an undecided sort of break in their tops. Instead of running regularly they seemed to hunch themselves up in little heaps, and throw off a tiny flutter of spray, which generally fell in the opposite direction to what little wind there was. The pigs and fowls felt the approaching change keenly, and manifested the greatest uneasiness, leaving their food and acting strangely. We were making scarcely any headway, so that the storm was longer making its appearance than it would have been had we been a swift clipper ship running down the Indian Ocean. For two days we were kept in suspense; but on the second night the gloom began to deepen, the wind to moan, and a very uncomfortable 'jobble' of a sea got up. Extra gaskets were put upon the sails and everything moveable about the decks was made as secure as it could be. Only the two close-reefed topsails and two storm-staysails were carried, so that we were in excellent trim for fighting the bad weather when it did come. The sky gradually darkened and assumed a livid green tint, the effect of which was most peculiar.

The wind blew fitfully in short gusts, veering continually back and forth over about a quarter of the compass. Although it was still light, it kept up an incessant mournful moan not to be accounted for in any way. Darker and darker grew the heavens, although no clouds were visible, only a general pall of darkness. Glimmering lightnings played continually about the eastern horizon, but not brilliant enough to show us the approaching storm-cloud. And so came the morning of the third day from the beginning of the change. But for the clock we should hardly have known that day had broken, so gloomy and dark was the sky. At last light came in the east, but such a light as no-one would wish to see. It was a lurid glare, such as may be seen playing over a cupola of Bessemer steel when the spiegeleisen is added, only on such an extensive scale that its brilliancy was dulled into horror. Then beneath it we saw the mountainous clouds fringed with dull violet and with jagged sabres of lightning darting from their solid black bosoms. The wind began to rise steadily but rapidly, so that by 8 a.m. it was blowing a furious gale from E.N.E. In direction it was still unsteady, the ship coming up and falling off to it several points. Now, great masses of torn ragged cloud hurtled past us above, so low down as almost to touch the mastheads. Still the wind increased, still the sea rose, till at last the skipper judged it well to haul down the tiny triangle of storm-staysail still set (the topsail and fore-staysail had been furled long before), and let her drift under bare poles, except for three square feet of stout canvas in the weather mizen-rigging. The roar of the wind now dominated every sound, so that it might have been thundering furiously, but we should not have heard it. The ship still maintained her splendid character as a sea-boat, hardly shipping a drop of water; but she lay over at a most distressing angle, her deck sloping off fully thirty-five to forty degrees. Fortunately she did not roll to windward. It may have been raining in perfect torrents, but the tempest tore off the surface of the sea, and sent it in massive sheets continually flying over us, so that we could not possibly have distinguished between fresh water and salt.

The chief anxiety was for the safety of the boats. Early on the second day of warning they had been hoisted to the topmost notch of the cranes, and secured as thoroughly as experience could suggest; but at every lee lurch we gave it seemed as if we must dip them under water, while the wind threatened to stave the weather ones in by its actual solid weight. It was now blowing a furious cyclone, the force of which has never been accurately gauged even by the present elaborate instruments of various kinds in use. That force is, however, not to be imagined by anyone who has not witnessed it, except that one notable instance is on record by which mathematicians may get an approximate estimate.

Captain Toynbee, the late highly respected and admired Marine Superintendent of the British Meteorological Office, has told us how, during a cyclone which he rode out in the *Hotspur* at Sandheads, the mouth of the Hooghly, the three naked topgallantmasts of his ship, though of well-tested timber a foot in diameter and supported by all the usual network of stays, and without the yards, were snapped off and carried away solely by the violence of the wind. It must, of course, have been an extreme gust which did not last many seconds, for no cable that was ever forged would have held the ship against such a cataclysm as that. This gentleman's integrity is above suspicion; so that no exaggeration could be charged against him, and he had the additional testimony of his officers and men to this otherwise incredible fact.

The terrible day wore on, without any lightening of the tempest, till noon, when the wind suddenly fell to a calm. Until that time the sea, although heavy, was not vicious or irregular, and we had not shipped any heavy water at all. But when the force of the wind was suddenly withdrawn, such a sea arose as I have never seen before or since. Inky mountains of water raised their savage heads in wildest confusion, smashing one another in whirlpools of foam. It was like a picture of the primeval deep out of which arose the new-born world. Suddenly out of the whirling blackness overhead the moon appeared, nearly in the zenith, sending down through the apex of a dome of torn and madly gyrating cloud a flood of brilliant light. Illumined by that startling radiance, our staunch and sea-worthy ship was tossed and twirled in the hideous vortex of mad sea until her motion was distracting. It was quite impossible to loose one's hold and attempt to do anything without running the imminent risk of being dashed to pieces. Our decks were full of water now, for it tumbled on board at all points; but as yet no serious weight of a sea had fallen upon us, nor had any damage been done. Such a miracle as that could not be expected to continue for long. Suddenly a warning shout rang out from somewhere – 'Hold on, all, for your lives!' Out of the hideous turmoil around arose, like some black fantastic ruin, an awful heap of water. Higher and higher it towered, until it was level with our lower yards, then it broke and fell upon us. All was blank. Beneath that mass every thought, every feeling, fled but one – 'How long shall I be able to hold my breath?' After what seemed a never-ending time, we emerged from the wave more dead than alive, but with the good ship still staunch underneath us, and Hope's lamp burning brightly. The moon had been momentarily obscured, but now shone out again, lighting up brilliantly our bravely battling ship. But, alas for others! men, like ourselves, whose hopes were gone. Quite near us was the battered remainder of what had been a splendid ship. Her masts were gone, not even the stumps being visible, and it seemed to our eager eyes as if she was settling down. It was even so, for as we looked, unmindful of our own danger, she quietly disappeared – swallowed up with her human freight in a moment, like a pebble dropped into a pond.

While we looked with hardly beating hearts at the place where she had sunk, all was blotted out in thick darkness again. With a roar as of a thousand thunders the tempest came once more, but from the opposite direction now. As we were under no sail, we ran little risk of being caught aback; but, even had we, nothing could have been done, the vessel being utterly out of control, besides the impossibility of getting about. It so happened, however, that when the storm burst upon us again, we were stern on to it, and we drove steadily for a few moments until we had time to haul to the wind again. Great heavens, how it blew! Surely, I thought, this cannot last long – just as we sometimes say of the rain when it is extra heavy. It did last, however, for what seemed an interminable time, although anyone could see that the sky was getting kindlier. Gradually, imperceptibly, it took off, the sky cleared and the tumult ceased, until a new day broke in untellable beauty over a revivified world.

Years afterwards I read, in one of the handbooks treating of hurricanes and cyclones, that 'in the centre of these revolving storms the sea is so violent that few ships can pass through it and live.' That is true talk. I have been there, and bear witness that but for the build and sea-kindliness of the *Cachalot* she could not have come out of that horrible cauldron again, but would have joined that nameless unfortunate whom we saw succumb, 'never again heard of'. As it was, we found two of the boats stove in, whether by breaking sea or crushing wind nobody knows. Most of the planking of the bulwarks was also gone, burst outward by the weight of water on deck. Only the normal quantity of water was found in the well on sounding, and not even a rope-yarn was gone from aloft. Altogether, we came out of the ordeal triumphantly, where many a gallant vessel met her fate, and the behaviour of the grand old tub gave me a positive affection for her, such as I have never felt for a ship before or since.

FRANK T. BULLEN: *The Cruise of the Cachalot*

More fell than anguish, hunger or the sea.

WILLIAM SHAKESPEARE: *Othello*

Shipwreck

Trawlermen

Trawlermen have the heart of lions. There was the case of the timber steamer *Fred Borchard*, for example, which foundered off the coast of Norway in the autumn of 1951 in a dreadful fury of the sea, littered with great baulks of timber broken from the *Borchard*'s decks. A little trawler, by name the *Boston Fury*, steamed among these baulks in that wild gale and literally fished twenty-seven of the twenty-nine men in the *Borchard*'s crew out of the sea, though the *Boston Fury* could launch no boats. Boats would be smashed up by the timber. But what about men? She put her men in the water, gale or no gale, and they swam among those murdering baulks, which were crashing, rolling and plunging in the violent turmoil of the sea. They got lines to the twenty-seven men, and they saved them. Men said afterwards that only fishermen could have carried out a rescue like that. The *Borchard* went down north of the Arctic Circle, too, and the month was October.

ALAN VILLIERS: *Posted Missing*

Dory Men

The *Joao Costa* was not an auxiliary schooner, but a full-powered motor-ship, carrying a little steadying sail. Like the other dory-fishermen, her business was to sail over from her home port in the early spring of the year, anchor on some convenient point on the Grand Banks (preferably on foul ground, in order to avoid the too numerous big trawlers which also work there) and, sending out her fifty-five dorymen in their fifty-five little boats each day for the following six or seven months, fill herself with fine fat cod which were salted down aboard. Then she brought this cargo home where it was treated and marketed. For six years the *Joao Costa* did this very well. She was commanded by a young master with the same name as the ship, though he did not own her. She was named for his father; not him. Like most of the modern masters he had not himself been a doryman, but he was a fine seaman and an able fisherman.

On the seventh voyage the *Joao Costa* foundered. She was coming back alone from the banks off the west coast of Greenland when she was caught in a very bad blow near the Azores. She opened up, took in more water than the pumps could cope with (she was deeply laden) and, within a few hours of the leak first becoming serious, she went down. At the time her radio was temporarily out of order, and before it could be repaired she was gone. So no message was sent away. As she was not due at Lisbon for four more days, she was not missed. She had been gone a week before a search was begun for her, for it was known that she must have passed through much bad weather and, at first, her failure to arrive was put down to delay caused by this.

A week after the *Joao Costa* had gone down, the American Liberty ship *Compass*, east-bound from the Atlantic seaboard of the United States towards the Mediterranean, chanced to steam into the area. The sea was still lumpy, after running high the whole week. Suddenly those in the *Compass* sighted a small boat adrift on the sea – three small boats, six small boats, dozens of them! They were strange little boats, painted yellow, each with a large number on its side, painted in white. In the boats were men, waving. The little boats were jumping and leaping in the sea so much that the *Compass* had difficulty in getting the men out of them, and the men had to jump for the bottom of a rope-ladder dangling in the sea. Thirty, forty, forty-five men were picked up. They were the dorymen of the *Joao Costa*, and they had been a week in those dories – a week without food and only such moisture as they could squeeze from the rain which soaked their stocking caps.

In the meantime, not far away, the German motorship *Henriette Schulte* was also finding herself suddenly among more of the dorymen adrift in the North Atlantic and she and the steamer *Steel Executive* – summoned by radio to assist – picked up the balance of the *Joao Costa*'s crew. Not just the survivors – *all* of them! The youthful master, a slim young man with a face like a priest, the deckboys, the handful of engineers, the cook and his mate, every single doryman, every single soul who had been aboard. The master had kept the majority of the men together, and the mate had led the rest when they were split up by the continuous bad weather.

Those men were not all skilled dorymen. The officers, the deck-boys, and the engineers rarely went in a dory on the Banks, because that was not their work. But they were all used to dories, all skilful small-boat sailors and superb seamen, used to hardship, and the dorymen were also used to accepting the risk of being adrift in a dory at sea. There was one other quality which kept these men together and helped them to survive. This was that they prayed and they believed in the praying.

ALAN VILLIERS: *Posted Missing*

Rintrah roars
And shakes his fires in the burden'd air;
Hungry clouds
Swag on the deep.

WILLIAM BLAKE: *Marriage of Heaven and Hell*

The Wreck

Storm and unconscionable winds once cast
On grinding shingle, masking gap-toothed rock,
This ancient hulk. Rent hull, and broken mast,
She sprawls sand-mounded, of sea-birds the mock.
Her sailors, drowned, forgotten, rot in mould,
Or hang in stagnant quiet of the deep;
The brave, the afraid into one silence sold;
Their end a memory fainter than of sleep.
She held good merchandise. She paced in pride
The uncharted paths men trace in ocean's foam.
Now laps the ripple in her broken side,
And zephyr in tamarisk softly whispers, Home.
The dreamer scans her in the sea-blue air,
And, sipping of contrast, finds the day more fair.

WALTER DE LA MARE

How Haidee found Don Juan

'Twas twilight, and the sunless day went down
    Over the waste of waters; like a veil,
Which, if withdrawn, would but disclose the frown
    Of one whose hate is masked but to assail.
Thus to their hopeless eyes the night was shown,
    And grimly darkled o'er the faces pale,
And the dim, desolate deep: twelve days had Fear
Been their familiar, and now Death was here.

At half-past eight o'clock booms, hencoops, spars,
    And all things, for a chance, had been cast loose,
That still could keep afloat the struggling tars,
    For yet they strove, although of no great use:

There was no light in heaven but a few stars,
    The boats put off o'er-crowded with their crews;
She gave a heel, and then a lurch to port,
And, going down head foremost – sunk, in short.

Then rose from sea to sky the wild farewell –
    Then shriek'd the timid and stood still the brave, –
Then some leap'd overboard with dreadful yell,
    As eager to anticipate their grave;
And the sea yawn'd around her like a hell,
    And down she suck'd with her the whirling wave,
Like one who grapples with his enemy,
And strives to strangle him before he die.

At first one universal shriek there rush'd,
    Louder than the loud ocean, like a crash
Of echoing thunder; and then all was hush'd,
    Save the wild wind and the remorseless dash
Of billows; but at intervals there gush'd,
    Accompanied with a convulsive splash,
A solitary shriek, the bubbling cry
Of some strong swimmer in his agony.

With twilight it again came on to blow,
    But not with violence; the stars shone out,
The boat made way; yet now they were so low
    They knew not where nor what they were about;
Some fancied they saw land, and some said, 'No!'
    The frequent fog-banks gave them cause to doubt –
Some swore that they heard breakers, others guns,
And all mistook about the latter once.

As morning broke, the light wind died away,
    When he who had the watch sung out and swore
If 'twas not land that rose with the sun's ray,
    He wish'd that land he never might see more;
And the rest rubb'd their eyes and saw a bay,

Or thought they saw, and shaped their course for
    shore;
For shore it was, and gradually grew
Distinct, and high, and palpable to view.

And then of these some part burst into tears,
    And others, looking with a stupid stare,
Could not yet separate their hopes from fears,
    And seem'd as if they had no further care;
While a few pray'd (the first time for some years),
    And at the bottom of the boat three were
Asleep: they shook them by the hand and head,
And tried to awaken them, but found them dead.

As they drew nigh the land, which now was seen
    Unequal in its aspect here and there,
They felt the freshness of its growing green
    That waved in forest-tops, and smooth'd the air.
And fell upon their glazed eyes like a screen
    From glistening waves, and skies so hot and bare –
Lovely seem'd any object that should sweep
Away the vast, salt, dread, eternal deep.

The shore look'd wild, without a trace of man,
    And girt by formidable waves; but they
Were mad for land, and thus their course they ran,
    Though right ahead the roaring breakers lay;
A reef between them also now began
    To show its boiling surf and bounding spray;
But finding no place for their landing better,
They ran the boat for shore – and overset her.

But in his native stream, the Guadalquiver,
    Juan to lave his youthful limbs was wont;
And having learnt to swim in that sweet river,
    Had often turned the art to some account:
A better swimmer you could scarce see ever,
    He could, perhaps, have passed the Hellespont,

As once (a feat on which ourselves we prided)
Leander, Mr Ekenhead, and I did.

So here, though faint, emaciated and stark,
   He buoyed his boyish limbs, and strove to ply
With the quick wave and gain, ere it was dark,
   The beach which lay before him, high and dry:
The greatest danger here was from a shark,
   That carried off his neighbour by the thigh;
As for the other two, they could not swim,
So nobody arrived on shore but him.

Nor yet had he arrived but for the oar,
   Which, providentially for him, was wash'd
Just as his feeble arms could strike no more,
   And the hard wave o'erwhelmed him as 'twas dash'd
Within his grasp; he clung to it, and sore
   The waters beat while he thereto was lash'd;
At last with swimming, wading, scrambling, he
Rolled on the beach, half senseless, from the sea;

There, breathless, with his digging nails he clung
   Fast to the sand, lest the returning wave,
From whose reluctant roar his life he wrung,
   Should suck him back to her insatiate grave:
And there he lay full-length, where he was flung,
   Before the entrance of a cliff-worn cave,
With just enough of life to feel its pain,
And deem that it was saved, perhaps, in vain.

With slow and staggering effort he arose,
   But sunk again upon his bleeding knee
And quivering hand; and then he look'd for those
   Who long had been his mates upon the sea;
But none of them appeared to share his woes,
   Save one, a corpse, from out the famish'd three,
Who died two days before, and now had found
An unknown barren beach for burial ground.

And as he gaz'd, his dizzy brain spun fast,
   And down he sunk; and as he sunk, the sand
Swam round and round, and all his senses pass'd;
   He fell upon his side, and his stretch'd hand
Droop'd dripping on the oar (their jury-mast),
   And, like a withered lily, on the land
His slender frame and pallid aspect lay
As fair a thing as e'er was form'd of clay.

How long in this damp trance young Juan lay
   He knew not, for the earth was gone for him,
And Time had nothing more of night nor day
   For his congealing blood and senses dim;
And how this heavy faintness pass'd away
   He knew not, till each painful pulse and limb
And tingling vein, seem'd throbbing back to life,
   For Death, though vanquish'd, still retired with strife.

His eyes he open'd, shut, again unclos'd,
   For all was doubt and dizziness; he thought
He still was in the boat, and had but dozed,
   And fell again with his despair o'erwrought,
And wish'd it death in which he had reposed,
   And then once more his feelings back were brought,
And slowly by his swimming eyes was seen
A lovely female face of seventeen.

'Twas bending close o'er his. . . .

LORD BYRON: Don Juan

The End of Steerforth

'Don't you think that,' I asked the coachman, in the first stage
out of London, 'a very remarkable sky? I don't remember to
have seen one like it.'

'Nor I – not equal to it,' he replied. 'That's wind, Sir. There'll be mischief done at sea, I expect, before long.'

It was a murky confusion – here and there blotted with a colour like the colour of the smoke from damp fuel – of flying clouds tossed up into most remarkable heaps, suggesting greater heights in the clouds than there were depths below them to the bottom of the deepest hollows in the earth, through which the wild moon seemed to plunge headlong, as if, in a dread disturbance of the laws of nature, she had lost her way and were frightened. There had been a wind all day; and it was rising then, with an extraordinary great sound. In another hour it had much increased, and the sky was more overcast, and it blew hard.

But as the night advanced, the clouds closing in and densely overspreading the whole sky, then very dark, it came on to blow harder and harder. It still increased, until our horses could scarcely face the wind. Many times, in the dark part of the night (it was then late in September, when the nights were not short) the leaders turned about, or came to a dead stop; and we were often in serious apprehension that the coach would be blown over. Sweeping gusts of rain came up before this storm, like showers of steel; and, at those times, when there was any shelter of trees or lee walls to be got, we were fain to stop in a sheer impossibility of continuing the struggle.

When the day broke, it blew harder and harder. I had been in Yarmouth when the seamen said it blew great guns, but I had never known the like of this, or anything approaching to it. . . . As we struggled on, nearer and nearer to the sea, from which this mighty wind was blowing dead on shore, its force became more and more terrific. Long before we saw the sea, its spray was on our lips, and showered salt rain upon us. The water was out, over miles and miles of the flat country adjacent to Yarmouth; and every sheet and puddle lashed its banks, and had its stress of little breakers setting heavily towards us. When we came within sight of the sea, the waves on the horizon, caught at intervals above the rolling abyss, were like glimpses of another shore with towers and buildings. When at last we got into the town, the people came out to their doors, all aslant, and with streaming hair, making a wonder of the mail that had come through such a night.

I put up at the old inn, and went down to look at the sea; staggering along the street, which was strewn with sand and seaweed, and with flying blotches of sea-foam; afraid of falling slates and tiles; and holding by people I met at angry corners. Coming near the beach, I saw, not only the boatmen, but half the people of the town, lurking behind buildings; some, now and then braving the fury of the storm to look away to sea, and blown sheer out of their course in trying to get zigzag back.

Joining these groups, I found bewailing women, whose husbands were away in herring or oyster boats, which there was too much reason to think might have foundered before they could run in anywhere for safety. Grizzled old sailors were among the people, shaking their heads, as they looked from water to sky, and muttering to one another; shipowners, excited and uneasy; children huddling together, and peering into older faces; even stout mariners, disturbed and anxious, levelling their glasses at the sea from behind places of shelter, as if they were surveying an enemy.

The tremendous sea itself, when I could find sufficient pause to look at it, in the agitation of the blinding wind, the flying stones and sand, and the awful noise, confounded one. As the high watery walls came rolling in, and, at their highest, tumbled into surf, they looked as if the least would engulf the town. As the receding wave swept back with a hoarse roar, it seemed to scoop out deep caves in the beach, as if its purpose were to undermine the earth. When some white-headed billows thundered on, and dashed themselves to pieces before they reached the land, every fragment of the late whole seemed possessed by the full might of its wrath, rushing to be gathered to the composition of another monster. Undulating hills were changed to valleys, undulating valleys (with a solitary storm-bird sometimes skimming through them) were lifted up to hills; masses of water shivered and shook the beach with a booming sound; every shape tumultuously rolled on, as soon as made, to change its shape and place, and beat another shape and place away; the ideal shore on the horizon, with its towers and buildings, rose and fell; the clouds flew fast and thick; I seemed to see a rending and upheaving of all nature.

Not finding Ham among the people whom this memorable wind – for it is still remembered down there as the greatest ever known to blow upon that coast – had brought together, I made my way to his house. It was shut; and as no-one answered to my knocking, I went, by back ways and bye-ways, to the yard where he worked. I learned there that he had gone to Lowestoft, to meet some sudden exigency of ship-repairing in which his skill was required; but that he would be back tomorrow morning, in good time.

I went back to the inn; and when I had washed and dressed, and tried to sleep, but in vain, it was five o'clock in the afternoon. I had not sat five minutes by the coffee-room fire, when the waiter coming to stir it, as an excuse for talking, told me that two colliers had gone down, with all hands, a few miles away; and that some other ships had been seen labouring hard in the Roads, and trying, in great distress, to keep off shore. . . . I was very much depressed in spirits; very solitary; and felt an uneasiness in Ham's not being there, disproportionate to the occasion. I was seriously affected, without knowing how much, by late events; and my long exposure to the fierce wind had confused me . . . there was a curious inattention in my mind, yet it was busy, too, with all the remembrances the place naturally awakened, and they were particularly distinct and vivid.

In this state, the waiter's dismal intelligence about the ships immediately connected itself, without any effort of my volition, with my uneasiness about Ham. I was persuaded that I had an apprehension of his returning from Lowestoft by sea, and being lost. This grew so strong with me, that I resolved to go back to the yard before I took my dinner, and ask the boat-builder if he thought his attempting to return by sea at all likely. He quite laughed when I asked him the question, and said there was no fear; no man in his senses, or out of them, would put off in such a gale of wind, least of all Ham Peggotty, who had been born to sea-faring!

So sensible of this, beforehand, that I had really felt ashamed of doing what I was nevertheless impelled to do, I went back to the inn. If such a wind could rise, I think it was rising. The howl and roar, the rattling of the doors and windows, the rumbling in the chimneys, the apparent rocking of the very house that sheltered me, and the prodigious tumult of the sea, were more fearful than in the morning. But there was now a great darkness besides; and that invested the storm with new terrors, real and fanciful.

I could not eat, I could not sit still, I could not continue steadfast to anything. Something within me, faintly answering to the storm without, tossed up the depths of my memory, and made a tumult in them. Yet, in all the hurry of my thoughts, wild running with the thundering sea – the storm and my uneasiness regarding Ham were always in the foreground.

My dinner went away almost untasted. . . . I walked to and fro, tried to read an old gazetteer, listened to the awful noises: looked at faces, scenes and figures in the fire. At length the steady ticking of the undisturbed clock on the wall tormented me to that degree that I resolved to go to bed. . . . For hours I lay there, listening to the wind and water; imagining, now, that I heard shrieks out at sea; now, that I distinctly heard the firing of signal guns; and now, the fall of houses in the town. I got up several times and looked out; but could see nothing except the reflection in the window-panes of the faint candle I had left burning, and of my own haggard face looking in at me from the black void.

At length my restlessness attained to such a pitch that I hurried on my clothes, and went downstairs. . . . I remained there, I dare say, two hours. Once, I opened the yard gate, and looked into the empty street. The sand, the seaweed and the flakes of foam were driving by; and I was obliged to call for assistance before I could shut the gate again and make it fast against the wind.

There was a dark gloom in my solitary chamber when I at length returned to it; but I was tired now, and, getting into bed again, fell – off a tower and down a precipice – into the depths of sleep. I have an impression that for a long time, though I dreamed of being elsewhere and in a variety of scenes, it was always blowing in my dream. At length I lost that feeble hold upon reality, and was engaged with two dear friends, but who they were I don't know, at the siege of some town in a roar of cannonading.

The thunder of the cannon was so loud and incessant, that I could not hear something I much desired to hear, until I made a great exertion and awoke. It was broad day – eight or nine o'clock; the storm raging, in lieu of the batteries; and someone knocking and calling at the door.

'What is the matter?' I cried.

'A wreck! Close by!'

I sprung out of bed, and asked what wreck?

'A schooner, from Spain or Portugal, laden with fruit and wine. Make haste, Sir, if you want to see her! It's thought, down on the beach, she'll go to pieces every moment.'

The excited voice went clamouring along the staircase; and I wrapped myself in my clothes as quickly as I could, and ran into the street. Numbers of people were there before me, all running in one direction, to the beach. I ran the same way, outstripping a good many, and soon came facing the wild sea.

The wind might by this time have lulled a little, though not more sensibly than if the cannonading I had dreamed of had been diminished by the silencing of half-a-dozen guns out of hundreds. But the sea, having upon it the additional agitation of the whole night, was infinitely more terrific than when I had seen it last. Every appearance it had then presented, bore the expression of being *swelled;* and the height to which the breakers rose, and, looking over one another, bore one another down, and rolled in in interminable hosts, was most appalling.

In the difficulty of hearing anything but wind and waves, and in the crowd and the unspeakable confusion, and my first breathless efforts to stand against the weather, I was so confused that I looked out to sea for the wreck and saw nothing but the foaming heads of the great waves. A half-dressed boatman, standing next me, pointed with his bare arm (a tattooed arrow on it, pointing in the same direction) to the left. Then, O great Heaven, I saw it, close in upon us.

One mast was broken short off, six or eight feet from the deck, and lay over the side, entangled in a mass of sail and rigging; and all that ruin, as the ship rolled and beat – which she did without a moment's pause and with a violence quite inconceivable – beat the side as if it would stave it in. Some efforts were even then being made to cut this portion of the wreck away; for, as the ship, which was broadside on, turned towards us in her rolling, I plainly descried her people at work with axes, especially one active figure with long curling hair, conspicuous among the rest. But a great cry, which was audible even above the wind and water, rose from the shore at this moment; the sea, sweeping over the rolling wreck, made a clean breach, and carried men, spars, casks, planks, bulwarks, heaps of such toys, into the boiling surge.

The second mast was yet standing, with the rags of a rent sail, and a wild confusion of broken cordage flapping to and fro. The ship had struck once, the same boatman hoarsely said in my ear, and then lifted in and struck again. I understood him to add that she was parting amidships, and I could readily suppose so, for the rolling and beating were too tremendous for any human work to suffer long. As he spoke, there was another great cry of pity from the beach; four men arose with the wreck out of the deep, clinging to the rigging of the remaining mast; uppermost, the active figure with the curling hair.

There was a bell on board; and as the ship rolled and dashed, like a desperate creature driven mad, now showing us the whole sweep of her deck as she turned on her beam-ends towards the shore, now nothing but her keel, as she sprung wildly over and turned towards the sea, the bell rang; and its sound, the knell of those unhappy men, was borne towards us on the wind. Again we lost her, and again she rose. Two men were gone. The agony on shore increased. Men groaned, and clasped their hands; women shrieked, and turned away their faces. Some ran wildly up and down along the beach, crying for help where no help could be. I found myself one of these, frantically imploring a knot of sailors whom I knew not to let those two creatures perish before our eyes.

They were making out to me, in an agitated way – I don't know how, for the little I could hear I was scarcely composed enough to understand – that the life-boat had been bravely manned an hour ago, and could do nothing; and that as no man would be so desperate as to attempt to wade off with a rope and establish a communication with the shore, there was nothing left to try; when I noticed that some new sensation moved the people on the beach, and saw them part, and Ham come breaking through them to the front.

I ran to him – as well as I know, to repeat my appeal for help. But, distracted though I was, by a sight so new to me and terrible, the determination in his face and his look, out to sea – exactly the same look as I remembered in connection with the morning after Emily's flight – awoke me to a knowledge of his danger. I held him back with both arms; and implored the men with whom I had been speaking not to listen to him, not to do murder, not to let him stir from off that sand.

Another cry arose on shore; and looking to the wreck, we saw the cruel sail, with blow on blow, beat off the lower of the two men, and fly up in triumph round the active figure left alone upon the mast.

Against such a sight, and against such determination as that of the calmly desperate man who was already accustomed to lead half the people present, I might as hopefully have entreated the wind. 'Mas'r Davy,' he said, cheerily grasping me by both hands, 'if my time is come, 'tis come. If 'tan't, I'll bide it. Lord above bless you, and bless all! Mates, make me ready. I'm a-going off.'

I was swept away, but not unkindly, to some distance, where the people around me bade me stay; urging, as I confusedly perceived, that he was bent on going, with help or without, and that I should endanger the precautions for his safety by troubling those with whom they rested. I don't know what I answered, or what they rejoined; but I saw hurry on the beach, and men running with ropes from a capstan that was there, and penetrating into a circle of figures that hid him from me. Then I saw him standing alone, in a seaman's frock and trousers; a rope in his hand, or slung to his wrist; another round his body: and several of the best men holding, at a little distance, to the latter, which he laid out himself, slack upon the shore, at his feet.

The wreck, even to my unpractised eye, was breaking up. I saw that she was parting in the middle, and that the life of the solitary man upon the mast hung by a thread. Still, he clung to it. He had a singular red cap on – not unlike a sailor's cap, but of a finer colour; and as the few yielding planks between him and destruction rolled and bulged, and his anticipative death-knell rung, he was seen by all of us to wave it. I saw him do it now, and thought I was going distracted, when his action brought an old remembrance to my mind of a once dear friend.

Ham watched the sea, standing alone, with the silence of suspended breath behind him, and the storm before, until there was a great retiring wave, when, with a backward glance at those who held the rope which was made fast round his body, he dashed in after it, and in a moment was buffeting with the water; rising with the hills, falling with the valleys, lost beneath the foam; then drawn again to land. They hauled in hastily.

He was hurt. I saw blood on his face, from where I stood; but he took no thought of that. He seemed hurriedly to give them some directions for leaving him more free – or so I judged from the motion of his arm – and was gone as before.

And now he made for the wreck, rising with the hills, falling with the valleys, lost beneath the rugged foam, borne in towards the shore, borne on towards the ship, striving hard and valiantly. The distance was nothing, but the power of the sea and wind made the strife deadly. At length he neared the wreck. He was so near that with one more of his vigorous strokes he would be clinging to it, when a high, green, vast hillside of water, moving on shoreward from beyond the ship, he seemed to leap up into it with a mighty bound, and the ship was gone!

Some eddying fragments I saw in the sea, as if a mere cask had been broken, in running to the spot where they were hauling in. Consternation was in every face. They drew him to my very feet – insensible – dead. He was carried to the nearest house; and, no-one preventing me now, I remained near him, while every means of restoration was tried; but he had been beaten to death by the great wave, and his generous heart was stilled for ever.

As I sat beside the bed, when hope was abandoned and all was done, a fisherman, who had known me when Emily and I were children, and ever since, whispered my name at the door.

'Sir,' said he, with tears starting to his weather-beaten face, which, with his trembling lips, was ashy pale, 'will you come over yonder?'

The old remembrance that had been recalled to me, was in his look. I asked him, terror-stricken, leaning on the arm he held out to support me:

'Has a body come ashore?'

He said, 'Yes.'

'Do I know it?' I asked then.

He answered nothing.

But he led me to the shore. And on that part of it where she and I had looked for shells, two children – on that part of it where some lighter fragments of the old boat, blown down last night, had been scattered by the wind – among the ruins of the home he had wronged – I saw him lying with his head upon his arm, as I had often seen him lie at school.

CHARLES DICKENS: *David Copperfield*

He rode upon a cherub and did fly; yea, he did fly upon the wings of the wind. He made darkness his secret place; his

pavilion round about him were dark waters and thick clouds
of the skies.

PSALM 18

Pity the castaway; sea-faring is an uncertain business.

PHOCYLIDES: *Fragment*

Sir Patrick Spens

i. THE SAILING

The king sits in Dunfermline town
    Drinking the blude-red wine;
'O whare will I get a skeely skipper,
    To sail this new ship o' mine?'

O up and spak an eldern knight,
    Sat at the king's right knee;
'Sir Patrick Spens is the best sailor
    That ever sail'd the sea.'

Our king has written a braid letter,
    And seal'd it with his hand,
And sent it to Sir Patrick Spens,
    Was walking on the strand.

'To Noroway, to Noroway,
    To Noroway o'er the faem;
The king's daughter o' Noroway,
    'Tis thou must bring her hame.'

The first word that Sir Patrick read
    So loud, loud laugh'd he;
The neist word that Sir Patrick read
    The tear blinded his e'e.

'O wha is this has done this deed
   And tauld the king o' me,
To send us out, at this time o' year,
   To sail upon the sea?

'Be it wind be it wet, be it hail, be it sleet,
   Our ship must sail the faem;
The king's daughter o' Noroway
   'Tis we must fetch her hame.'

They hoysed their sails on Monenday morn
   Wi' a' the speed they may;
They hae landed in Noroway
   Upon a Wodensday.

ii. THE RETURN

'Mak ready, mak ready, my merry men a'.
   Our gude ship sails the morn.'
'Now ever alack, my master dear,
   I fear a deadly storm.

'I saw the new moon late yestreen
   Wi' the auld moon in her arm;
And if we gang to sea, master,
   I fear we'll come to harm.'

They hadna sail'd a league, a league,
   A league but barely three,
When the lift grew dark, and the wind blew loud,
   And gurly grew the sea.

The ankers brak, and the topmast lap,
   It was sic a deadly storm;
And the waves came owre the broken ship
   Till a' her sides were torn.

'Go fetch a web o' the silken claith,
  Another o' the twine,
And wap them into our ship's side,
  And let nae the sea come in.'

They fetch'd a web o' the silken claith,
  Another o' the twine,
And they wrapp'd them round that gude ship's
    side,
  But still the sea came in.

O laith, laith were our gude Scots lords
  To wet their cork-heel'd shoon;
But lang or a' the play was played
  They wat their hats aboon.

And mony was the feather bed
  That flattered on the faem;
And mony was the gude lord's son
  That never mair cam hame.

O lang, lang may the ladies sit
  Wi' their fans into their hand,
Before they see Sir Patrick Spens
  Come sailing to the strand.

And lang, lang may the maidens sit
  Wi' their gowd cames in their hair,
A-waiting for their ain dear loves –
  For them they'll see nae mair.

Half-owre, half-owre to Aberdour
  'Tis fifty fathoms deep;
And there lies gude Sir Patrick Spens
  Wi' the Scots lords at his feet.

ANON.

The Drowning of Lycidas

He ask'd the waves, and ask'd the Fellon winds,
What hard mishap hath doom'd this gentle swain?
And questioned every gust of rugged winds
That blows from off each beaked Promontory,
They knew not of his story,
And sage Hippotades their answer brings,
That not a blast was from his dungeon stray'd,
The Ayr was calm, and on the level brine
Sleek Panope with all her sisters play'd.
It was that fatal and perfidious Bark,
Built in th' eclipse, and rigg'd with curses dark,
That sunk so low that sacred head of thine.

JOHN MILTON: *Lycidas*

St Paul is Wrecked on the Island of Malta

Now when much time was spent, and when sailing was now dangerous because the fast was now already past, Paul admonished them, and said unto them, 'Sirs, I perceive that this voyage will be with hurt and much damage, not only of the lading and the ship, but also of our lives.'

Nevertheless the centurion believed the master and the owner of the ship more than those things which were spoken by Paul. And because the haven was not commodious to winter in, the more part advised to depart thence also, if by any means they might attain to Phenice, and there to winter, which is an haven of Crete, and lieth toward the south-west and north-west. And when the south wind blew softly, supposing that they had obtained their purpose, loosing thence, they sailed close by Crete. But not long after there arose against it a tempestuous wind, called Euroclydon; and when the ship was caught, and could not bear up into the wind, we let her drive, and, running under a certain island which is called Clauda, we had much work to come by the boat; which when they had taken up, they used helps, undergirding the ship, and fearing lest they should fall into the quicksands, strake sail, and so were driven.

And we being exceedingly tossed with a tempest, the next day they lightened the ship, and the third day we cast out with our own hands the tackling of the ship. And when neither sun nor stars in many days appeared, and no small tempest lay on us, all hope that we should be saved was then taken away. But after long abstinence Paul stood forth in the midst of them and said: 'Sirs, ye should have hearkened unto me, and not have loosed from Crete, and to have gained this harm and loss. And now I exhort you to be of good cheer; for there shall be no loss of any man's life among you, but of the ship. For there stood by me this night the angel of God, whose I am and whom I serve, saying "Fear not, Paul, thou must be brought before Caesar; and lo! God hath given thee all them that sail with thee." Wherefore, Sirs, be of good cheer, for I believe God that it shall be even as it was told me. Howbeit, we must be cast upon a certain island.'

But when the fourteenth night was come, as we were driven up and down in Adria, about midnight the shipmen deemed that they drew near to some country, and sounded, and found it twenty fathoms; and when they had gone a little further, they sounded again and found it fifteen fathoms. Then fearing lest we should have fallen upon rocks, they cast four anchors out of the stern and wished for the day. And as the shipmen were about to flee out of the ship, when they had let down the boat into the sea, under colour as though they would have cast anchors out of the foreship, Paul said to the centurion and to the soldiers, 'Except these abide in the ship, ye cannot be saved.' Then the soldiers cut off the ropes of the boat and let her fall off.

And while the day was coming on, Paul besought them all to take meat, saying, 'This day is the fourteenth day that ye have tarried and continued fasting, having taken nothing. Wherefore I pray you to take some meat, for this is for your health, for there shall not an hair fall from the head of any of you.'

And when he had thus spoken, he took bread and gave thanks to God in presence of them all; and when he had broken it he began to eat. Then they were all of good cheer, and they also took some meat. And we were in all in the ship two hundred three score and sixteen souls.

And when they had eaten enough, they lightened the ship and cast out the wheat into the sea; and when it was day, they knew not the land; but they discovered a certain creek with a shore, into the which they were minded, if it were possible, to thrust in the ship. And when they had taken up the anchors, they committed themselves unto the sea, and loosed the rudder-bands and hoisted up the mainsail to the wind, and made toward shore. And falling into a place where two seas met, they ran the ship aground; and the fore part stuck fast and remained unmoveable, but the hinder part was broken with the violence of the waves. And the soldiers' counsel was to kill the prisoners, lest any of them should swim out and escape; but the centurion, willing to save Paul, kept them from their purpose, and commanded that they which could swim should cast themselves first into the sea, and get to land, and the rest, some on boards and some on broken pieces of the ship. And so it came to pass that they escaped all safe to land.

ACTS: ch. 27

The Tempest

On a ship at sea. A tempestuous noise of thunder and lightning heard.

Enter a SHIPMASTER *and a* BOATSWAIN

MAST. Boatswain!

BOATS. Here, master: what cheer?

MAST. Good, speak to the mariners; fall to't, yarely, or we run ourselves aground. Bestir, bestir.

(exit)

Enter MARINERS

BOATS. Heigh, my hearts! Cheerly, cheerly, my hearts! Yare, yare! Take in the topsail. Tend to the master's whistle. Blow till thou burst thy wind, if room enough!

Enter ALONSO, SEBASTIAN, ANTONIO, FERDINAND, GONZALO, *and others*

ALON. Good boatswain, have care. Where's the master? Play the men.

BOATS. I pray now, keep below.

ANT. Where is the master, boatswain?

BOATS. Do you not hear him? You mar our labour. Keep your cabins. You do assist the storm.

GON. Nay, good, be patient.

BOATS. When the sea is. Hence! What cares these roarers for the name of king? To cabin; silence! Trouble us not.

GON. Good, yet remember whom thou hast aboard.

BOATS. None that I love more than myself. You are a counsellor, if you can command these elements to silence, and work the peace of the present, we will not hand a rope more. Use your authority; if you cannot, give thanks you have lived so long and make yourself ready in your cabin for the mischance of the hour, if it so hap. Cheerly, good hearts! Out of our way, I say.

(exit)

GON. I have great comfort from this fellow, methinks he hath no drowning mark upon him; his complexion is perfect gallows. Stand fast, good fate, to his hanging: make the rope of his destiny our cable, for our own doth little advantage. If he be not born to be hanged, our case is miserable.

(exeunt)

Re-*enter* BOATSWAIN

BOATS. Down with the topmast! Yare! Lower, lower! Bring her to try with main course. (*A cry within*) A plague upon

this howling! They are louder than the weather or our
office.

Re-enter SEBASTIAN, ANTONIO *and* GONZALO

Yet again! What do you here? Shall we give o'er and
drown? Have you a mind to sink?

SEB. A pox o' your throat, you bawling, blasphemous,
incharitable dog!

BOATS. Work you then.

ANT. Hang, cur! hang, you whoreson, insolent noise-maker!
We are less afraid to be drowned than thou art.

GON. I'll warrant him for drowning; though the ship were
no stronger than a nutshell and as leaky as an unstaunched
wench.

BOATS. Lay her a-hold, a-hold! Set her two courses. Off to
sea again. Lay her off.

Enter MARINERS *wet*

MAR. All lost! to prayers, to prayers! All lost!

BOATS. What, must our mouths be cold?

GON. The king and prince at prayers! Let's assist them, for
our case is as theirs.

SEB. I'm out of patience.

ANT. We are merely cheated of our lives by drunkards:
This wide-chapped rascal – would thou might'st lie
drowning. The washing of ten tides!

GON. He'll be hanged yet, Though every drop of water
swear against it. And gape at widest to glut him.
(*A confused noise within: 'Mercy on us! We split, we split!
Farewell my wife and children! Farewell, brother! We split,
we split, we split!*)

ANT. Let's all sink with the king.

SEB. Let's take leave of him.

(*Exeunt* ANT. *and* SEB.)

GON. Now would I give a thousand furlongs of sea for an

acre of barren ground, long heath, brown furze, any thing.
The wills above be done! but I would fain die a dry death.

(*Exeunt*)

WILLIAM SHAKESPEARE: *The Tempest* (xiii)

The Loss of Sir Humphrey Gilbert

And as it was God's ordinance upon him, even so the vehement
perswasion and intreatie of his friends could nothing availe to
divert him from a wilfull resolution of going through in his
Frigat, which was overcharged upon their deckes, with fights,
nettings, and small artillerie, too cumbersome for so small a
boate, that was to pass through the Ocean sea at that season of
the yere, when by course we might expect much storme of
foule weather, whereof indeed we had enough.

But when he was intreated by the Captaine, Master and other
his well-willers of the *Hinde* not to venture in the Frigat, this
was his answere: I will not forsake my little company going
homeward, with whom I have passed so many stormes and
perils. And in very trueth, hee was urged to be so over hard,
by hard reports given of him, that he was afraid of the sea,
albeit this was rather rashness, than advised resolution, to
preferre the wind of a vaine report to the weight of his owne
life.

Seeing he would not bend to reason, he had provision out of
the *Hinde*, such as was wanting aboord his Frigat. And so we
committed him to God's protection, and set him aboord his
Pinnesse, we being then more than 300 leagues onward of our
way home.

By that time we had brought the Islands of Açores south of
us, yet we then keeping much to the North, until we had got
into the height and elevation of England: we met with very
foule weather, and terrible seas, breaking short and high
Pyramid wise. The reason whereof seemed to proceede either

of hilly grounds high and low within the sea (as we see hills and dales upon the land) upon which the seas do mount and fall: or else the cause proceedeth of diversitie of winds, shifting often in sundry points: at which having power to move the great Ocean, which againe is not presently setled, so many seas do encounter together, as there had been diversitie of winds. Howsoever it commeth to passe, men which all their life time had occupied the Sea, never saw more outragious Seas. We had also upon our maine yard, an apparition of a little fire by night, which seamen do call Castor and Pollux. But we had onely one, which they take an evill sign of more tempest: the same is usuall in stormes.

Munday the ninth of September, in the afternoone, the Frigat was neere cast away, oppressed by waves, yet at that time recovered: and giving foorth signes of joy, the Generall sitting abaft with a booke in his hand, cried out unto us in the *Hinde* (so oft as we did approach within hearing), We are as neere to heaven by sea as by land. Reiterating the same speech, well beseeming a souldier, resolute in Jesus Christ, as I can testifie he was.

The same Monday night, about twelve of the clocke, or not long after, the Frigat being ahead of us in the *Golden Hinde*, suddenly her lights were out, whereof as it were in a moment we lost the sight, and withall our watch cryed, the Generall was cast away, which was too true. For in that moment, the Frigat was devoured and swallowed up of the Sea. Yet still we looked out all that night, and ever after, untill we arrived upon the coast of England: omitting no small saile at sea, unto which we gave not the tokens betweene us, agreed upon, to have perfect knowledge of each other, if we should at any time be separated.

In great torment of weather, and perill of drowning, it pleased God to send safe home the *Golden Hinde*, which arrived in Falmouth, the 22nd day of September, being Sonday, not without as great danger escaped in a flaw, comming from the Southeast, with such thicke mist, that we could not discerne land, to put in right with the Haven.

HAKLUYT: *The English Voyages*

The same day I went on board we set sail, standing away to the northward upon our own coasts, with design to stretch over for the African coast, when they came into about ten or twelve degrees of northern latitude; which, it seems, was the manner of their course in those days. We had very good weather, only excessively hot, all the way upon our own coast, till we came to the height of Cape St Augustino; from whence, keeping farther off at sea, we lost sight of land, and steered as if we were bound for the Isle Fernando de Noronha, holding our course N.E. by N., and leaving those isles on the east. In this course we passed the line in about twelve days time, and were, by our last observation, in seven degrees twenty-two minutes northern latitude, when a violent tornado, or hurricane, took us quite out of our knowledge. It began from the south-east, came about to the north-west, and then settled into the north-east; from whence it blew in such a terrible manner, that for twelve days together we could do nothing but drive, and, scudding away before it, let it carry us wherever fate and the fury of the winds directed; and during these twelve days, I need not say that I expected every day to be swallowed up; nor did any in the ship expect to save their lives.

In this distress we had, besides the terror of the storm, one of our men died of the calenture, and a man and a boy washed overboard. About the twelfth day, the weather abating a little, the master made an observation as well as he could, and found that he was in about eleven degrees of north latitude, but that he was twenty-two degrees of longitude difference west from Cape St Augustino; so that he found he was gotten upon the coast of Guiana, or the north part of Brazil, beyond the river Amazones, towards that of the river Oroonoque, commonly called the Great River; and now he began to consult with me what course he should take; for the ship was leaky and very much disabled, and he was for going directly back to the coast of Brazil.

I was positively against that, and looking over the charts of the sea-coast of America with him, we concluded there was no inhabited country for us to have recourse to till we came within the circle of the Carribbee Islands, and therefore resolved to stand away for Barbadoes; which, by keeping off at sea, to avoid the in-draught of the bay or gulf of Mexico, we might easily perform, as we hoped, in about fifteen days sail; whereas we could not possibly make our voyage to the coast of Africa without some assistance both to our ship and to ourselves.

With this design we changed our course, and steered away N.W. by W., in order to reach some of our English islands, where I hoped for relief; but our voyage was otherwise determined; for, being in the latitude of twelve degrees eighteen minutes, a second storm came upon us, which carried us away with the same impetuosity westward, and drove us so out of the way of all human commerce, that had all our lives been saved as to the sea, we were rather in danger of being devoured by savages than ever returning to our own country.

In this distress, the wind still blowing very hard, one of our men early one morning cried out, 'Land!' and we had no sooner run out of the cabin to look out, in hopes of seeing whereabouts in the world we were, than the ship struck upon a sand, and in a moment, her motion being so stopped, the sea broke over her in such a manner, that we expected we should all have perished immediately; and we were even driven into our close quarters, to shelter us from the very foam and spray of the sea.

It is not easy for anyone who has not been in the like condition to describe or conceive the consternation of men in such circumstances. We knew nothing where we were, or upon what land it was we were driven; whether an island or the main, whether inhabited or not inhabited. As the rage of the wind was still great, though rather less than at first, we could not so much as hope to have the ship hold many minutes without breaking in pieces, unless the winds, by a kind of miracle, should turn immediately about. In a word, we sat looking upon one another, and expecting death every moment, and every man acting accordingly, as preparing for another world; for there was little or nothing more for us to do in this; that which was our present comfort, and all the comfort we had, was that, contrary to our expectation, the ship did not break yet, and that the master said the wind began to abate.

Now, though we thought the wind did a little abate, yet the ship having thus struck upon the sand, and sticking too fast for us to expect getting her off, we were in a dreadful condition indeed, and had nothing to do but to think of saving our lives as well as we could. We had a boat at our stern just before the storm, but she was first staved by dashing against the ship's rudder, and in the next place she broke away, and either sunk or was driven off to sea; so there was no hope from her. We had another boat on board, but how to get her off into the sea was a doubtful thing; however, there was no room to debate, for we fancied the ship would break in pieces every minute, and some told us she was actually broken already.

In this distress, the mate of our vessel laid hold of the boat, and with the help of the rest of the men they got her flung over the ship's side; and getting all into her, let go, and committed ourselves, being eleven in number, to God's mercy and the wild sea: for though the storm was abated considerably, yet the sea went dreadfully high upon the shore, and might well be called *den wild Zee*, as the Dutch call the sea in a storm.

And now our case was very dismal indeed; for we all saw plainly, that the sea went so high that the boat could not escape, and that we should be inevitably drowned. As to making sail, we had none, nor, if we had, could we have done anything with it; so we worked at the oar towards the land, though with heavy hearts, like men going to execution; for we all knew that when the boat came near the shore, she would be dashed in a thousand pieces by the breach of the sea. However, we committed our souls to God in the most earnest manner; and the wind driving us towards the shore, we hastened our destruction with our own hands, pulling as well as we could towards land.

What the shore was, whether rock or sand, whether steep or shoal, we knew not; the only hope that could rationally give us the least shadow of expectation, was, if we might happen into some bay or gulf, or the mouth of some river, where by great chance we might have run our boat in, or got under the lee of the land, and perhaps made smooth water. But there was nothing of this appeared; but as we made nearer and nearer the shore, the land looked more frightful than the sea.

After we had rowed, or rather driven, about a league and a half, as we reckoned it, a raging wave, mountain-like, came rolling astern of us, and plainly bade us expect the *coup de grâce*. In a word, it took us with such a fury, that it overset the boat at once; and separating us as well from the boat as from one another, gave us not time hardly to say, 'O God!' for we were all swallowed up in a moment.

Nothing can describe the confusion of thought which I felt, when I sank into the water; for though I swam very well, yet I could not deliver myself from the waves so as to draw breath, till that wave having driven me, or rather carried me, a vast way on towards the shore, and having spent itself, went back, and left me upon the land almost dry, but half dead with the water I took in. I had so much presence of mind, as well as breath left, that seeing myself nearer the main land than I expected, I got upon my feet, and endeavoured to make on towards the land as fast as I could, before another wave should return and take me up again; but I soon found it was impossible to avoid it; for I saw the sea come after me as high as a great hill, and as furious as an enemy, which I had no means or strength to contend with: my business was to hold my breath, and raise myself upon the water, if I could; and so by swimming to preserve my breathing, and pilot myself towards the shore if possible, my greatest concern now being, that the wave, as it would carry me a great way towards the shore when it came on, might not carry me back again with it when it gave back towards the sea.

The wave that came upon me again buried me at once twenty or thirty feet deep in its own body, and I could feel myself carried with a mighty force and swiftness towards the shore a very great way; but I held my breath, and assisted myself to swim still forward with all my might. I was ready to burst with holding my breath, when as I felt myself rising up, so, to my immediate relief, I found my head and hands shoot out above the surface of the water; and though it was not two seconds of time that I could keep myself so, yet it relieved me greatly, gave me breath and new courage. I was covered again with water a good while, but not so long but I held it out; and finding the water had spent itself, and began to return, I struck forward against the return of the waves, and felt ground again with my feet. I stood still a few moments to recover breath, and till the waters went from me, and then took to my heels, and ran with what strength I had, farther towards the shore. But neither would this deliver me from the fury of the sea, which came pouring in after me again; and twice more I was lifted up by the waves and carried forwards as before, the shore being very flat.

The last time of these two had well nigh been fatal to me; for the sea having hurried me along, as before, landed me, or rather dashed me, against a piece of rock, and that with such force as it left me senseless, and indeed helpless, as to my own deliverance; for the blow taking my side and breast, beat the breath as it were quite out of my body; and had it returned again immediately, I must have been strangled in the water; but I recovered a little before the return of the waves, and seeing I should be covered again with the water, I resolved to hold fast by a piece of the rock, and so to hold my breath, if possible, till the wave went back. Now, as the waves were not so high as at first, being nearer land, I held my hold till the wave abated, and then fetched another run, which brought me so near the shore, that the next wave, though it went over me, yet did not so swallow me up as to carry me away; and the next run I took, I got to the main land; where, to my great comfort, I clambered up the cliffs of the shore, and sat me down upon the grass, free from danger, and quite out of the reach of the water. . . . I walked about on the shore, lifting up my

hands, and my whole being, as I may say, wrapt up in a con-
templation of my deliverance; making a thousand gestures and
motions, which I cannot describe; reflecting upon all my
comrades that were drowned, and that there should not be one
soul saved but myself; for, as for them, I never saw them afterwards, or any sign of them, except three of their hats, one cap,
and two shoes that were not fellows.

DANIEL DEFOE: *Robinson Crusoe*

The waters saw thee, O God, the waters saw thee; they were
afraid; the depths also were troubled. The clouds poured out
water, the skies sent out a sound; thine arrows also went
abroad. The voice of thy thunder was in the heaven, the
lightnings lightened the world; the earth trembled and shook.

Thy way is in the sea, and thy path in the great waters, and
thy footsteps are not known.

PSALM 77

Epitaphs from the Greek Anthology

(i)

Your body lies in foreign earth, Cleisthenes. On the Black
Sea your ship was driving when death took you; and cheated
of the sweet delight of your home-coming, you never returned
to sea-girt Chios.

SIMONIDES

(ii)

Not earth nor the weight of a little stone is Erasippus' tomb,
but the whole sea here before your eyes. He went down with
his ship, and where his bones are rotting only the sea-birds
know.

GLAUCUS

(iii)

This is a sailor's grave. Sail on, friend; for when I was drowned, the ships that accompanied me held on their course.

THEODORIDES

(iv)

Ask not, sailor, whose body lies here. I wish you better luck than mine, and a kindlier sea.

ANON.

The Day's Work

A Nineteenth Century Merchant Seaman's Day

Nothing is more common than to hear people say: 'Are not sailors very idle at sea? What can they find to do?' This is a very natural mistake and being very frequently made, it is one which every sailor feels interested in having corrected. In the first place, then, the discipline of the ship requires every man to be at work upon *something* when he is on deck, except at night and on Sundays. Except at these times, you will never see a man on board a well-ordered vessel standing idle on deck, sitting down, or leaning over the side. It is the officer's duty to keep everyone at work, even if there is nothing to be done but to scrape the rust from the chain cables. In no state prison are the convicts more regularly set to work and more closely watched. No conversation is allowed amongst the crew at their duty, and though they frequently do talk when aloft or when near one another, yet they always stop when an officer is nigh.

With regard to the work upon which the men are put, it is a matter which probably would not be understood by one who has not been at sea. When I first left port, and found that we were kept regularly employed for a week or two, I supposed that we were getting the vessel into sea trim, and that it would soon be over, and that we should have nothing to do but to sail the ship; but I found that it continued so for two years, and at the end of the two years there was as much to be done as ever. As has often been said, a ship is like a lady's watch, always out of repair. When first leaving port, studding-sail gear is to be rove, all the running rigging to be examined, that which is unfit for use to be got down and new rigging rove in its place; then the standing rigging is to be overhauled, replaced, and repaired, in a thousand different ways; and wherever any of the numberless ropes or the yards are chafing or wearing upon it, there 'chafing gear', as it is called, must be put on. This chafing gear consists of worming, parcelling, roundings, battens, and service of all kinds – both rope-yarns, spun-yarns, marline and seizing-stuffs. Taking off, putting on, and mending the chafing gear alone, upon a vessel, would find constant employment for two or three men, during working hours, for a whole voyage.

The next point to be considered is, that all the 'small stuffs' which are used on board a ship – such as spun-yarn, marline, seizing-stuff, etc. etc. – are made on board. The owners of a vessel buy up incredible quantities of 'old junk' which the sailors unlay, after drawing out the yarns, knot them together and roll them up in balls. These 'rope-yarns' are constantly used for various purposes, but the greater part is manufactured into spun-yarn. For this purpose every vessel is furnished with a 'spun-yarn winch,' which is very simple, consisting of a wheel and spindle. This may be heard constantly going on deck in pleasant weather; and we had employment, during a great part of the time, for three hands in drawing and knotting yarns and making spun-yarn.

Another method of employing the crew is 'setting up' rigging. Whenever any of the standing rigging becomes slack (which is continually happening), the seizings and coverings must be taken off, tackles got up, and, after the rigging is bowsed well taut, the seizings and coverings replaced, which is a very nice piece of work. There is also such a connection between different parts of a vessel, that one rope can seldom be touched without altering another. You cannot stay a mast aft by the back-stays without slacking up the head-stays etc. etc. If we add to this all the tarring, greasing, oiling, varnishing, painting, scraping and scrubbing which are required in the course of a long voyage, and also remember that this is all to be done in *addition* to watching at night, steering, reefing, furling, bracing, making and setting sail, and pulling, hauling, and climbing in every direction, one will hardly ask, 'What can a sailor find to do at sea?'

162

If, after all this labour – after exposing the lives and limbs in storms, wet and cold,

> *Wherein the cub-drawn bear would couch;*
> *The lion and the belly-pinched wolf*
> *Keep their furs dry,*

the merchants and captains think that they have not earned their twelve dollars a month (out of which they clothe themselves) and their salt beef and hard bread, they keep them picking oakum – *ad infinitum*. This is the usual resource upon a rainy day, for then it will not do to work upon rigging, and when it is pouring down in floods, instead of letting the sailors stand about in sheltered places, and talk, and keep themselves comfortable, they are separated to different parts of the ship, and kept at work picking oakum. I have seen oakum stuff placed about in different parts of the ship, so that the sailors might not be idle in the *snatches* between the frequent squalls upon crossing the equator. Some officers have been so driven to find work for the crew in a ship ready for sea, that they have set them to pounding the anchors (often done) and scraping the chain cables. The 'Philadelphia catechism' is:

> *Six days shalt thou labour and do all thou art able,*
> *And on the seventh – holystone the decks and scrape the cable.*

Before leaving this description, I would state, in order to show landsmen how little they know of the nature of a ship, that a *ship-carpenter* is kept in constant employ during good weather on board vessels which are in what is called perfect sea order.

R. H. DANA: *Two Years Before the Mast*

The First Chase of the White Whale

Like noiseless nautilus shells, their light prows sped through the sea; but only slowly they neared the foe. As they neared him, the ocean grew still more smooth; seemed drawing a carpet over its waves; seemed a noon-meadow, so serenely it spread. At length the breathless hunter came so nigh his seemingly unsuspecting prey, that his entire dazzling hump was distinctly visible, sliding along the sea as if an isolated thing, and continually set in a revolving ring of finest, fleecy, greenish foam. He saw the vast, involved wrinkles of the slightly projecting head beyond. Before it, far out on the soft, Turkish-rugged waters, went the glistening white shadow from his broad, milky forehead, a musical rippling playfully accompanying the shade; and behind, the blue waters interchangeably flowed over into the moving valley of his steady wake; and on either hand bright bubbles arose and danced by his side. But these were broken again by the light toss of hundreds of gay fowls softly feathering the sea, alternate with their fitful flight; and like to some flag-staff rising from the painted hull of an argosy, the tall but shattered pole of a recent lance projected from the white whale's back; and at intervals one of the cloud of soft-toed fowls hovering, and to and fro skimming like a canopy over the fish, silently perched and rocked on this pole, the long tail feathers streaming like pennons.

A gentle joyousness – a mighty mildness of repose in swiftness, invested the gliding whale. Not the white bull Jupiter swimming away with ravished Europa clinging to his graceful horns, his lovely, leering eyes sideways intent upon the maid, with smooth bewitching fleetness rippling straight for the nuptial bower in Crete; not Jove, not that great Majesty Supreme, did surpass the glorified White Whale as he so divinely swam.

On each soft side – coincident with the parted swell, that but once leaving him, then flowed so wide away – on each bright side, the whale shed off enticings. No wonder there had been some among the hunters who namelessly transported and allured by all this serenity, had ventured to assail it; but had fatally found that quietude but the vesture of tornadoes. Yet calm, enticing calm, oh, whale! thou glidest on, to all who for the first time eye thee, no matter how many in that same way thou may'st have bejuggled and destroyed before.

And thus, through the serene tranquillities of the tropical sea, among waves whose hand-clappings were suspended by exceeding rapture, Moby Dick moved on, still withholding from sight the full terrors of his submerged trunk, entirely hiding the wrenched hideousness of his jaw. But soon the fore part of him slowly rose from the water; for an instant his whole marbleised body formed a high arch, like Virginia's natural bridge, and warningly waving his bannered flukes in the air, the grand god revealed himself, sounded, and went out of sight. Hoveringly halting, and dipping on the wing, the white sea-fowls longingly lingered over the agitated pool that he left.

With oars apeak, and paddles down, the sheets of their sails adrift, the three boats now stilly floated, awaiting Moby Dick's reappearance.

'An hour,' said Ahab, standing rooted in his boat's stern; and he gazed beyond the whale's place, towards the dim blue spaces and wide wooing vacancies to leeward. It was only an instant; for again his eyes seemed whirling round in his head as he swept the watery circle. The breeze now freshened; the sea began to swell.

'The birds! The birds!' cried Tashtego.

In long Indian file, as when herons take wing, the white birds were now all flying towards Ahab's boat; and when within a few yards began fluttering over the water there, wheeling round and round, with joyous, expectant cries. Their vision was keener than man's; Ahab could discover no sign in the sea. But suddenly as he peered down and down into its depths, he profoundly saw a white living spot no bigger than a white weasel, with wonderful celerity uprising, and magnifying as it rose, till it turned, and then there were plainly revealed two long crooked rows of white, glistening teeth, floating up from the undiscoverable bottom. It was Moby Dick's open mouth and scrolled jaw; his vast, shadowed bulk still half blending with the blue of the sea. The glittering mouth yawned beneath the boat like an open-doored marble tomb; and giving one sidelong sweep with his steering oar, Ahab whirled the craft aside from this tremendous apparition. Then, calling upon Fedallah to change places with him, went forward to the bows, and seizing Perth's harpoon, commanded his crew to grasp their oars and stand by to stern.

Now, by reason of this timely spinning round the boat upon its axis, its bow, by anticipation, was made to face the whale's head while yet under water. But as if perceiving this stratagem, Moby Dick with that malicious intelligence ascribed to him, sidelingly transplanted himself, as it were, in an instant, shooting his pleated head lengthwise beneath the boat.

Through and through; through every plank and each rib, it thrilled for an instant, the whale obliquely lying on his back, in the manner of a biting shark, slowly and feelingly taking its bows full within his mouth, so that the long, narrow, scrolled lower jaw curled high up into the open air, and one of the teeth caught in a rowlock. The bluish pearl-white of the inside of the jaw was within six inches of Ahab's head, and reached higher than that. In this attitude the White Whale now shook the slight cedar as a mildly cruel cat her mouse. With unastonished eyes Fedallah gazed, and crossed his arms; but the tiger-yellow crew were tumbling over each other's heads to gain the uttermost stern.

And now, while both elastic gunwales were springing in and out, as the whale dallied with the doomed craft in this devilish way; and from his body being submerged beneath the boat, he could not be darted at from the bows, for the bows were almost inside of him, as it were; and while the other boats involuntarily paused, as before a quick crisis impossible to withstand, then it was that monomaniac Ahab, furious with this tantalising vicinity of his foe, which placed him all alive and helpless in the very jaws he hated; frenzied with all this, he seized the long bone with his naked hands and wildly strove to wrench it from its gripe. As now he thus vainly strove, the jaw slipped from him; the frail gunwales bent in, collapsed, and snapped, as both jaws like an enormous shears, sliding further aft, bit the craft completely in twain, and locked themselves fast again in the sea, midway between the two floating wrecks. These floated aside, the broken ends drooping, the crew at the stern-wreck clinging to the gunwales, and striving to hold fast to the oars to lash them across.

At that preluding moment, ere the boat was yet snapped, Ahab, the first to perceive the whale's intent, by the crafty upraising of its head, a movement that loosed his hold for the time; at that moment his hand had made one final effort to push the boat out of the bite. But only slipping further into the whale's mouth, and tilting over sideways as it slipped, the boat had shaken off his hold upon the jaw; spilled him out of it, as he leaned to the push; and so he fell flat-faced upon the sea.

Rippingly withdrawing from his prey, Moby Dick now lay at a little distance, vertically thrusting his oblong white head up and down in the billows; and at the same time slowly revolving his whole spindled body; so that when his vast wrinkled forehead rose – some twenty or more feet out of the water – the now rising swells, with all their confluent waves, dazzlingly broke against it, vindictively tossing their shivered spray still higher into the air. So, in a gale, the but half baffled Channel billows only recoil from the base of the Eddystone, triumphantly to overleap its summit with their scud.

But soon resuming his horizontal attitude, Moby Dick swam swiftly round and round the wrecked crew; sideways churning the water in his vengeful wake, as if lashing himself up to still another and more deadly assault. The sight of the splintered boat seemed to madden him, as the blood of grapes and mulberries cast before Antiochus' elephants in the book of Maccabees. Meanwhile Ahab half smothered in the foam of the whale's insolent tail, and too much of a cripple to swim – though he could still keep afloat, even in the heart of such a whirlpool as that; helpless Ahab's head was seen, like a tossed bubble which the least chance shock might burst. From the boat's fragmentary stern, Fedallah incuriously and mildly eyed him; the clinging crew, at the other drifting end, could not succour him; more than enough was it for them to look to themselves. For so revolvingly appalling was the White Whale's aspect, and so planetarily swift the ever-contracting circles he made, that he seemed horizontally swooping upon them. And though the other boats, unharmed, still hovered hard by, still they dared not pull into the eddy to strike, lest that should be the signal for the instant destruction of the jeopardised castaways, Ahab and all; nor in that case could they themselves hope to escape. With straining eyes, then, they remained on the outer edge of the direful zone, whose centre had now become the old man's head.

Meantime, from the beginning all this had been descried from the ship's mastheads; and squaring her yards, she had borne down upon the scene; and was now so nigh, that Ahab in the water hailed her: – 'Sail on the . . .' but at that moment a breaking sea dashed on him from Moby Dick, and whelmed him for the time. But struggling out of it again, and chancing to rise on a towering crest, he shouted: 'Sail on the whale! Drive him off!'

The Pequod's prow was pointed; and breaking up the charmed circle, she effectually parted the white whale from his victim. As he sullenly swam off, the boats flew to the rescue.

HERMAN MELVILLE: *Moby Dick*

Fram; A Strong Ship

Everything of course was done to make the sides of the ship as strong as possible. The frame timbers were of choice Italian oak that had originally been intended for the Norwegian navy, and had lain under cover at Horten for 30 years. They were all grown to shape and 10-11 inches thick. The frames were built in two courses or tiers, closely wrought together, and connected by bolts, some of which were riveted. The frames were about 21 inches wide and were placed close together, with only about an inch or an inch and a half between; and these interstices were filled with pitch and saw-dust mixed, from the keel to a little distance above the water-line, in order to keep the ship moderately watertight even should the outer skin be chafed through.

The outside planking consists of three layers. The inner one is of oak 3 inches thick, fastened with spikes and carefully caulked; outside this another oak sheathing 4 inches thick, fastened with through bolts and caulked; and outside these comes the ice-skin of greenheart which like the other planking runs right down to the keel. At the water-line it is 6 inches thick, gradually diminishing towards the bottom to 3 inches . . . The lining inside the frame timbers is of pitch-pine planks, some 4, some 8 inches thick; it was also carefully caulked once or twice.

The total thickness of the ship's sides is, therefore, from 24 to 28 inches of solid, watertight wood. It will readily be understood that such a ship's side, with its rounded form, would of itself offer a very good resistance to the ice; but to make it still stronger the inside was shored up in every possible way, so that the hold looks like a cobweb of balks, stanchions and braces. In the first place there are two rows of beams, the upper deck and between decks, principally of solid oak, partly also of pitch-pine; and all of these are further connected with each other, as well as with the sides of the ship, by numerous supports. The diagonal stays are, of course, placed as nearly as possible at right angles to the sides of the ship, so as to strengthen them against external pressure and to distribute its force. The vertical stanchions between both tiers of beams and between the lower beams and keelson are admirably adapted for this latter object. All are connected together with strong knees and iron fastenings, so that the whole becomes, as it were, a single coherent mass.

FRIDTJOF NANSEN: Farthest North (xiv)

Billy Budd

On the gun-decks of the *Indomitable* the general estimate of his nature and its unconscious simplicity eventually found rude utterance from another foretopman, one of his own

watch, gifted as some sailors are with an artless poetic tempera-
ment. The tarry hands made some lines, which, after circulating
among the shipboard crew for a while, finally got rudely
printed at Portsmouth as a ballad. The title given to it was the
sailor's.

Billy in the Darbies

Good of the chaplain to enter Lone Bay
And down on his marrow-bones here and pray
For the likes just o' me, Billy Budd – But look:
Through the port comes the moonshine astray!
It tips the guard's cutlass and silvers this nook,
But 'twill die in the dawning of Billy's last day.
A jewel-block they'll make of me to-morrow,
Pendent pearl from the yard-arm end .
Like the ear-drop I gave to Bristol Molly –
Oh 'tis me, not the sentence, they'll suspend.
Ay, ay, all is up; and I must up too
Early in the morning, aloft from alow.
On an empty stomach, now, never it would do;
They'll give me a nibble – bit o' biscuit ere I go.
Sure, a messmate will reach me the last parting cup;
But turning heads away from the hoist and the belay,
Heaven knows who will have the running of me up!
No pipe to those halyards – but aren't it all sham?
A blur's in my eyes; it is dreaming that I am.
A hatchet to my panzer? all adrift to go?
The drum roll to grog, and Billy never know?
But Donald he has promised to stand by the plank;
So I'll shake a friendly hand ere I sink.
But – no! It is dead then I'll be, come to think.
I remember Taff the Welshman when he sank;
And his cheek it was like the budding pink.
But me, they'll lash me in hammock, drop me deep

Fathoms down, fathoms down, how I'll dream fast asleep.
I feel it stealing now. Sentry, are you there?
Just ease these darbies at the wrist,
And roll me over fair.
I am sleepy, and the oozy weeds about me twist.

HERMAN MELVILLE: Billy Budd

Look-Out

Nothing in these Rules shall exonerate any vessel, or the owner, or master, or crew thereof, from the consequences of any neglect to carry lights or signals, or of any neglect to keep a proper look-out, or of the neglect of any precaution which may be required by the ordinary practice of seamen, or by the special circumstances of the case.

Regulations for Preventing Collisions at Sea. Article 29

Torn Mainsail

The main-sail, by the squall so lately rent,
In streaming pendants flying, is unbent:
With brails refixed, another soon prepared,
Ascending, spreads along beneath the yard.
To each yard-arm the headrope they extend,
And soon their earrings and their robans bend.
That task performed, they first the braces slack,
Then to the chesstree drag the unwilling tack.
And, while the lee clue-garnet's lowered away,
Taught aft the sheet they tally, and belay.

WILLIAM FALCONER: The Shipwreck

Man Overboard

Everyone who has been much at sea must remember the peculiar sounds which pervade a ship when a man is known to have fallen overboard. The course steered is so suddenly altered, that as she rounds-to the effect of the sails is doubled; the creaking of the tiller-ropes and rudder next strike the ear; then follows the pitter-patter of several hundred feet in rapid motion, producing a singular tremor, fore and aft. In the midst of these ominous noises may be heard, over all, the shrill startling voice of the officer of the watch, generally betraying in its tone more or less uncertainty of purpose. Then the violent flapping of the sails, and the mingled cries of 'Clear away the boats!' 'Is the lifebuoy gone?' 'Heave that grating after him!' 'Throw that hen-coop over the stern!' 'Who is it, do you know?' 'Where did he fall from?' 'Can he swim?' 'Silence!' An impetuous, and too often an ill-regulated rush now succeeds to gain the boats, which are generally so crowded that it becomes dangerous to lower them down, and more time is lost in getting the people out again than would have manned them twice over, if any regular system had been prepared, and rendered familiar and easy by practice beforehand.

I could give a pretty long list of cases which I have myself seen, or have heard others relate, where men have been drowned while their shipmates were thus struggling on board who should be first to save them, but who, instead of aiding, were actually impeding one another by their hurry-skurry and general ignorance of what really ought to be done. I remember, for example, hearing of a line-of-battle-ship, in the Baltic, from which two men fell one evening, when the ship's company were at quarters. The weather was fine, the water smooth, and the ship going about seven knots. The two lads in question who were furling the fore-royal at the time, lost their hold, and were jerked far in the sea. At least a dozen men, leaving their guns, leaped overboard from different parts of the ship, some dressed as they were, and others stripped. Of course, the ship

was in a wretched state of discipline where such frantic pro-
ceedings could take place. The confusion soon became worse
confounded; but the ship was hove aback, and several boats
lowered down. Had it not been smooth water, daylight, and
fine weather, many of these absurd volunteers must have
perished. I call them absurd, because there is no sense in merely
incurring a great hazard, without some useful purpose to guide
the exercise of courage. These intrepid fellows merely knew
that a man had fallen overboard, and that was all; so away they
leaped out of the ports and over the hammock-nettings, without knowing whereabouts the object of their Quixotic heroism
might be. The boats were obliged to pick up the first that presented themselves, for they were all in a drowning condition;
but the two unhappy men who had been flung from aloft,
being furthest off, went to the bottom before their turn came.

CAPT. BASIL HALL, R.N., F.R.S.:
The Lieutenant and Commander

Value of the Lead

In thick or hazy weather, St George's channel must be
approached with extreme caution, and no vessel should
confidently run for it without having first made the Tuskar or
the Smalls, or the land in their vicinity.

Although the necessity of an unremitting attention to the
use of the lead in thick weather has been before noticed, it may
be repeated here that such attention is of the greatest importance, as it affords the mariner the only certain indication of his
safety or danger, and contributes to relieve his mind in some
degree from the anxiety he must feel while his vessel
continues within the limits of this dangerous navigation.

A vessel from the westward, having arrived in the vicinity
of the Saltees, and making a lighthouse in hazy weather, must
be careful to ascertain whether it is the Hook or the Tuskar

before she alters her course, an error in this respect having proved fatal to some vessels, while others have become dangerously embayed and entangled among Saltee rocks. Hook lighthouse may be known by its three *red* belts; the Tuskar is a *white* tower. By attention to the lead, however, this mistake may at all times be avoided, as the water is much deeper in the vicinity of the Tuskar than at an equal distance from the Hook.

By not shoaling the water to less than 35 fathoms, a vessel will pass 7 or 8 miles to the southward of Coningbeg light-vessel, and by sounding at proper intervals will know when she is crossing the belt of fine dark sand and mud before alluded to. In her progress to the eastward she will deepen her water. Should a vessel advance so far as to increase the depth to 60 fathoms, it will be an indication of having neared the Smalls, and she must accordingly haul to the northward, proceeding with the utmost caution until her position is ascertained. From Coningbeg light-vessel, an East course for 19 miles will carry a ship about 2½ miles to the southward of the South rock of the Tuskar, and about the same distance from the Brandies and Barrels. It must be borne in mind, however, that the east-going stream sets towards these dangers, for which, particularly in light winds, due allowance must be made. Do not approach within 2 miles of the Tuskar until it bears northward of N. by E. ½ E., to clear South rock. In fine weather a vessel may pass half a mile to the eastward of the Tuskar. In thick weather approach it no nearer than the depth of 40 fathoms.

Irish Coast Pilot

Queequeg's Request

He called one to him in the grey morning watch, when the day was just breaking, and taking his hand said that while in Nantucket he had chanced to see certain little canoes of dark wood, like the rich war-wood of his native isle; and upon enquiry he had learned that all whalemen who died in Nantucket were laid in those same dark canoes, and that the fancy of being so laid had much pleased him; for it was not unlike the custom of his own race, who, after embalming a dead warrior, stretched him out in his canoe, and so left him to be floated away to the starry archipelagoes; for not only do they believe that the stars are isles, but that far beyond all visible horizons, their own mild, uncontinented seas interflow with the blue heavens, and so form the white breakers of the milky way. He added, that he shuddered at the thought of being buried in his hammock, according to the usual sea custom, tossed like something vile to the death-devouring sharks. No: he desired a canoe like those of Nantucket, all the more congenial to him, being a whaleman, that like a whale-boat these coffin-canoes were without a keel; though that involved but uncertain steering, and much leeway adown the dim ages.

HERMAN MELVILLE: *Moby Dick*

Raft under Sail

No officer can tell how soon he may be called upon to place his crew on a raft, should his ship be wrecked; and yet, unless he has been previously made aware of some method of steering it, no purpose may be answered but that of protracting the misery of the people under his charge. Nothing can be more simple, or more easy of application, than the South American contrivance. Near both ends of the centre spar there is cut a perpendicular slit, about a couple of inches wide by one or two feet in length. Into each of these holes a broad plank, called guaras by the natives, is inserted in such a way that it may be thrust down to the depth of ten or twelve feet, or it may be drawn up entirely. The slits are so cut, that, when the raft is in motion, the edges of these planks shall meet the water. It is clear, that if both the guaras be thrust quite down, and held fast in a perpendicular direction, they will offer a broad surface towards the side, and thus, by acting like the leeboards of a river barge, or the keel of a ship, prevent the balsa from drifting sidewise or dead to leeward. But while these guaras serve the purpose of a keel, they also perform the important duty of a rudder, the rationale of which every sailor will understand, upon considering the effect which must follow upon pulling up either the guara in the bow or that in the stern. Suppose, when the wind is on the beam, the foremost one drawn up, that end of the raft will instantly have a tendency to drift to leeward, from the absence of the lateral support it previously received from its guara or keel at the bow; or, in sea language, the balsa will immediately 'fall off', and in time she will come right before the wind. On the other hand, if the foremost guara be kept down while the sternmost one is drawn up, the balsa's head, or bow, will gradually come up towards the wind, in consequence of that end retaining its hold of the water by reason of its guara, while the stern end, being relieved from its lateral support, drifts to leeward. Thus, by judiciously raising or lowering one or both the guaras, the raft may not only be steered with the greatest nicety, but may be tacked or wore, or otherwise directed, with precision.

I never shall forget the sensation in a ship I commanded one evening on the coast of Peru, as we steered towards the road-stead of Payta. An immense balsa was dashing out before the land-wind, and sending a snowy wreath of foam before her like that which curls up before the bow of a frigate in chase. As long as she was kept before the wind, we could understand this in some degree; but when she hauled up in order to round the point, and having made a stretch along-shore, proceeded to tack, we could scarcely believe our eyes. Had the celebrated Flying Dutchman sailed past us, our wonder could hardly have been more excited.

CAPT. BASIL HALL, R.N., F.R.S.:
The Lieutenant and the Commander

Fire

If at sea and the ship takes fire, immediately stop her; if the fire is aft try and keep head to wind, but do not give her any more way than you can help as it increases the draught; if the fire is forward, keep her right before the wind and stop the engines; if any of the hatches are off, batten them down immediately, and block up the mouths of the ventilators. While this is being done, if the seat of the fire cannot be reached, screw on the deck hose, cut a small hole in either the deck or in the hatchway large enough to admit the nozzle of the hose, and keep playing upon the place where you surmise the fire is situated; open the sluices so that the water will find its way into the engine room and be discharged overboard.

If the fire decreases, be very careful in taking the hatches off, as the least air might fan a smouldering fire into a blaze; try to find where the fire originated, and throw any smouldering cargo overboard, if it can be got at.

If the hose is insufficient, connect the steam pipe with the hold under a good pressure of steam. Do not apply steam and water at the same time, as the water will condense the steam.

If the fire still gains when all the deck hoses or steam pipes are on, get the boats provisioned, and see all clear for saving life. If the vessel is in a position to be run on shore and the fire is gaining rapidly, then run her on shore. Open all the sluices and sea cocks to scuttle her, which perhaps will save the ship; this, of course, is a last resource.

REED'S *Seamanship*

Old Papa

But it was the last outrage, the murder of a poor old Italian, which caused the San Francisco trial.

'Old Papa', as he was called by the men, one day failed to show up on watch. It was the afternoon watch, and Bully

Waterman, like a tiger in search of blood, accompanied his mate forward in order to fetch the Dago out of the foc's'le. Pounding on the scuttle with his heaver, the irate skipper yelled for Old Papa, and when the man appeared asked him why he was not standing watch. By way of reply Old Papa mumbled something in Italian and pointed to his feet. They were black with mortification! Someone had stolen his only pair of boots, and he had been compelled to go bare foot through the bitter weather of the Horn, with the result that his feet had been frozen.

But as soon as he began to mumble Italian, Bully Waterman let fly.

'Curse you, speak English, can't you?' he yelled and straightway struck the wretched old man over the head with his heaver.

The Dago dropped as if he had been pole-axed.

At this, the captain roared to the steward to bring some hot whisky forward.

'You don't need any whisky,' said the mate calmly, 'the man's dead.'

BASIL LUBBOCK: *The China Clippers*

The Sailor's Life

Voyages of purchase or reprisals, which are now grown a common traffic, swallow up and consume more sailors and mariners than they breed, and lightly not a slop of a rope-hauler they send forth to the Queen's ships but he is first broken to the sea in the herring-man's skiff or cockboat, where having learned to brook all waters, and drink as he can out of a tarry can, and eat poor John out of sooty platters, when he may get it, without butter or mustard, there is no ho with him, but, once heartened thus, he will needs be a man of war, or a tobacco taker, and wear a silver whistle. Some of these for their haughty climbing come home with wooden legs, and some with none, but leave body and all behind. Those that escape to bring news tell of nothing but eating tallow and young blacka-mores, of five and five to a rat in every mess and the ship-boy to the tail, of stopping their noses when they drank stinking water that came out of the pump of the ship, and cutting a greasy buff jerkin in tripes and broiling it for their dinners. Divers Indian adventures have been seasoned with direr mishaps, not having for eight days' space the quantity of a candle's-end among eight score to grease their lips with; and landing in the end to seek food, by the cannibal savages they have been circumvented and forced to yield their bodies to feed them.

THOMAS NASHE: Lenten Stuffe

England's Mariners

To speake a word of that just commendation which our nation doe indeed deserve: it can not be denied, but as in all former ages, they have been men full of activity, stirrers abroad, and searchers of the remote parts of the world, so in this most famous and peerlesse governement of her most excellent Majesty, her subjects through the speciall assistance, and bless-ing of God, in searching the most opposite corners and quarters of the world, and to speake plainly, in compassing the vaste globe of the earth more than once, have excelled all the nations and peoples of the earth. For, which of the kings of this land before her Majesty, had theyr banners ever seene in the Caspian sea? Which of them hath ever dealt with the Emperor of Persia, as her Majesty hath done, and obtained for her merchants large and loving privileges? Who ever saw before this regiment, an English Ligier in the stately porch of the Grand Signor at Constantinople? Who ever found English consuls and agents at Tripolis in Syria, at Aleppo, at Babylon, at Balsara, and which is more, who ever heard of Englishmen at Goa before now? What English shippes did heeretofore ever anker in the mighty river of Plate? passe and repasse the unpassable (in former opinion) straight of Magellan, range along the coast of Chili, Peru, and all the backside of Nova Hispania, further then any christian ever passed, travers the mighty bredth of the South Sea, land upon the Luzones in despight of the enemy, enter into alliance, amity, and trafficke with the princes of the Moluccaes, and the Isle of Java, double the famous Cape of Bona Speranza, arive at the Isle of Santa Helena, and last of al returne home most richly laden with the commodities of China, as the subjects of this now flourishing monarchy have done?

RICHARD HAKLUYT: from the *Epistle Dedicatorie*
to his *Principal Navigations:* 1589

The Elizabethan Navy

The navy of England may be divided into three sorts, of which the one serveth for the wars, the other for burden, and the third for fishermen which get their living by fishing on the sea. How many of the first order are maintained within the realm, it passeth my cunning to express. Certes there is no prince in Europe that hath a more beautiful or gallant sort of ships than the Queen's majesty of England at this present, and those generally are of such exceeding force that two of them being well appointed and furnished as they ought, will not let to encounter with three or four of those of other countries, and either bouge them or put them to flight, if they may not bring them home. Neither are the moulds of any foreign barks so conveniently made, to brook so well one sea as another, lying upon the shore of any part of the continent, as those of England. And therefore the common report that strangers make of our ships amongst themselves is daily confirmed to be true, which is that for strength, assurance, nimbleness, and swiftness of sailing, there are no vessels in the world to be compared with ours.

WILLIAM HARRISON: *The Description of England* (1587)

Sard Tries to Rejoin His Ship

'Upon them that *hope*,' he thought, 'is His mercy.' He ran at his steady pace, which, as he knew, he could keep for miles.

Though it seemed so near, that shining on the sands, which he knew to be the river, was a full half-mile away. Before he had gone three hundred yards of it, he saw that the sand just ahead of him was darker and shinier than the sand under his feet. A memory of another dangerous sand, far away on an English sea-coast, shot into his mind on the instant, but the footing failed before he could stop. The sand gave beneath the one foot and let in the other; ooze of water shot up to the surface: he flung himself backwards violently, and got out, but fell, and saw, or thought he saw, the surface of the sand shaking as though it were laughing at him. He rolled himself clear, then rose and looked at it. 'That's a pretty bad quicksand,' he said. 'I might get through, but from the pull on that foot, I think that it would pull me down. Probably I can get round the shoreward end of it.'

He tried, but failed: the shoreward end of the quicksand was tropical bog.

'Very well,' he said. 'I'll swim round the seaward end. It is only a hundred yards. I need not go far out. It will be something to have the swamp washed off me again.' He went knee-deep into the sea, with some misgivings, for the shallows of all that coast are haunted with sand sharks, which came right in to have the warmth of the sand. He splashed as he went, to scare them. He had gone about thigh-deep into the water and was just setting down to swim, when there came suddenly an agonizing pain in his left foot.

His first thought was, 'I'm on a thorn,' then 'I'm on a snake'; then, as the pain ran in a long, hot, stabbing streamer up his leg, he knew the truth, that he had trodden on a sting-ray. He hopped out of the water to the shore, feeling all the blood in his foot turn to vitriol and come surging along, as vitriol, to his heart. Most excruciating agony made him fling himself down. He tried to hold out his leg, but that was unendurable torment. He tried to kneel upon it, while he put a ligature above the knee, but the pain made him so sick that he could not bear it. He tried to lie down, but that was unbearable. He rolled over and over, moaning: then staggered up, and hopped and hopped, gasping with pain, until he fell. He had never known any pain in his life, except the bangs and knocks of his profession, but now he tasted a full measure.

Although he fell, the pain did not stop, it hit him when he was down, it grew worse. The cold, deadly, flat thing in the sand had emptied his horn into him. He buried his face in the sand: he dug his hands into the sand. Then the poison seemed to swing him round and double him up. It seemed to burn every vein and shrivel every muscle and make every nerve a message of agony.

He managed to cast loose the wrapping from the foot. The foot no longer looked like a foot, but like something that would burst. In his deadly sickness he thought that his foot was a pollard willow tree growing to the left of the road. He wondered why he was not on his bicycle. He said that his foot was dead, that it had died of the gout, and would drop from his body and never grow again.

All the venom came in pain on to his abdominal muscles; then he felt it come swimming along like little fiery rats round the carcase of his heart. He saw his heart for a moment or two like a black pig caught in a bog; the rats came all round it together, from every side, they closed in on it and bit it, bit it, bit it.

When he came to himself a little, he said something about the stars being too many, altogether too many, for the job in hand. He said that he could not pick up the guiding lights.

Then he felt that every star was a steamer's masthead light, and that all those myriads of steamers were bearing down upon him without sidelights. 'Their look-out men are all asleep,' he said, 'I can't see how they are bearing, and I have no lights at all. I must find a flare and burn them off.' He groped for a flare, but found only his wet clothes pressing on his body. 'The flares are all damp,' he said, 'the flares won't burn. It is my fault; I stored them in the pickle-house. They ought to have been in the chart-room with the flags.' He wandered off in his thoughts far away from the lights of the stars. He lost all knowledge that he was lying on the sand three or four thousand miles from home. His main thought was that he was wandering along corridors in search of doors. He knew that it was very important to find doors, but whenever he found any, they closed in his face and became parts of the walls.

After a long time he roused himself up, feeling weak and sick. He knew at once, from the feel of things, that it was midnight. A sense of his position came to him. The *Pathfinder* must have sailed: he had lost his passage: he was miles from anywhere: he had lost Richard's bicycle. All these things had happened because of his dream, because of Los Xicales. He sat up, but saw no light in the direction of the house. Over the spit with the pine trees there came a sort of flashing glimmer twice a minute as the light swung round in the tower of Manola point. . . . The closeness in the air was gone; a breeze was blowing the rain straight along the beach. The trees inshore were whistling and rustling: the seas broke as though they were cross, with a sharp smash instead of the relenting wash of twilight. All sorts of little life was scuttering about the sand; white owls, or sea-birds, cruised overhead as silently as sails.

Sard sat up and tried his left leg. It was numb and much swollen. He could not feel anything in it from his mid-thigh to his toe. It had become as dead as a leg of clay or mutton. When he dinted the flesh by pressing on it, the dint remained.

With a little difficulty he stood up on one leg. He then felt for the first time that he had only one leg, that the other would

183

not act. He could move it, but not bend it; when he put it on the sand, the thing ceased to be his; it neither obeyed nor rebelled, it failed. He was so cold that he felt that he would die. He sat for twenty minutes working to restore his leg. He no longer felt pain in it, the pain was gone, but it was as though the poison had burnt out the life. In some ways he would rather have had the pain than this deadness.

'Now I am in a bad way,' he said, 'for not many come to this beach, and none in this State will wander about looking for me. If I could only reach Los Xicales. . . . However, I can't reach Los Xicales this way: the quicksand bars the land and I'm not going to risk another sting in the sea. But I might crawl along the beach to that man who has the horses, Miguel, with the good heart, near the salt-pans. . . .'

He was suffering much: the leech-bites in his right leg itched like mosquito-bites, but were also hot and stinging; his mouth had fur in it, which tasted like brown paper; he felt that he was dying of cold. His blood seemed to have changed within him to something grey and slow. Worse than his bodily state was the thought that he had broken his word to Captain Cary and missed his passage; 'mizzled his dick,' as Pompey Hopkins called it.

'She'll be sailed by this time,' he thought. 'Whatever grace Captain Cary gave me, she'll have gone by this.'

He stood up to look about him: he now realised, for the first time, the change in the weather.

The northern section of the heaven was covered with intense darkness. Over the blackness a sort of copper-coloured wisp, like smoke, was driving at a great speed. The blackness was lit up continually by lightning, which burned sometimes in steady glows, sometimes in sharp stabs of light. The wind had risen; directly Sard crossed the sandy spit, it struck him with fury, driving sand and fragments of shell against his face and down his neck. The sea was not yet breaking with any violence upon the beach. It was white as far as the eye could see, as though the heads of every wave have been whipped off and flogged into foam which shone as though with moonlight from the phosphorescence. Washes of breaker burst and rushed up the sand to Sard's feet, like washes of fire in which all the marvellous shells of which the beach was composed, were lit up like jewels. Far away to the right, out at sea on the edge of the sky, there was, as it were, a shaking wall of white from the sea already running upon the Rip-Raps. He could see it waver, but it never seemed to change. There was a roller there before the last had gone.

'This is the norther,' Sard thought. 'I hope the old man did not wait too long for me, but got clear of the Rip-Raps before it came on.'

He rebandaged his foot, picked some stakes from among the driftwood to serve as walking sticks, and with the help of these set out towards the salt-pans to borrow a horse. He hobbled forward, dead into the teeth of the gale. The worst thing about the gale was the cold. Far south as it was, the wind came down directly from the northern ice-fields. Sard stumbled along against it, keeping his direction by the pale flame of the breakers which roared at his side and flung their fire at his feet. . . . A flat road is a long road at best; against a gale it is a bad road.

Nearly all the way a great white bird (whether an owl or some sea-bird, he could not tell) flew above and ahead of him. It seemed to him that this bird shone. Perhaps the poison had upset his eyes, or perhaps his eyes never lost the shine of the sea breaking beside him. In his shaken state, this bird seemed like a luminous swan, guiding him to quiet.

JOHN MASEFIELD: *Sard Harker*

Going Aloft

'Main upper t'gallant buntlines!'

My turn had come.

With, I flatter myself, an altogether to be admired imitation of enthusiasm and spontaneity, I leapt into the main weather rigging and began climbing towards the main futtock shrouds. Everybody went about their jobs with the most elaborate assumptions of non-awareness and nonchalance but they didn't deceive me; the solo flight of an apprentice is always a matter of speculation and interest particularly to the ship's officers. As I climbed into the shrouds and made my way up the lower rigging I was conscious of that heightening of tension which always occurs as the orchestra is just obviously about to bring the overture to a conclusion and the curtain to go up. The back-draught from the mains'l was blowing about me in disturbing eddies but I couldn't be certain that it was this and not my apprehension that was crinkling my flesh. The ship was heeled ever so slightly to port and climbing was easy, the ratlines were firm and evenly spaced and with difficulty I suppressed an inclination to run up them in order not to be accused of trying to show off. As the mains'l bellied and emptied the buntlines made a soft drumming upon the canvas like the patter of countless feet. The rigging was full of strange, mute noises as if it were lived in and I became conscious of millions of tensions, and movement as of people going about their business, and the small interaction of everyday things. It was possible to conceive of it as you would a city teeming to the activities of countless draughts and currents drumming along carefully conceived arteries and highways, pressing dumbly upon barriers, surging down corridors designed for it, through flumes and into funnels, as intricately disposed and channelled as the runnels of an irrigation system: musical as a fountain, inevitable as death.

I reached the futtock shrouds and swung up over them without so much as a tremor and stood in the main top. The lower tops'l, sheeted home to the main yard-arms, was as tight as a buttock and just straining, just surging forward with a suggestion of effort. The tight, graceful curve of the bunt swept below me, just below eye-level, thrumming with wind like the over-activated, overcharged hum of a dynamo, almost aggressively potent, and I started up the topmast shrouds half afraid of it, as if it might pursue me. The topmast shrouds were secured to the top with bottle-screws and the ratlines were of rope and sagged in the middle when you put your foot in them, drawing the shrouds together and sort of pillowing your feet. This didn't give any sense of security. It was more like having to pull your feet out of a trap at each step. The topmast shrouds led to the crosstrees.

As I went up I became more than ever aware of penetrating into a densely populated area where, on the higher levels, life became for the inhabitants more attenuated perhaps but certainly fiercer. It was subjected to keener draughts of competition, tensions were more intense. The evidences of occupation which from on deck and in the lower rigging were but a low murmur as of highly civilised communities living in integrated cohesion with each other, muted and gentle, here had a strain of hysteria. It was like a sort of inverted underworld where ruled the knife, the razor and the broken bottle. And above the crosstrees lurked sinister entities, dealing out death. Once or twice, when I was tempted to look down, I was overcome with vertigo. The pressure of wind on the body had increased and was inclined to pluck at clothes with an aggressive and resentful hand like a half-intimidated mob with the intention of lynching you which yet lacks a little of its courage to do so. But there was no mistaking its intent: there was no getting away from the presence of the wind. It had body, was solid. In the topmast rigging the wind was no zephyr, but an entity with purpose pouring out of the west as tangible as water from a conduit, and with unimaginable power and gusto tossing its mane, saying Ha! Ha! stamping like a stallion. I was quite unable to come to any sort of terms with it. The wind pressed me against the rigging and impeded my steps. Unlike the lower shrouds, the topmast shrouds were almost vertical, and although not aggressively loose, were loose enough. The sensation of having to pull your feet out of ratlines as though they were bird snares implied a hostility towards effort on the part of the entities who lived there that was not encouraging to confidence. Here, only the most expert were welcomed with any sort of gladness, let alone hospitality. The spirit of the rigging, cantankerous and aloof, brooded; it was ready to pounce upon the smallest relaxation, the slightest mitigation of effort, a least error, one's tiniest slip.

I reached the crosstrees and without pausing a moment to look around me or take stock of my position, plunged into the t'gallant shrouds. . . . After the massive stability of the tubular steel topmasts and lower masts it was with absolute terror one projected oneself on to the t'gallant mast to feel it whip and quibble. The t'gallant mast was a spar of massive Oregon stepped into the topmast below the crosstrees through steel rings. I couldn't make out where or how it was secured and in examining it I suddenly became aware I was gazing down a mast that bent and whipped like a hazel. The whole stupendous spar was leaning to leeward, away from the wind and swaying with it, as the wind increased or slackened. As the ship worked and rolled, rolled back against the wind, the t'gallant shrouds set up a shrill screaming in protest, doubly high, doubly intensified, echoing through the mind and giving rise to a sort of horrified attention and setting afoot all sorts of panic trembling as echoes awoke in sympathy, in harmony, in protest, and the mad jangling goes on echoing ceaselessly in the jangling, echoing corridors of one's own consciousness. It is of this that I am afraid.

Somewhere at hand, the wind is trapped within an aperture making that peculiar moaning sound, like a genie in a bottle, tu-whoo, tu-whoo, talking away to itself now high, now lower, with the prattling insistency of a dotty child. All these small talking voices carry on mad conversations with each other, perfectly insensitive to the human – this is something that affronts sense and before which the mind reels with antagonism. But it's what goes on up there where they are all as mad as hell and blind to one's existence and talking away nineteen to the dozen like Bedlam.

The ship rolled. The t'gallant mast screamed across the sky in arcs of movement, the wind prowled through the rigging like hounds baying a stag, and I was the animal: they were baying at me. For a second, appalled at the danger and powerless, as I felt, to do anything to meet it, I clung to the rigging like a child to its parent. The t'gallant mast lurched sickeningly away from me – back; the shrouds suddenly slackened. I was left swinging nerveless. Then slowly they twisted upon themselves and crossed over and I found myself facing seawards, away from the mast, two hundred feet up. It was a moment of pure beauty and terror, like coming upon a precipice – the abyss opening at your feet. I was gazing upon a view of sky and seascape extensive and grand beyond the wildest dreams of imagination. Over there, not so very far away, was the French coast. A grey-blue cloud was piling up and up over France like a mythical swan, downy with cumulus. Immeasurably higher, streamers of alto-cirrus poured from the wind's eye, dazed by the sun. The inclination was to raise one's hands in admiration, adoration of it and drop into it, into Abraham's bosom, to recline in one of those clouds as on a couch. I might have done this for I was sufficiently unhinged by everything to be beyond entirely rational consideration. I was interrupted by a shout. Wrenching my eyes from the fabulous prospect in the sky above and before me, I came back to earth and searched on deck. The Mate was on the poop, gesticulating and carrying on in a manner that left me in no doubt as to his meaning, namely that I was to get up and get on with it. . . . I gave the rigging a wild shake like a petulant schoolboy. To my astonishment it shot round and untwisted, almost shooting me off. The ship had rolled lazily to port, the t'gallant mast whipped over to leeward, the weather shrouds were brought up taut with a jerk. The ship had simply completed one wallow in a seaway. It might have been a life-time. Making the most of my opportunity while the ship was still heeled over, I scrambled hastily up the rest of the way to the upper t'gallant yard in a great hurry and sat breathless, more from emotion, the strangeness of my position and the slight queasiness of vertigo than from exertion, astride the yard itself.

FRANK BAINES: *In Deep*

It grew lighter in the sky, but no lighter to landward; they were running in a blind and moving seascape not a thousand yards across, all cloud and water, both mad. The ship strode into it, and streaked her way across it, smashing on to the greyness a track of a paleness and a greenness of many million bubbles, over which the petrels scuttered.

Where they were Cruiser did not know, and did not much care. The exultation that was so movingly in the ship was in himself. They were getting up Channel with a marvellous slant, and who could tell that they were not leading the fleet. It would clear up presently, and they would see where they were, or pass something that would tell them.

'Forward there,' he called. 'Up there two of you, and get a good burton on the foreyard. Lively now, I'm going to give her a stunsail.'

'Burton on the foreyard: ay, ay, Sir.'

He turned to the helmsmen. Coates, who had the weather spokes, was enjoying it; he loved to see a ship driven; but Bauer at the lee wheel was scared.

'How is she, Coates?' he asked.

'She's begun to be a bit kittenish,' Coates said, 'but nothing to hurt, Sir.'

'You're keeping a good course. You can steer, Coates.'

'Yes, Sir. And she can kick, I tell you.'

'Keep your eyes forward, Bauer,' Cruiser said. 'There's nothing for you to look at behind you.'

There was, though. There was a toppling, running array of heaping water ever slipping over at the top.

'If you let her broach to, Bauer,' he said, 'you'll be the first man drowned and the last man God will forgive and that's what you'll get by it.'

Bauer smiled a sickly smile, and licked his dry lips and said: 'Yes, Sir.'

'All ready the burton, forward.'

'All ready, Sir.'

'Bowse it well taut.' He went forward to see to the setting of the sail.

As the courses of the *Bird of Dawning* were very deep as well as square, the lower studding-sail was a great sail, needing much care in the setting, in such a wind as was blowing. The boom was run forward and guyed. All hands mustered to the job. They well knew that if it were not done smartly, the sail would go. A wild sea spread from under their feet into the hurrying cloud, but those there felt, from the push of the rain that came down upon them, that the greyness was about to go. The rain that had streamed from all things relented suddenly and died into a pattering.

'Let her go,' Cruiser called. The tackles skirled as the men went away with them; he paid out the tripping line as they ran. The boom dipped under as it went and the great sail darkened with the wet half up it. As the stops came adrift, the sail lifted and strove to flog itself clear, but the checks of the gear came on to it and stayed it. One instant before it had been a bulge of canvas, flapping at folds where the wind could catch it, now it was a straining curve of sail, held by check and countercheck, leaning like a wing to the ship over all that hurry of leaping sea. She put down her foot, and the foot of the sail stooped into it, as a gull stoops upon the wing. She rose, with the water dripping from the scoop, and again plunged and arose shaking.

'That's got her where she lives,' Clutterbucke said. 'That's made her lift her feet.'

The effect on the ship was instantaneous. She had been leaping, now she seemed to lift from sea to sea, and to tread down their crests into subjection.

'I think she'll stand a topmast stunsail,' Cruiser said to himself.

He went aft to watch the steering, which was grown the livelier for the sail. From the poop, he had a new impression of the power of her drive: she was swooping and swerving like a thing alive; in fact, she was a thing alive: she had ceased to be wood and iron, laden with cases: she was something of the spirit of the wind, and of the kindled wit of man, that laughed as she flew.

Suddenly as he stood by the wheel, watching her head, and letting his eyes run aloft to the curves of the leaches under strain, the greyness in the heaven parted as though the sheets had given, with the effect of a sail suddenly let go and clued up. The cloud tattered itself loose to windward and rived itself apart, and blue sky showed and spread. Instantly, a blueness and a brightness came upon the water. To leeward before them the storm passed away like a scroll. There to port, far away, was the Chesil Beach, with the Needles beyond it, and the far and faint line of England stretching astern to the Start. The sun appeared and beauty came with him, so that all the tumbling and heaping brightness rejoiced.

One of the first things revealed was a fine clipper ship two miles ahead, lying almost the same course. On the starboard quarter, perhaps two miles away, another lofty ship came racing up channel, and far astern a third showed. This third was perhaps not one of the China fleet.

'We've turned into the straight,' Cruiser said. 'There seem to be three left in it.'

'Yes, Sir,' Fairford said, 'unless the race is already won.'

'We'll learn soon enough if it's already won,' Cruiser said. 'Get a tackle on the yardarm there,' he called. 'All hands set studding sails.' The mate and the men marvelled, but they leaped to the order. They were now as keen as Cruiser to bring their ship home. Not a man thought that perhaps the race had been already won by someone; to them the race was now beginning.

Cruiser was on the foc's'le head with the telescope trying to make out the ship ahead. Under the tapering clouds of sail he could see a dark green hull, with an old-fashioned transom look about her stern. She could be no other than the *Caer Ocvran*. She had been running with prudence, not knowing where she was; now that the sky had cleared she was making sail.

'All ready, the fore-topmast stunsail, Sir,' Mr Fairford

reported, adding under his breath, 'if you think she'll stand them, Sir.'

'No time for prudence how,' Cruiser said, 'hoist away there – lively now.'

One at a time the mighty wings of studding sail swayed aloft and shook themselves out of their bundles with a roaring into service. Cruiser saw the topsail yard lift and the booms buckle as the strain came upon them; but the gear held. A whiteness boiled along the *Bird's* side and flew in a sheet over the waist as she felt the new power given to her. Cruiser watched for a minute, standing well forward, eyeing the straining booms. 'They'll hold,' he thought, 'as long as the wind keeps steady and the helmsmen behave.' He crossed the foc's'le and eyed the ship ahead. She had set her lower studding sail, and no doubt was setting more as fast as the men could move, but the *Bird of Dawning* seemed sailing two feet to her one.

He watched for half a moment; Fairford and others were at his side, staring.

'Ah, she's holding us,' Fairford said suddenly. 'Yes, she's holding us. There go her topmast studding sails: beautifully done too. She's got forty hands at stations. It's something to have a full crew.'

'We've got twelve,' Cruiser said. 'Twelve good men upset the Roman Empire. Get the top gallant stunsails on her.'

The men ran to it: he slipped aft with the telescope, partly to con the ship, partly to see what the ship astern might be. He steadied the glass against a mizen shroud and stared at the ship astern. She was on the starboard quarter, and plainly much nearer than she had been. She was not more than a mile and a half away. Not much of her showed except a tower of leaning sail, winged out with studding sails, a jibboom poising and bowing, and a roll of white water under her bows. He broke off from his staring to rate Bauer at the lee wheel. 'Never mind what's astern of you,' he called. 'Watch your steering or you'll have the masts out of her and we'll skin you alive.'

He looked again at the ship astern. Someone forward had said that she was the *Min and Win*. He was satisfied that she was not the *Min and Win*, but a much bigger and newer ship, the *Fu-Kien*, commanded by a reckless daredevil known as Bloody Bill China. 'Well, what Bill can carry we can drag,' he said, so he leaped down into the waist, to the job of getting more sail on to a ship that already had plenty.

'She's gaining on us though,' Cruiser muttered. He could see now plainly her anchors over the bows dripping brightness whenever she rose from the sea. 'Well, I'll try what the skysail will do. Up there, one of you, and loose the skysail.'

They loosed and hoisted it, and had the sight of the pole bending like a whip of whalebone to the strain. Bill replied by loosing his main skysail, which blew away in the setting. They raced on now, hardly changing position. They raced in the laughing morning, while the coast slipped by them, all the landmarks long looked for.

Cruiser had had prepared for two days on the poop a contrivance for sending letters and telegrams ashore in case of luck or need. He had lashed to a ship's lifebuoy in upright positions two blue and white boat flags, which the *Bird of Dawning's* boats had borne in the Foochow Regatta. He had then bent to the buoy a long line of small stuff ready to lower it over the side. To this buoy he now lashed with great care two bottles of brandy, frapped with bagwrinkle, and a canvas pack sewn up in oilskin, which contained a sovereign, and an urgent appeal to the finder to send two telegrams there plainly written out, ready to be sent.

[Not long after] a big smack, under a reefed mainsail and jib, hove up, all gleaming, ahead. She was crossing their bows, making for some point on the Hampshire coast. It was what Cruiser had most longed for during that morning. He signalled to her with a red weft that he wished to speak, and luckily the fishermen understood, and hove up into the wind with a shaking sail to let the *Bird of Dawning* pass.

As the great ship surged by, Cruiser in the mizen rigging shouted to the smack through his speaking trumpet asking them to send off the telegrams. He pointed to the buoy, which the mate smartly lowered to the sea and paid out upon. They saw the buoy lift high on the sea, with its flags blowing clear, and in an instant it was tossed away upon the following surge to the smack's bows. A man leaned over with a boathook, fished for it, caught it and hove it inboard, then bent over it as the sail filled. Cruiser saw the bottles pass from hand to hand while the skipper looked at the writing. The skipper presently waved vigorously to show that he understood.

'I only hope that he does understand,' Cruiser thought; 'and that nobody else has worked the same traverse.' One telegram was to the London and Dover Tug Company to have two tugs for the *Bird of Dawning* off the South Foreland, the other was to his brother, now a young lawyer in London, to meet the ship in the Downs and advise about the claims for salvage.

'Mike is the only lawyer I know,' Cruiser thought. 'And I've been abroad for a year: if he should have died, I shall be up a gum-tree.'

As he had expected, the change of the lifting of the gale brought with it a lessening of the wind and a shifting of it two points to the northward. All three ships had now set every sail that they could carry, to the royal studding sails and trust-to-gods. Cruiser had guyed out a boom below the jibboom and had set a spritsail: Bloody Bill China had bonnets on his courses and contrivances that he called puff-balls in the roaches of his topsails. What the *Caer Ocvran* was doing they could not clearly see: she was almost dead ahead of them. The three ships were drawing nearer to each other, the *Caer Ocvran* coming back, the *Fu-Kien* coming on. If the race had not been already won by some ship in ahead of them, it was the finest finish seen since the China prize was raced for.

. . . As the day drew on, the tide slackened and the wind dropped and shifted still more to the north: it gave them a beam sea and much anxiety for their gear, which held, but only just held.

At one that afternoon, as they passed Beachy all three ships began to feel the turn of the tide; the flying kites had to come in lest they should pitch the spars away. Then in little short spells of twenty minutes the wind would lull and the kites would be set again; and in this kind of sailing Bloody Bill China had an advantage: as Cruiser could see, he had the boys aloft in the tops all the time ready to race up to loose the light sails or take them in. He was creeping up a little and a little, and was now only about a mile astern, having gained certainly a mile and a half in five hours. In another five hours the *Fu-Kien* would be half a mile ahead, having the pick of the tugs at the South Foreland. The *Caer Ocvran* was at a slight disadvantage, being not quite so happy in fresh or clearing weather as in light airs. However, her captain was fighting for every inch she lost. Cruiser with his small crew had only the miracle of the ship in his favour. He felt more and more keenly every instant that the ship was the best ship in the race. In other voyages she may not have been so; in this race all had conspired together, her builder and some happy combination in her trim, to make her supreme, but now she was short of hands, unable to do her best.

A darkness gathered into the heaven astern of them as the secondary moved up. The hours of the afternoon dragged by as the ships strained up Channel, all drawing nearer, all watched by thousands ashore, who now guessed that those three moving beauties were the clippers of the China fleet.

Just off the Fairlight a little steamer, going with coals for Fowey, edged close in to the *Bird of Dawning*, so as to have a good look at her. Cruiser hailed her through the trumpet.

'Ahoy, there, the *Chaffinch*, what China ship won the Race?'

'No ship,' the *Chaffinch*'s skipper shouted back. 'You are the race. Go in and win.'

'Thank you,' Cruiser shouted. 'Is that straight?'

'Yes. Get to it. Knock the bastards silly.'

This was greeted by a cheer from all hands: they had a chance still.

There came a sudden hurrying greyness astern: it sent before it a hissing noise which put Cruiser's heart into his boots. He shouted out, 'Let go your royal halyards. Stand by topgallant braces,' and had let fly the main royal halyards as a rain squall swept over them and blotted out ships, sea and land in a deluge that filled the scupper. Out of the deluge there came wind in a gust that tore the flying royals into tatters. Something more than the royals went, the topgallant stunsails went at tack and halyards, blew out in the rain like dirty flags, flogged once, twice and away, with whips of their gear lashing round anything they touched. The masts bent, the yards curved at the arms under the pull of the sheets, and the ship leapt forward as though suddenly lashed.

The men ran to the gear: nothing more was lost: the split sails were cleared and new ones bent but not set. The rain made a darkness about them for twenty minutes, during which Cruiser had two men on the foc's'le looking out.

As the squall cleared off, the sun drawing to the west shone out and made a rainbow upon its darkness. Under the arch of colours they saw the *Caer Ocvran* not two hundred yards from them on the starboard bow. She seemed to be stuck there in tossing waters that whitened about her in a great bubble.

Through the glass Cruiser could plainly see her captain, pacing his weather poop, glancing quickly aloft and at the *Bird of Dawning*. 'Ah, yes, Sir,' Fairford said as he watched, 'you can glance and you can curse the helmsman, but the *Bird of Dawning*'s got you beat to the wide.'

'That's Captain Winstone,' Cruiser said. 'He was mate of the *Bidassoa* when I was in her. Look at that now: did you ever see a ship so wet?'

'She's famous for it, Sir, the *Caer*. A fine ship, too.'

Presently they were abreast of her, and forging ahead upon her, so that they could see her in her glory. She had a straight sheer and a transome stern, having been built upon the lines of the famous French frigate, *L'Aigle*. In a light air no ship of her time could touch her, and she could run with the swiftest. She had a name through the seven seas for being wet, her decks now were running bright; for she was a caution in a head sea. They were watching and tending her now, getting some of her after sail off her to keep her from burying her bow. Cruiser dipped his colours to her as he passed, but would not hail his old captain. As he drew clear, he saw her famous figurehead of Queen Gwenivere bowing down into the smother, then rising and pausing, then plunging down till the foc's'le-rail was lipping green.

'Look at that,' Cruiser said. 'Did you ever see a ship pitch like that?'

As he spoke, she took a deeper scend than usual, and rose with a snapped stunsail boom lifting on a loose wing.

The *Fu-Kien* drew clear of the *Caer Ocvran* on her lee side, she was now a quarter of a mile away and gaining perhaps twenty yards a minute. Dungeness lay ahead, distant perhaps eight miles, and somewhere about Dungeness there would be pilots and perhaps tugs. There or thereabout the race would be decided, another hour would see it out. Cruiser's men had been hard at it all day, and were showing signs of wear. They drank strong tea, syrupy with sugar and laced with brandy, as they got their hawsers ready forward and eyed the distant winning post.

All the issue from the gate of the Channel were about them: all the ships of a tide or two before from London and Antwerp, all the fishermen of Kent and Sussex. Every seaman who came past had no eyes for anything but those two superb clippers disputing for pride of place.

When the squall had passed by both had set every rag that could be brought to draw: they were now straining under clouds of canvas with a strong beam wind and a head tide. Tarlton, who had been in the *Fu-Kien*, was not encouraging. 'Just the wind she likes most,' he said; 'she's a glutton for it.' All the marvellous evening shone out mile after mile as they raced: the French coast plain as far as Calais, England white to windward, with occasional windows flashing like jewels, and a darkness of passing storm beyond. Occasional violent gusts kept men in both ships at the upper halyards, and still the *Fu-Kien* gained.

Cruiser was watching her now, she was not more than a hundred yards astern and to leeward, her decks full of men, and spare sails, all made up for bending, on each hatch, and the ship herself a picture of perfection, all bright for port, the paint-work and tarring finished, the hull black, with a white sheer-straik to set off her sheer, the yards black, man-of-war fashion, but with white yard-arms, and her masts all scraped clean with glass, of shining yellow pine. All her brass was bright, and the scroll below her bowsprit had been freshly gilt. She was driving on easily with great laughing leaps. Cruiser could see, in the bearing of the men in her, their certainty that they were winning. Both ships were hauling their wind now to turn the bend. Both could see now, coming out from Dungeness, the pilot-cutter, standing towards them, not two miles away, and beyond, making for them what seemed to be tugs, but might be small coasters.

'Too bad, Sir,' old Fairford said. 'We'd have done it if we'd had a bit more luck.'

Cruiser was feeling broken-hearted at being passed on the post, but he could not take this view of it. 'No, no,' he said. 'We've had such luck as sailors never had before. Think of what has come to us.' All the same, he had to move away. When he was on the lee poop staring at the *Fu-Kien*, old Fairford could not see how bitterly he felt.

As they hauled their wind, the *Fu-Kien* forged ahead upon them, standing close in upon them, intending to weather upon them and drive across their bows. Bloody Bill China was there on his poop, an unmistakeable big figure with a hard tall grey hat jammed sideways on his head and a long pistol in his right hand. 'That's Bloody Bill, Sir,' Tarlton said to Mr Fairford. 'Bloody Bill China, Sir, the Captain. You'll see him send a bottle of brandy out to the yardarm in a moment.'

Sure enough a lad with a line went up the mizen rigging and out to the crojick yard with it, rove it through a jewel block at the yardarm, and brought it down on deck. A bottle of brandy was hauled to the yardarm upon it and dangled there. 'That's Bloody Bill's way, Sir,' Tarlton said. 'If ever he weathers on a ship he shoots a bottle of brandy at the yardarm and then splits another on all hands.'

Twenty faces stared at the *Bird of Dawning* from the *Fu-Kien*'s side. Those men of the sea, negroes, Malays and Europeans, grinned and cheered as their ship slid past.

Bloody Bill China, who was certainly half-drunk, shouted something to his steward, who was standing near the break of the poop beside a grog-kid. The steward put a corkscrew into the cork of a bottle which he held. Bloody Bill strode to the ship's rail, and yelled at Cruiser, whom he took to be Captain Miserden, 'Give my love to the Prophet Habakkuk.'

Voices from the *Fu-Kien*'s waist, eager for the promised grog and full of joy in their victory, shouted 'Habakkuk, Yah, Yah, Habakkuk,' and instantly the *Fu-Kien*'s mainmast was ahead of the *Bird of Dawning*'s mizen, and at once the *Fu-Kien*'s crew manned the rail and cheered, and beat the fire signal on both her bells. Bloody Bill China brandished his pistol above his head, brought it down, and fired it as it fell: the bottle at the yardarm was shattered – the brandy spilled. Instantly the steward drew his cork and Bloody Bill China shouted, 'Grog-oh! The *Fu-Kien* wins the China race.'

She tore past the *Bird of Dawning*. She cleared her by a cable, then by three hundred yards. 'Look out, Sir,' Tarlton cried to Cruiser. 'He'll cross your bows as sure as God made Sunday.'

And instantly Bloody Bill China did, he luffed up out of bravado, so as to get to windward of the *Bird of Dawning*.

He was going to cross her bows, just to show her. As he luffed, one of the violent gusts beat down upon both ships. Cruiser saw it coming and let go in time, but it caught the *Fu-Kien* fairly, and whipped her topgallant masts clean off in succession as one might count one, two, three. The great weight of the gear swung to and fro on each mast, the fore-upper topsail went at the weather clew, the main-upper topsail halyards parted and the yard coming down brought the lower topsail with it, bending the truss and cockbilling the yard. The helmsman let her go off, she fell off, thumping and thrashing while gear came flying down from the ruin. With a crash the wreck of the foretopgallant mast, with its three yards, the stunsail booms and weight of sail and half a mile of rigging, collapsed about the forehatch.

It had all happened in a moment. Cruiser had been warned and had just time to heave the helm up. The *Bird of Dawning* always steered like a bird: she answered to a touch, she answered to it now, but the *Fu-Kien* was right athwart her hawse not three hundred yards away, falling off and coming down on her, with all the wreck on her mainmast visibly shaking the whole mast. One active dare-devil soul was already racing with an axe to the splintered masthead, to hack through the shrouds.

Cruiser saw her come round almost on her heel, straight at the *Bird of Dawning*. For about half a minute it seemed certain .that the two would go into each other and sink each other. The mizen royal yard slid out of its bands and smote the *Fu-Kien*'s deck end-on like a harpoon. The terrified helmsman hove the helm hard down; the ship, having still way on her, swung back into the wind; with a running, ripping, walloping crash, her main top-gallant wreck came down into her waist, going through the bunt of the mainsail as it went.

The *Bird of Dawning* went passed her and missed her by thirty yards. As they passed, Bloody Bill China leaped on to the top of the wheel-box, hurled his hard hat at Cruiser, and while it was still in the air, settling to the sea, put three bullets through it with his pistol; he then hurled his pistol after it and leaped down cursing on to the main-deck to clear the wreck.

Cruiser left him to clear it; there, ranging down upon him, was the pilot-cutter. In another minute that graceful boat rounded to with her pilot, who caught the tackle flung, and in an instant was swung high and brought upon the *Bird of Dawning*'s deck.

JOHN MASEFIELD: *The Bird of Dawning*

San Juan de Ulloa

Shortly after this the 16 of September we entered the port of Saint John de Ullua and in our entrie the Spaniardes thinking us to be the fleete of Spaine, the chiefe officers of the Countrey came aboord us, which being deceived of their expectation were greatly dismayed: but immediately when they sawe our demand was nothing but victuals, were recomforted. I found also in the same Port twelve ships which had in them by report two hundred thousand pound in gold and silver, all which (being in my possession, with the Kings Iland as also the passengers before in my way thitherward stayed) I set at libertie, without taking from them the waight of a groat; onely because I would not be delayed of my dispatch, I stayed two men of estimation and sent post immediately to Mexico, which was two hundred miles from us, to the Presidentes and Councell there, shewing them of our arrivall there by the force of weather, and the necessitie of the repaire of our shippes and victuals, which wantes we required as friends to King Philip to be furnished of for our money: and that the Presidents and Councell there should with all convenient speede take order, that at the arrivall of the Spanish fleete, which was dayly looked for there might no cause of quarrell rise betweene us and them, but for the better maintenance of amitie, their commandement might be had in that behalfe. This message being sent away the sixteenth day of September at night, being the very day of our arrivall, in the next morning we sawe open of the Haven thirteene great shippes, and understanding them to bee the fleete of Spaine, I sent immediately to advertise the Generall of the fleete of my being there, doing him to understand, that before I would suffer them to enter the Port, there should some order of conditions passe betweene us for our safe being there, and maintenance of peace.

Now it is to be understood that this Port is made by a little Iland of stones not three foote above the water in the highest place, and but a bowshoot of length any way, this Iland standeth from the maine land two bow shootes or more, also it is to be understood that there is not in all this coast any other place for ships to arrive in safety, because the North winde hath there such violence, that unlesse the shippes be very safely moored with their ankers fastened upon this Iland, there is no remedie for these North windes but death:

also the place of the Haven was so little, that of necessitie the shippes must ride one aboord the other, so that we could not give place to them, nor they to us: and here I beganne to bewaile that which after followed, for now, said I, I am in two dangers, and forced to receive the one of them. That was, either I must have kept out the fleete from entring the Port, the which with Gods helpe I was very well able to doe, or else suffer them to enter in with their accustomed treason, which they never faile to execute, where they may have opportunitie, to compasse it by any meanes: if I had kept them out, then there had bene present shipwrecks of all the fleete which amounted in value to sixe Millions, which was in value of our money 1,800,000 li, which I considered I was not able to answer, fearing the Queenes Majesties indignation in so waightie a matter. Thus with myself revolving the doubts I thought rather better to abide the Jutt of the uncertainty, then the certaintie. The uncertaine doubt I account was their treason which by good policie I hoped might be prevented, and therefore as chusing the least mischiefe I proceeded to conditions. . . .

Thus following our demand, we required victuals for our money, and licence to sell as much ware as might furnish our wants, and that there might be of either part twelve gentlemen as hostages for the maintenance of peace: and that the Iland for our better safetie might be in our own possession, during our abode there, and such ordinance as was planted in the same Iland which were eleven peeces of brass: and that no Spaniard might land in the Iland with any kind of weapon. These conditions at the first he somewhat disliked, chiefly the guard of the Iland to be in our own keeping, which if they had had, we had soone knowen our fare: for with the first North winde they had cut our cables and our ships had gone ashore: but in the end he concluded to our request, with a writing from the Viceroy signed with his hands and sealed with his seale, and forthwith a trumpet blowen with commandment that none of either part should be meane to violate the peace upon paine of death.

Thus at the end of 3 days all was concluded and the fleete entered the Port, saluting one another as the manner of the sea doth require. Then we laboured 2 daies placing the English ships by themselves and the Spanish ships by themselves, the captaines of ech part and inferior men of their parts promising great amitie of al sides: which even as with al fidelitie it was ment on our part, so the Spaniards ment nothing less on their parts, but from the maine land had furnished themselves with a supply of men to the number of 1000, and ment the next Thursday being the 23 of September at dinner time to set upon us on all sides.

The same Thursday in the morning the treason being at hand, some appearance showed, as shifting of weapon from ship to ship, planting and bending of ordinance from the ships to the Iland where our men warded, passing too and fro of companies of men more then required for their necessary business, and many other ill likelihoods, which caused us to have a vehement suspition, and therewithal sent to the Viceroy to enquire what was ment by it, which sent immediately straight commandement to unplant all things suspicious, and also sent word that he in the faith of a Viceroy would be our defence from all villanies. Yet we being not satisfied with this answere, because we suspected a great number of men to be hid in a great ship of 900 tunnes, which was mored next unto the Minion, sent againe to the Viceroy the master of the Jesus which had the Spanish tongue, and required to be satisfied if any such thing were or not.

The Viceroy now seeing that the treason must be discovered, foorthwith stayed our master, blew the Trumpet, and of all sides set upon us: our men which warded ashore being stricken with sudden feare, gave place, fled, and sought to recover succour of the ships; the Spaniards being before provided for the purpose landed in all places in multitudes from their ships which they might easily doe without boates, and slewe all our men ashore without mercie, a fewe of them escaped aboord the Jesus. The great ship which had by estimation three hundred men placed in her secretly, immediately fell aboord the Minion, but by Gods appointment, in the time of the suspicion we had, which was onely one halfe houre, the Minion was made readie to avoide, and so leesing her hedfasts, and hayling away by the sternfastes she was gotten out: thus with Gods help she defended the violence of the first brunt of these three hundred men.

The Minion being passed out, they came aboord the Jesus, which also with very much adoe and the losse of manie of our men were defended and kept out. Then there were also two other ships that assaulted the Jesus at the same instant, so that she had hard getting loose, but yet with some time we had cut our headfastes and gotten out by the stern-fastes.

Now when the Jesus and the Minion were gotten about two shippes length from the Spanish fleete, the fight beganne so hotte on all sides that within one houre the Admirall of the Spaniards was supposed to be sunke, their Viceadmirall burned and one other of their principall ships supposed to be sunke, so that the shippes were little able to annoy us.

Then it is to be understood, that all the Ordinance upon the Iland was in the Spaniardes handes, which did us so great annoyance, that it cut all the mastes and yardes of the Jesus, in such sort that there was no hope to carrie her away: also it sunke our small shippes, whereupon we determined to place the Jesus on that side of the Minion, that she might abide all the batterie from the land, and so be a defence for the Minion till night, and then to take such reliefe of victuall and other necessaries from the Jesus as the time would suffer us, and to leave her.

As we were thus determining, and had placed the Minion from the shot of the land, suddenly the Spaniards had fired two great shippes which were coming directly with us, and having no meanes to avoide the fire, it bredde among our men a marvellous feare, so that some sayd, let us depart with the Minion, other said, let us see whither the winde will carrie the fire from us. But to be short, the Minion's men which had alwayes their sayles in a readinesse, thought to make sure worke, and so without either consent of the Captaine or Master cut their saile, so that very hardly I was received into the Minion.

The most part of the men that were left alive in the Jesus, made shift and followed the Minion in a small boat, the rest which the little boate was not able to receive, were inforced to abide the mercy of the Spaniards (which I doubt was very little), so with the Minion only and the Judith (a small barke of 50 tunne) we escaped, which barke the same might forsooke us in our great miserie. . . .

Having a great number of men and little victuals our hope of life waxed lesse and lesse: some desired to yeeld to the Spaniards, some rather desired to obtaine a place where they might give themselves to the Infidels, and some had rather abide with a little pittance the mercie of God at sea. So thus with many sorowful hearts we wandred in an unknowen Sea by the space of 14 dayes, till hunger inforced us to seek the land, for hides were thought very good meat, rats, cats, mice, and dogs, none escaped that might be gotten, parrots and monkeys that were had in great price were thought there very profitable if they served the turne one dinner. Thus in the end the 8 day of October we came to the land in the botome of the same bay of Mexico in 23 degrees and a halfe, where we hoped to have found inhabitants of the Spaniards, reliefe of victuals, and place for the repaire of our ship, which was so sore beaten with shot from our enemies and brused with shooting off our ordinance, that our wearie and weake armes were scarce able to defende and keepe out water. But all things happened to the contrary, for we found neither people, victuall, nor haven of relief, but a place where having faire weather with some perill we might land a boat: our people being forced with hunger desired to be set on land, whereunto I consented.

And such as were willing to land I put them apart, and such as were desirous to goe homewardes, I put them apart, so that they were indifferently parted a hundred of one side and a hundred of the other side: these hundred men we set aland with all diligence in this little place beforesaid, which being landed, we determined there to take in fresh water, and so with our little remaine of victuals to take the sea.

The next day there arose an extreame storme, so that in three dayes we could by no meanes repaire aboord our ship: the ship also was in such perill that every houre we looked for shipwracke.

But yet God againe had mercie on us, and sent faire weather, we had aboord our water, and departed the sixteenth day of October, after which day we had faire and prosperous weather till the sixteenth day of November, which day God be praised we were cleere from the coast of the Indies, and out of the chanell and gulfe of Bahama.

After this growing neere to the colde countrey, our men being oppressed with famine, died continually, and they that were left grew into such weakenesse that we were scantly able to manage our shippe, and the winde being always ill for us to recover England, we determined to go with Galicia in Spaine, with intent there to relieve our company and other extreame wantes. And being arrived the last day of December in a place neere unto Vigo called Ponte Vedra, our men with excesse of fresh meate grew into miserable diseases, and died a great part of them. With all speede possible we departed to Vigo where we had some helpe of certaine English ships and twelve fresh men, wherewith we repaired our wants as we might, and departing the 20 day of January 1568 arrived in Mounts bay in Cornewall the 25 of the same moneth, praised be God therefore.

If all the miseries and troublesome affaires of this sorowfull voyage should be perfectly and throughly written, there should neede a painefull man with his pen, and as great a time as he had that wrote the lives and deathes of the Martyrs.

JOHN HAWKINS: in Hakluyt's *The English Voyages* (xv)

Boarding Officer

Personally, provided that we had plenty of sea room, and that I had full confidence in the Master of my own [Examination] vessel, I never saw the weather in which I was unwilling to go away on boat duty. Some stirring times came my way in consequence, but it was all useful experience.

Sometimes, while an examination was being carried out, the ship being examined would get out of position, and, either from carelessness or for some other reason, her lee side would become her weather one just as the boarding officer was ready to leave her. This would make things exceedingly lively, both for the boarding officer and for the crew of the boat towing alongside. We did our best under the circumstances, always remembering that, if humanly possible, we must not do anything to endanger the safety of the vessel being examined. Occasionally, the vessel being examined would get out of position while the boarding officer was actually stepping on to the Jacob's ladder in the act of boarding, and then the life of the boarding officer was not a happy one for the next few minutes.

One day, while a big sea was running, I had just stepped on to the Jacob's ladder on the lee side of a vessel of about four thousand tons, when there was a cry of 'Look out, sir!' from the coxswain of my boat. Thinking that the warning meant that the boat was likely to swing in and crush me, I looked down, so as to be ready to jump from the ladder back into the boat before she could strike me. There were twenty rungs of the ladder between where I was and the deck above, far too many for me to be able to get up before the boat could reach me.

The moment occupied in looking down was my undoing. As I had stepped on to the ladder, so had the ship got out of position, and, unobserved by me, she was now head to wind. The warning shout from the coxswain was to draw my attention to a huge wave which, rolling along the ship's side from forward, almost reached to the height of the deck. It was on and over me almost before I saw it. Clinging on to that ladder like a limpet, I was completely overwhelmed, and was washed aft along the ship's side to the extreme limit of the length of the ladder, for all the world as though I had been a mere chestnut hanging on the end of a string.

As I was washed aft the wave rolled me round and round. Now the ladder would be between the ship and myself, and again I would be between the ladder and the ship, until I was almost dizzy. Arrived at the full scope of the ladder, the wave passed and left me unsupported, high up within a few feet of the deck. With my own weight, back I swung, still being rolled round and round, but in the reverse direction, almost as far the other way, as though I were a pendulum. Reaching my forward limit, the next wave hit me and repeated the process. Backwards and forwards I swung, three times, before the ship was once again brought round so as to put me on the lee side. Then the crew untwisted the ladder from on deck, so that once more the ladder was between me and the side of the ship, and I made my way in safety to the rail and was helped on board, to carry out my examination as per programme.

What of my boat, while this performance was in progress? She had seen what was happening in sufficient time to take the necessary action, and sheering away to the full extent of her boat-rope, she had kept clear of me, and had ridden more or less successfully over the waves which had dealt so unkindly with my unfortunate self. This time my boat's crew enjoyed all the fun of the fair without contributing in any way to the general entertainment, but things did not by any means always so turn out.

*   *   *

Another day I was detailed to board a large and deeply laden foreign steamer. The weather being moderate, I went away in No. 5's motor-boat, and having crossed the bows of the oncoming steamer, started to round-to under her lee, in order to drop alongside. Then, and not till then, did I discover that she was not losing headway as rapidly as I had anticipated would be the case, even though her engines were going full astern. We were only about half through our turn when I made the discovery – that is to say, we were heading directly for the ship at almost right angles to her course. To my horror, I then noted that, under the combined action of her reversed propeller and a strong wind which was blowing, she was coming down bodily on top of us, in such a way that I should not have room to complete my turn before her propeller would be abreast of us. At once I put our boat full speed astern, but this had only the effect of keeping us the same relative distance from the ship's side, while she steadily forged ahead.

Though her propeller was deeply immersed, such was the power of her engines that the propeller, in turning astern, created a huge vortex, or whirlpool, similar in character to the funnel-shaped whirl to be observed over the plughole of an emptying bath. Nearer and nearer to us approached that wicked-looking cavity which appeared to have a depth of at least ten feet, until the bow of our boat, still going astern for all the engine was worth, overhung its extreme edge. I told the two members of my crew to get as far aft as possible, in the hope of deferring a nose dive into the vortex to the last possible moment. At the same time I did my best to attract the attention of those in charge of the steamer, so that they might stop her engines before it should be too late. Nothing was to be gained by jumping out of the boat, as no swimmer could possibly have swum more quickly away from the vortex than the boat was already travelling, under the influence of her reversed propeller.

Every second seemed to me to be ages long, but after what appeared a lapse of several hours, my frantic signals were observed from the bridge of the steamer. A clanging of bells, her propeller ceased to revolve, the vortex filled up, and we were saved!

H. IAN MAC IVER: *Amateurs Afloat*

Searchlights

About 7 p.m. on Monday, February 11th, 1929, it was blowing a strong gale from the north-east, bringing a heavy sea into Dover harbour, and during this the steamer *Ville de Liege*, of about 2,000 tons, belonging to the Belgian State Railways, arrived from Ostend with forty-eight passengers and mails. As she was making for the inner berth of the Admiralty Pier she was struck by a heavy sea on the port quarter, being knocked round broadside on to the sea and driven on the rocks about two hundred feet from the Inner Harbour entrance. Fortunately her broadside position to the sea caused her to act as a kind of breakwater, and this enabled some of her port boats to be lowered and take the passengers into the harbour, where, though wet through, they landed in safety.

As usually happens in such circumstances, the vessel's electric installation failed and the steamer was in darkness. To remedy this I telephoned to the Officer in Charge of the Searchlights at the Admiralty Pier, asking him to turn the lights on the steamer. His reply was that he could not do so without orders. I am afraid that my language was not so polite as it might have been as I told him to hurry up and get orders or I would make trouble. For the benefit of those who read this I have left out the actual words I used. In any case the printers would have substituted dashes, I think.

However, the searchlight authorities got their own back a bit, for a few days later I received an account made out on official blue paper in duplicate for the sum of fivepence, this being the cost of telephone calls asking permission for the searchlights to be turned on.

CAPT. JOHN IRON: *Keeper of the Gate*

Signals

Well, we left for the precious place [Surinam], and in due course arrived off the river about 8 o'clock one evening. Although I stood in to twenty-four feet, I could see nothing, so I anchored and went up into the mizen top, whence I could just make out a small light abeam from which I took a bearing. At daylight I stood in towards it, and then the fun began.

I made a signal to the Lightship asking what water was on the bar. They dipped their ensign, which I took to mean 'come on', but at once touched and had to make sail and drive the ship into deep water again. While I was doing this, the Lightship signalled, 'Anchor immediately.' But I was not so big an ass as to do so until I was well afloat again.

After anchoring I sent one of our boats away to the ship to get a pilot, and in due course the boat returned with a native. I asked him what they meant by dipping the ensign when I asked what water they had. His reply was rich.

'Well, captain,' he said, 'the rats have eaten our signal-book, and we thought by dipping the ensign you would stop.'

'And what did you mean by telling me to anchor when on the bar?' I asked.

'I told our captain that was the wrong signal,' said the man. 'We meant to tell you to send a boat for a pilot.'

CAPT. JOHN IRON: *Keeper of the Gate*

The Bell Rock

'You see that mark there, sir, on Smith's Ledge?' said Mr Long to me one day, 'that was the place where the forge stood; and the ledge beyond, with the old bit of iron on it, is the "*last hope*", where Mr Stevenson and his men were so nearly lost.' Then he went on to tell me the following incident, as illustrating one of the many narrow escapes made by the builders [of the Bell Rock Lighthouse].

One day, soon after the men had commenced work, it began to blow hard, and the crew of the boat belonging to the attending vessel, named the *Smeaton*, fearing that her moorings might be insufficient, went off to examine them. This was wrong. The workmen on the rock were sufficiently numerous to completely fill three boats. For one of these, to leave the rock was to run a great risk, as the event proved. Almost as soon as they reached the *Smeaton*, her cables parted and she went adrift, carrying the boat with her away to leeward, and although sail was instantly made, they found it impossible to regain the rock against wind and tide. Mr Stevenson observed this with the deepest anxiety, but the men (busy as bees about the rock) were not aware of it at first.

The situation was terrible. There were thirty-two men left on a rock which would in a short time be overflowed to a depth of twelve or fifteen feet by a stormy sea, and only two boats in which to remove them. These two boats, if loaded to the gunwales, could have held only a few more than the half of them.

While the sound of the numerous hammers and the ring of the anvil were heard, the situation did not appear so hopeless; but soon the men at the lowest part of the foundation were driven from work by the rising tide, then the forge-fire was extinguished, and the men generally began to make towards their respective boats for their jackets and dry socks. When it was discovered that one of the three boats was gone not a word was uttered, but the men looked at each other in evident perplexity. They seemed to realise their position at once.

In a few minutes some of that band must inevitably be left to perish, for the absent boat and vessel were seen drifting farther and farther away to leeward. Mr Stevenson knew that in such a case, where life and death were in the balance, a desperate struggle among the men for precedence would be certain. Indeed he afterwards learned that the picket had resolved to stick by their boat against all hazards. While they were thus gazing in silence at each other and at the distant vessel, their enterprising leader had been casting about in his mind as to the best method of at least attempting the deliverance of his men, and he finally turned round to propose, as a forlorn hope, that all hands should strip off their upper clothing, that every unnecessary article should be removed from the boats, that a specified number should get into each, and that the remainder should hang on by the gunwales, and thus be dragged through the water while they were rowed cautiously towards the *Smeaton*! But when he tried to speak his mouth was so parched that his tongue refused utterance! and then he discovered (as he says himself) 'that saliva is as necessary to speech as the tongue itself!' Turning to a pool, he moistened his lips with sea-water, and found immediate relief. He was again about to speak when someone shouted 'a boat! a boat!' and, sure enough, a large boat was seen through the haze making towards the rock. This timely visitor was James Spink, the Bell Rock pilot, who had come off express from Arbroath with letters. His visit was altogether an unusual one, and his truly providential appearance unquestionably prevented loss of life on that critical occasion. This is one specimen – selected from innumerable instances of danger and risk – which may give one some idea of what is encountered by those who build such lighthouses as the Bell Rock.

R. M. BALLANTYNE: *Personal Reminiscences*

Reminiscences

We ran into bad weather in the Bay of Biscay. The sea was very rough when I went on watch one night, and as we had no cargo the ship was bouncing about like a cork. The engines raced in a most alarming way whenever the propeller was lifted out of the water, and I expected to see them collapse in front of me at any moment. Suddenly, the nuts which held down one of the main bearing covers jumped right off with a report like a gun. I rang the bridge telegraph and stopped the engine. The chief's room opened off the engine-room and he came tearing down the ladders in his pyjamas. He shouted at me, 'Who the hell authorized you to stop the engines?' I said I thought the main shaft was broken. He paid no attention and started the engines again, but when I pointed to the nuts he shut off the steam and we had a look at them. The threads had been corroded so much with the water running constantly on the bearing that the nuts had stripped off. Mr Gregg wrapped canvas round the bolts and screwed the nuts on again. I never for a moment thought they would hold, but they did.

One of my firemen was an Irishman named John Coyle. He was a little shrivelled man, like a monkey, and he was said to be seventy years old, but as he lived for thirty years longer, I do not suppose he was much over fifty. He was famous in the Company because once when the Customs had made a great haul of smuggled cheroots he claimed to be the culprit. He was tried and sentenced to, I think, six months' imprisonment, but the real owners paid the fine, amounting to £54, and he was liberated. John got a small present for his trouble, but he always held that he had arranged to go to prison and get the amount of the fine when he came out. It was the sorrow of his life. He was a very good fireman, and I used to go into the stokehold every watch for lessons – firing is not nearly such a simple matter as many people imagine.

I have never forgotten the fright Rankin gave me after everything had been closed up in preparation for running the engines next day. I had opened the air-pump for inspection. This pump was worked by the main engines, and a good deal of dismantling had to be done before it could be inspected. We were having tea in the mess-room when Rankin said, 'Are you sure you took all your tools out of that pump before you closed it up?'
I said I was quite sure, and then I began to feel nervous.

215

I knew if something had been left inside there would be a smash when the engines were started, so I said, 'Look here, I'll open it up again and make sure.'

'No, you won't,' said Rankin.

I begged him to allow me to work all night, but he was inexorable, and I did not sleep a wink. I think I never had a more miserable moment than when the engines made their first revolution. Everything went well and Rankin said to me, 'I hope this will be a lesson to you. Always make sure of your work the first time. Half the people in the world are scared stiff because they are never sure of anything.'

On our way home that voyage we stopped for only a few hours at Colombo, and to keep me employed Davie told me to adjust one of the crankpin bearings. This was a comparatively big job, for the shaft was eighteen inches diameter. However, I got the bearing opened up, and showed it to NcNab, who agreed that it was all right. As Davie was ashore, I closed it up and was just finishing when he came down below. He was very angry that he had not seen it and was certain that I had put it up too tight, and insisted that I should slacken back the nuts. I told him I was sure it would start knocking if I did what he wanted, and McNab was called in. He always was a broken reed and never contradicted Davie, so, as it was nearly sailing time, there was nothing for it but to do what he said. The result was that we started out across the Indian Ocean with something like a steam hammer bumping away in the bottom of the ship. Davie would never stop at sea, but even he did not seem to like the idea of going on to Aden, and he said it was all my fault and gave me a very bad time. However, something happened the first day out that pleased him more than if he had got a fortune. A passenger had been brought on board very ill at Colombo, and the day after we sailed Davie came down on my afternoon watch looking almost genial. 'That man's dead, Mister,' he said, 'and they are buryin' him to-morrow after breakfast. I'll have to go to the funeral, but I'll get Sammy to take as long as he can, and you'll have everything ready, and nip up these nuts. You'll only have about five minutes, mind, so see you don't waste any time. They'll be down any minute now asking you for a pair of firebars to sink him with, and see you don't give them new ones. I always keep a lot of old burned ones on the starboard stringer for jobs like this.' Next day he said to me after the funeral, 'Man, when they were slingin' him off the plank, I heard you laying on with the big hammer, and I says to him, "I don't know you, but good luck to you".'

I realized that the rose box must be choked. I sent the greaser for the serang, whose duty it was to see to these things. He came down in a little and I told him to have the rose box cleared. He said that he was on duty only from 7 till 5, and that if I wanted him at night I must ask the Burra Sahib, meaning Davie. I began to lose my temper, and when after some more argument I saw him smile to the greaser I hit him with the back of my hand just below the ear. So far as I know I did not hit him very hard, but he went down. He did not stagger, but he just closed up like a concertina and lay on the floor plates in a heap. I straightened him out, but he seemed quite dead. I knew what adepts these people are at shamming, so I got out the fire hose and played it on him. The force was so great that his body moved along the floor plates. I was now in a dreadful panic and I ran up to the doctor's room. He was, of course, asleep, and it took me a long time to persuade him that it was not a joke. When he came down to the engine-room and felt the man's heart, he said, 'I think he's dead, but I can do nothing with him down here. It's far too hot. We must get him on deck.' I am not a particularly strong man, but I was in such a state of terror that I picked the serang up and carried him up the ladders in my arms. I never knew how I did it. I put him down on the deck and the doctor got busy. I leant against the bulwarks and watched the doctor and listened to the noise of the propeller as it got louder and died away when the ship dived and rose again on the gentle swell. I knew quite well how strict the law is about officers striking men, and I remembered that Captain Kidd was hanged, not because he was a pirate, but because he had struck a gunner, just as I had struck the serang. The doctor sat back on his heels and said, 'Well, old fellow, I'm sorry for you – this man's dead.' I said, 'Well there's only one thing to do. We'll dump him overboard.' And just then the serang opened his eyes. We never knew whether he was shamming or whether it was just a coincidence, but there is no doubt he would have been overboard within the next minute if he had not wakened up. The serang was very civil to me after that, and old Abdul told me that I had done him a lot of good.

The destroyer's trials continued to go very well, but Nevinsky did not become any more affable. One day, however, we had a mishap which made a great difference. We were about to carry out astern trials, and Nevinsky said he wished to go full speed astern for fifteen minutes. I told him we must go outside the islands, as there was no room where we were. He said, 'We can put the rudder over to keep clear.' I told him it would be dangerous to use the rudder at full speed astern, and I incautiously added, 'Even the British Admiralty do not ask people to do that.' He fired up at once and said, 'You mean that if they cannot do it, we cannot do it.' That, of course, was just what I did mean, but I could not say so and I kept quiet.

'Well,' he said, 'you have my order.'

We had a Finnish pilot, a very good man. I told him what Nevinsky wanted and I felt he was not displeased to think we were going to wreck the ship. I asked him where he thought we would go ashore, and told him to send the tugboat which attended us to wait for us there. I then told him not to move the rudder till he was certain we were going on the rocks, as I was sure the steering-gear would carry away. We went off and were soon travelling at a great speed. I went down to the engine-room and told them to stop both engines the moment I blew my whistle. I then went up on deck again. We were throwing up a great wave at our stern, and it was difficult to see where we were going. I stayed at the engine-room hatch and could not see Nevinsky or the pilot, as the funnels were in the way. Some of the Russians were looking very uneasy, and I did not feel too happy myself. Suddenly the ship swung round – I blew my whistle, and the engines stopped. We heeled over and a great wave broke over the stern and came rushing up the deck. Then we righted ourselves and lay rocking in absolute silence. The tug had us in tow before any of the Russians knew what had happened.

Nevinsky came to me looking very pale, and asked if much damage had been done. I said I did not know how bad it was, but that the steering-gear had carried away and I thought the rudder had struck one of the propellers. The engine-room telegraphs were still standing at 'full astern', and when he saw me looking at them he was very humiliated. We went down to the ward-room and he was extraordinarily nice about the whole incident, and took all the blame. He sent for the others and they all seemed to think I had saved their lives. He said, 'Now tell me your father's name.' When I told him, he kissed me. 'You are now,' he said, 'Wassilief Famitch – William, son of Thomas.'

I felt very embarrassed – it was like something in the Bible.

W. G. RIDDELL: Adventures of an Obscure Victorian

Dr Johnson at Sea

Joseph reported that the wind was still against us. Dr Johnson said, 'A wind, or not a wind? that is the question'; for he can amuse himself at times with a little play of words or rather sentences. I remember when he turned his cup at Aberbrothick, where we drank tea, he muttered, *claudite iam rivos, pueri*. I must again and again apologise to fastidious readers for recording such minute particulars. They prove the scrupulous fidelity of my *Journal*.

While we were chatting in the indolent stile of men who were to stay here all this day at least, we were suddenly roused at being told that the wind was fair, that a little fleet of herring-busses was passing by for Mull, and that Mr Simpson's vessel was about to sail. Hugh McDonald, the skipper, came to us, and was impatient that we should get ready, which we soon did. Dr Johnson, with composure and solemnity, repeated the observation of Epictetus, that, 'as man has the voyage of death before him, – whatever may be his employment, he should be ready at the master's call; and an old man should never be far from the shore, lest he should not be able to get himself ready.' He rode, and I and the other gentlemen walked, about an English mile to the shore, where the vessel lay. Dr Johnson said, he should never forget Skye, and returned thanks for all civilities. We were carried to the vessel in a small boat which she had, and we set sail very briskly about one o'clock.

I was much pleased with the motion for many hours. Dr Johnson grew sick, and retired under cover, as it rained a good deal. I kept above, that I might have fresh air, and finding myself not affected by the motion of the vessel, I exulted in being a stout seaman, while Dr Johnson was quite in a state of annihilation. But I was soon humbled; for after imagining that I could go with ease to America or the East Indies, I became very sick, but kept above board, though it rained hard.

As we had been detained so long in Skye by bad weather, we gave up the scheme that Col had planned for us of visiting several islands, and contented ourselves with the prospect of seeing Mull, and Icolmkill and Inchkenneth, which lie near to it.

Mr Simpson was sanguine in his hopes for awhile, the wind being fair for us. He said, he would land us at Icolmkill that night. But when the wind failed, it was resolved we should make for the sound of Mull, and land in the harbour of Tobermorie. We kept near the five herring vessels for some time; but afterwards four of them got before us, and one little wherry fell behind us. When we got in full view of the point of Ardnamurchan, the wind changed, and was directly against our getting into the sound. We were then obliged to tack, and get forward in that tedious manner.

As we advanced the storm grew greater, and the sea very rough. Col then began to talk of making for Egg, or Canna, or his own island. Our skipper said, he would get us into the Sound. Having struggled for this a good while in vain, he said, he would push forward till we were near the land of Mull, where we might cast anchor, and lie till the morning; for although, before this, there had been a good moon, and I had pretty distinctly seen not only the land of Mull, but up the Sound, and the country of Morven as at one end of it, the night was now grown very dark.

Our crew consisted of one McDonald, our skipper, and two sailors, one of whom had but one eye; Mr Simpson himself, Col, and Hugh McDonald his servant, all helped. Simpson said, he would willingly go for Col, if young Col or his servant would undertake to pilot us to a harbour; but, as the island is low land, it was dangerous to run upon it in the dark, Col and his servant appeared a little dubious. The scheme of running for Canna seemed then to be embraced; but Canna was ten leagues off, all out of our way; and they were afraid to attempt the harbour of Egg. All these different plans were successively in agitation. The old skipper still tried to make for the land of Mull; but then it was considered that there was no place there where we could anchor in safety. Much time was lost in striving against the storm. At last it became so rough, and threatened to be so much worse, that Col and his servant took more courage, and said they would undertake to hit one of the harbours in Col.

'Then let us run for it in God's name,' said the skipper; and instantly we turned towards it.

The little wherry which had fallen behind us had hard work. The master begged that, if we made for Col, we should put out a light to him. Accordingly one of the sailors waved a glowing peat for some time. The various difficulties that were started, gave me a good deal of apprehension, from which I was relieved, when I found we were to run for a harbour before the wind. But my relief was but of short duration; for I soon heard that our sails were very bad, and were in danger of being torn in pieces, in which case we should be driven upon the rocky shore of Col. It was very dark, and there was a heavy and incessant rain. The sparks of the burning peat flew so much about, that I dreaded the vessel might take fire. Then, as Col was a sportsman and had powder on board, I figured that we might be blown up. Simpson and he appeared a little frightened, which made me more so; and the perpetual talking, or rather shouting, which was carried on in Erse, alarmed me still more. A man is always suspicious of what is saying in an unknown tongue; and, if fear be his passion at the time, he grows more afraid. Our vessel often lay so much on one side, that I trembled lest she should be overset, and indeed they told me afterwards that they had run her sometimes to within an inch of the water, so anxious were they to make what haste they could before the night should be worse.

I now saw what I never saw before, a prodigious sea, with immense billows coming upon a vessel, so as that it seemed hardly possible to escape. There was something grandly horrible in the sight. I am glad I have seen it once.

Amidst all these terrifying circumstances, I endeavoured to compose my mind. It was not easy to do it; for all the stories I had heard of the dangerous sailing among the Hebrides, which is proverbial, came full upon my recollection. When I thought of those who were dearest to me, and would suffer severely, should I be lost, I upbraided myself as not having a sufficient cause for putting myself in such danger. Piety afforded me comfort; yet I was disturbed by the objections that have been made against a particular providence, and by the arguments of those who maintain that it is in vain to hope that the petitions of an individual, or even of congregations, can have any influence with the Deity; objections which have been often made, and which Dr Hawkesworth has lately revived in his Preface to the *Voyages to the South Seas*; but Dr Ogden's excellent doctrine on the efficacy of intercession prevailed.

It was half an hour after eleven before we set ourselves in the course for Col. As I saw them all busy doing something, I asked Col, with much earnestness, what I could do. He, with a happy readiness, put into my hand a rope, which was fixed to the top of one of the masts, and told me to hold it till he bade me pull. If I had considered the matter, I might have seen that this could not be of the least service; but his object was to keep me out of the way of those who were busy working the vessel, and at the same time to divert my fear, by employing me, and making me think that I was of use. Thus did I stand firm to my post, while the wind and rain beat upon me, always expecting a call to pull my rope.

The man with one eye steered; old McDonald, and Col and his servant, lay upon the fore-castle, looking sharp out for the harbour. It was necessary to carry much *cloth*, as they termed it, that is to say much sail, in order to keep the vessel off the shore of Col. This made violent plunging in a rough sea. At last they spied the harbour of Lochiern, and Col cried, 'Thank God we are safe!' We ran up till we were opposite to it, and soon afterwards we got into it, and cast anchor.

Dr Johnson had all this time been quiet and unconcerned. He had lain down on one of the beds, and having got free from sickness, was satisfied. The truth is, he knew nothing of the danger we were in; but, fearless and unconcerned, might have said, in the words which he has chosen for the motto of his *Rambler*,

Quo me cunque rapit tempestas, deferor hospes.

Once, during the doubtful consultations, he asked whither we were going; and upon being told that it was not certain whether to Mull or Col, he cried, 'Col for my money!'

I now went down, with Col and Mr Simpson, to visit him. He was lying in philosophick tranquillity with a greyhound of Col's at his back, keeping him warm. Col is quite the *iuvenis qui gaudet canibus*: he had five dogs with him.

I was very ill, and very desirous to get to shore. When I was told that we could not land that night, as the storm had now increased, I looked so miserably, as Col afterwards informed me, that what Shakespeare has made the Frenchman say of the English soldiers, when scantily dieted, 'Piteous they will look, like drowned mice!' might, I believe, have been well applied to me.

There was in the harbour, before us, a Campbelltown vessel, the *Betty*, Kenneth Morison master, taking in kelp, and bound for Ireland. We sent our boat to beg beds for two gentlemen, and that the master would send his boat, which was larger than ours. He accordingly did so, and Col and I were accommodated in his vessel till the morning.

JAMES BOSWELL: *Journal of a Tour to the Hebrides*

John Oxenham of Plymouth

There was another Englishman, who hearing of the spoyle that Francis Drake had done upon the coast of Nueva Espanna, and of his good adventure and safe returne home, was thereby provoked to undertake the like enterprise, with a ship of 140 tunnes and 70 men, and came thither, and had also conference with the foresaide Negros; and hearing that the gold and silver which came upon the mules from Panama to Nombre de Dios was now conducted with souldiers, he determined to do that which never any man before enterprised; and landed in that place where Francis Drake before had had his conference with the Negros.

This man covered his ship after he had brought her aground with boughes of trees, and hid his great Ordinance in the ground, and so not leaving any man in his ship, he tooke two small pieces of ordinance, and his calivers, and good store of victuals, and so went with the Negros about twelve leagues into the maine land, to a river that goeth to the South sea, and there he cut wood and made a Pinnesse, which was five and fortie foote by the keele, and having made this Pinnesse, he went into the South Sea, carrying sixe Negros with him to be his guides, and so went to the Iland of Pearles, which is five and twenty leagues from Panama, which is in the way that they come from

Peru to Panama, and there he was ten dayes without showing himselfe to any man, to see if he might get any ship that came from Peru.

At last there came a small Barke by, which came from Peru from a place called Quito, which he tooke and found in her sixtie thousand pezos of gold, and much victuals. But not contenting himself with this prize, hee stayed long without sending away his prize or any of the men, and in the ende of sixe dayes after he tooke another Barke which came from Lima, in which he tooke an hundred thousand pezos of silver in barres, with the which he thought to have gone, and entred the river; but first he went into the Islands to see if he could find any pearles: where he found a few, and so returned to his pinnesse againe, and so sailing to the river from whence he came, and comming neere to the mouth of the sayd river, hee sent away the two prizes that hee tooke, and with his pinnesse he went up the river.

The Negros that dwelt in the Island of pearls, the same night that he went from them, went in Canoas to Panama, and the Governour within two dayes sent foure barkes 100 men, 25 in every one, and Negros to row with the Captain John de Ortega, which went to the Iland of pearles, and there had intelligence which way the English men were gone, and following them he met by the way the ships which the English men had taken, of whom he learned that the English men had gone up the river, and he going thither, when he came to the mouth of the river, the captaine of Panama knew not which way to take, because there were three partitions in the river to go up in; and being determined to goe up the greatest of the three rivers, he saw comming downe a lesser river many feathers of hennes, which the Englishmen had pulled to eate, and being glad thereof, hee went up that river where hee saw the feathers; and after that he had bene in that river foure daies, he descried the Englishmens pinnesse upon the sands, and coming to her, there were no more than sixe Englishmen, whereof they killed one, and the other five escaped away, and in the pinnesse he found nothing but victuals.

But this captaine of Panama not herewith satisfied, determined to seeke out the Englishmen by land, and leaving twenty men in his pinnesses, hee with 80 shot went up the countrey. Hee had not gone halfe a league, but hee found a house made of boughs, where they found all the Englishmens goods, and the gold and silver also, and carrying it backe to their pinnesses, the Spaniards were determined to goe away, without following the English men any further.

But at the end of three dayes, the English Captaine came to the river with all his men, and above 200 Negros, and set upon the Spaniards with great fury; but the Spaniards having the advantage of trees which they stood behind, did easily prevaile, and killed eleven Englishmen and five Negros, and tooke other seven Englishmen alive, but of the Spaniards two were slaine and five sore hurt.

Among other things, the Spaniards enquired of the Englishmen which they tooke, why they went not away in fifteen dayes liberty which they had. They answered, that their captaine had commanded them to carie all that gold and silver which they had to the place where they had left their shippe, and they had promised him to carie it, although they made three or foure journeys of it, for hee promised to give them part of it besides their wages, but the mariners would have it by and by, and so their Captaine being angry because they would not take his word, fell out with them, and they with him, in so much that one of the company would have killed the Captaine, so that the Captaine would not have them to carie the treasure, but sayd hee would seeke Negros to carie it, and so he went and sought for Negros, and bringing those Negros to carie it, hee met with the five English men that hee had left in his pinnesse which ranne from the Spaniards, and the rest also which ran from the house, and they told him what the Spaniards had done, and then making friendship with all his men, he promised them halfe of all the treasure if they got it from the Spaniards, and the Negros promised to helpe him with their bowes and arrowes, and thereupon they came to seeke the Spaniards, and now that some of his company were killed and taken, hee thought it best to returne to his ship, and to passe backe for England. The Spanish captaine hearing this, having buried the dead bodies, and having gotten all things into his barkes, and taking the English men and their pinnesse with him, he returned to Panama: so the voyage of that English man did not prosper with him, as hee thought it would have done.

Nowe when the foure barkes were come to Panama, they sent advice also to Nombre de Dios, and they of Nombre de Dios sent also from them other foure barkes which (as the Spaniards say) found the English ship where she was hid, and brought her to Nombre de Dios: and that the viceroy of Peru not thinking it good to suffer fiftie English men to remaine in the country, sent a servant of his called Diego de Frees, with a hundred and fiftie shot into the mountaines to seeke them out, who found them making of certain Canoas to goe into the North Sea, and there to take some barke or other. Some of them were sicke, and were taken, and the rest fled with the Negros, who in the end betrayed them to the Spaniards, so that they were brought to Panama. And the Justice of Panama asked the English captaine whether hee had the Queenes licence, or the licence of any other Prince or Lord for his attempt. And he answered he had none, whereupon hee and all his company were condemned to dye, and so were all executed, saving the Captaine, the Master, the Pilot, and five boyes which were caried to Lima, and there the Captaine was executed with the other two, but the boyes be yet living.

LOPEZ VAZ: in Hakluyt *The English Voyages* (xvi)

The Castaway

Obscurest night involved the sky,
The Atlantic billows roar'd,
When such a destined wretch as I,
Wash'd headlong from on board,

Of friends, of hope, of all bereft
His floating home for ever left.

No braver chief could Albion boast
    Than he with whom he went,
Nor ever ship left Albion's coast
    With warmer wishes sent.
He loved them both, but both in vain,
Nor him beheld, nor her, again.

Not long beneath the whelming brine,
    Expert to swim, he lay;
Nor soon he felt his strength decline
    Or courage die away;
But waged with death a lasting strife,
Supported by despair of life.

He shouted: nor his friends had fail'd
    To check the vessel's course,
But so the furious blast prevailed,
    That pitiless perforce,
They left their outcast mate behind,
And scudded still before the wind.

Some succour yet they could afford;
    And, such as storms allow,
The cask, the coop, the floated cord,
    Delayed not to bestow.
But he (they knew) nor ship nor shore,
Whate'er they gave, should visit more.

Nor, cruel as it seem'd, could he
    Their haste himself condemn,
Aware that flight, in such a sea,
    Alone could rescue them;
Yet bitter felt it still to die
Deserted, and his friends so nigh.

He long survives, who lives an hour
   In ocean, self-upheld;
And so long he, with unspent power,
   His destiny repell'd;
And ever as the minutes flew,
Entreated help, or cried – 'Adieu!'

At length, his transient respite past,
   His comrades, who before
Had heard his voice in every blast,
   Could catch the sound no more:
For then, by toil subdued, he drank
The stifling wave, and then he sank.

No poet wept him; but the page
   Of narrative sincere,
That tells his name, his worth, his age,
   Is wet with Anson's tear:
And tears by bards or heroes shed
Alike immortalize the dead.

I therefore purpose not, or dream,
   Descanting on his fate,
To give the melancholy theme
   A more enduring date:
But misery still delights to trace
Its semblance in another's case.

No voice divine the storm allay'd,
   No light propitious shone,
When, snatch'd from all effectual aid,
   We perish'd, each alone:
But I beneath a rougher sea,
And whelm'd in deeper gulfs than he.

WILLIAM COWPER (xvii)

Steeving

Having filled the ship up to within four feet of her beams, the process of steeving commenced, by which a hundred hides are got into a place where one could not be forced by hand, and which presses the hides to the utmost, sometimes starting the beams of the ship, resembling in its effects the jackscrews which are used in stowing cotton. Each morning we went ashore, and beat and brought off as many hides as we could steeve in the course of the day, and, after breakfast, went down into the hold, where we remained at work until night. The whole length of the hold, from stem to stern, was floored off level, and we began with raising a pile in the after part, hard against the bulkhead of the run, and filling it up to the beams, crowding in as many as we could by hand and pushing in with oars; when a large 'book' was made of from twenty-five to fifty hides, doubled at the backs, and put into one another, like the leaves of a book. An opening was then made between two hides in the pile, and the back of the outside hide in the book inserted. Two long, heavy spars, called steeves, made of the strongest wood, and sharpened off like a wedge at one end, were placed with their wedge ends into the inside of the hide which was the centre of the book, and to the other end of each straps were fitted, into which large tackles were hooked, composed each of two huge purchase blocks, one hooked to the strap on the end of the steeve, and the other into a dog, fastened into one of the beams, as far aft as it could be got. When this was arranged, and the ways greased upon which the book was to slide, the falls of the tackles were stretched forward and all hands tallied on, and bowsed away until the book was well entered, when these tackles were nipped, straps and toggles clapped upon the falls, and two more luff tackles hooked on, with dogs, in the same manner, and thus, by luff upon luff, the power was multiplied, until into a pile in which one hide more could not be crowded by hand, a hundred or a hundred and fifty were often driven in by this complication of purchases. When the last luff was hooked on, all hands were called to the rope – cook, steward and all – and ranging ourselves at the falls, one behind the other, sitting down on the hides, with our heads just even with the beams, we set taut upon the tackles, and striking up a song, and all lying back at the chorus, we bowsed the tackles home, and drove the large books chock in out of sight.

R. H. DANA: *Two Years Before the Mast*

Slipping the Cable

This night, after sundown, it looked black at the southward and eastward, and we were told to keep a bright look-out. Expecting to be called up, we turned in early. Waking up about midnight, I found a man who had just come down from his watch, striking a light. He said that it was beginning to puff up from the south-east, and that the sea was rolling in, and he had called the captain; and as he threw himself down on his chest with all his clothes on, I knew that he expected to be called. I felt the vessel pitching at her anchor, and the chain surging and snapping, and lay awake expecting an instant summons. In a few minutes it came – three knocks on the scuttle, and 'All hands ahoy! Bear – a – hand – up and make sail.' We sprang up for our clothes, and were about half-way dressed, when the mate called out, down the scuttle, 'Tumble up here, men! tumble up! before she drags her anchor.' We were on deck in an instant. 'Lay aloft and loose the topsail!' shouted the captain, as soon as the first man showed himself. Springing into the rigging, I saw that the *Ayacucho*'s topsails were loosed, and heard her crew singing out at the sheets as they were hauling them home. This had probably started our captain, as 'old Wilson,' the captain of the *Ayacucho*, had been many years on the coast and knew the signs of the weather.

We soon had the topsails loosed; and one hand remaining,

as usual, in each top to overhaul the rigging and light the sail out, the rest of us laid down to man the sheets. While sheeting home, we saw the *Ayacucho* standing athwart our bows, sharp upon the wind, cutting through the head-sea like a knife, with her raking masts and sharp bows running up like the head of a greyhound. It was a beautiful sight. She was like a bird which had been frightened and had spread her wings in flight.

After the topsails had been sheeted home, the head-yards braced aback, the fore-topmast staysail hoisted, and the buoys streamed, and all ready forward for slipping, we went aft and manned the slip-rope, which came through the stern port with a turn round the timber-heads. 'All ready forward?' asked the captain. 'Ay ay, Sir; all ready,' answered the mate. 'Let go!' 'All gone, Sir;' and the iron cable grated over the windlass and through the hawse-hole, and the little vessel's head swinging off from the wind under the force of her backed head sails, brought the strain upon the slip-rope.

'Let go aft!' Instantly all was gone, and we were under way. As soon as she was well off from the wind, we filled away the head yards, braced all up sharp, set the foresail and trysail, and left our anchorage well astern, giving the points a good berth.

It now began to blow fresh; the rain fell fast and it grew very black; but the captain would not take in sail until we were well clear of the point. As soon as we left this on our quarter and were standing out to sea, the order was given, and we sprang aloft, double reefed each topsail, furled the foresail and double reefed the trysail, and were soon under easy sail. In these cases of slipping for south-easters, there is nothing to be done, after you have got clear of the coast, but to lie-to under easy sail and wait for the gale to be over, which seldom lasts more than two days and is often over in twelve hours; but the wind never comes back to the southward until a good deal of rain has fallen.

'Go below the watch,' said the mate; but here was a dispute which watch it should be, which the mate soon, however, settled by sending his watch below, saying that we should have our turn the next time we got under way. We remained on deck till the expiration of the watch, the wind blowing very fresh and the rain coming down in torrents. When the watch came up we wore ship and stood on the other tack, in towards land. When we came up again, which was at four in the morning, it was very dark, and there was not much wind, but it was raining as I thought I had never seen it rain before. We had on oil-cloth suits and south-wester caps, and had nothing to do but to stand bolt upright and let it pour down upon us. There are no umbrellas and no sheds to go under, at sea.

Toward morning the captain put his head out of the companionway and told the second-mate, who commanded our watch, to look out for a change of wind, which usually followed a calm and heavy rain; and it was as well that he did; for in a few minutes it fell dead calm, the vessel lost her steerage-way, and the rain ceased. We hauled up the trysail and courses, squared the afteryards, and waited for the change, which came in a few minutes, with a vengeance, from the north-west, the opposite point of the compass. Owing to our precautions, we were not taken aback, but ran before the wind with square yards. The captain coming on deck we braced up a little, and stood back for our anchorage. With the change of wind came a change of weather, and in two hours the wind moderated into the light steady breeze which blows down the coast the greater part of the year, and, from its regularity, might be called a trade-wind. The sun came out bright, and we set royals, skysails and studding-sails, and were under fair way for Santa Barbara.

R. H. DANA: *Two Years Before the Mast*

The Athenian Fleet Sails for Sicily

It was about midsummer when the expedition to Sicily began. Orders had already been issued to most of the allied contingents together with the light boats, food transports and miscellaneous odds and ends, to assemble at Corcyra ready to cross in company to the heel of Italy. The Athenians themselves, with such allied troops as were still on the spot, went down to Peiraeus at dawn on the day appointed and boarded their ships in readiness for putting to sea. The fighting forces were accompanied to the harbour by a motley crowd consisting of almost everyone left in the town, citizens and strangers alike: those who were natives of Athens came to bid God speed to friends, kinsmen or sons; conflicting emotions tore their hearts – hope of profit should all go well, and grief when they could not but think of how far away Sicily was and that they might never see their loved ones again. Indeed, now the decisive moment had come, the hazards and perils of the venture were much more vividly present to every mind than when the resolution to undertake the expedition had originally been passed in the Assembly, though some comfort was given to all by the magnitude of the assembled armament and the mere spectacle of the numbers of ships and men. The foreigners who flocked with them to the harbour, and the nameless mob who had nothing personally at stake, came simply as sight-seers; for the occasion was a memorable one and the object of the expedition far exceeded all reasonable expectation.

This first expedition, a Greek force raised by a single Greek city, was indeed the most costly and the most splendidly equipped which had ever been seen. Previous ones had equalled it in numerical strength of ships and fighting men: the expedition against Epidaurus, for instance, or Potidaea. . . . but in both those cases the passage involved was a short one and the equipment of the fleet in no way remarkable. But how different the occasion of which I now speak! Now everything pointed to a protracted term of service for both ships and men, and all possible contingencies had been provided for: the fleet had been brought to perfection at a vast expenditure of both public and private funds; the treasury was paying the seamen a drachma a day and had provided sixty warships and forty troop-transports, while the Trierarchs assumed responsibility for securing the best crews for their particular vessels, and contributed additional pay for the master-rowers and petty officers; each vessel had the best of gear regardless of cost and a figure-head as splendid as could be; and there was not a commander who failed to do his utmost to ensure the pre-eminence of his vessel as much in her trim as in her efficiency. The soldiers were all picked men, each the rival of the rest for supreme excellence in his weapons and personal equipment; each in his station did his utmost to outshine his fellows, so that the whole enterprise, in the eyes of Greece generally, looked more like a demonstration of Athenian power and resources than a planned attack upon a hostile state. The expense involved was indeed enormous and a heavy drain both on the treasury and on individuals. The state, in addition to its original expenditure, paid out further sums for the current use of the commanding officers; individuals had lavished money on their equipment and trierarchs on their ships, and they were all to spend more before they were done; every man, apart from the ordinary needs of campaigning, and over and above his pay, had to provide himself for a long period of foreign service, not to mention such funds as both soldiers and merchants took with them against the chances of doing business in the course of the campaign. If all this were reckoned up, it would amount to a pretty sum being taken from the city's resources.

In effect it was not so much the superiority of the actual forces engaged, but the daring and brilliance of this expedition, which called forth the astonishment and admiration of Greece, added to the fact that its objective involved a longer voyage than ever before and carried with it prospects more splendid, for a state like Athens, than any ever known.

When the crews were aboard and the vessels fully loaded with all their gear and supplies, a trumpet was blown and silence fell. The customary prayers before sailing were offered up not on each ship separately but, at the herald's bidding, as a single prayer rising in unison from all; from one end of the fleet to the other the bowls were filled with wine, and captains and men-at-arms poured libations from cups of silver and gold.

The crowds on shore joined in the prayers, Athenians and strangers alike – all, indeed, who wished them well. Then the Victory song was sung, the pouring of libations brought to an end, and the fleet moved in column from the harbour. Once open water was reached, they broke formation and raced each other to Aegina, whence they pressed on with all speed for Corcyra, to effect the junction with their allies.

THUCYDIDES: *History of Peloponnesian War* (xviii)

Beware of Dreams

Two men that wolde han passed over see,
For certeyn cause, into a fer contree,
If that the wynd ne hadde been contrarie,
That made hem in a citee for to tarie
That stood ful myrie upon an haven syde;
But on a day, agayn the even-tyde,
The wynd gan chaunge, and blew right as hem leste.
Jolif and glad they wente unto hir reste,
And casten hem ful erly for to saille.
    But to that o man fil a greet mervaille;
That oon of hem in slepyng as he lay,
Hym mette a wonder dreem, agayn the day:
Him thought a man stood by his beddes side
And hym comanded that he sholde abyde,
And seyde hym thus: 'If thou tomorwe wende,
Thou shalt be dreynt: my tale is at an ende.'
    He wook, and tolde his felawe what he mette,
And preyde hym his viage for to lette;
As for that day, he preyde hym to byde.
His felawe, that lay by his beddes syde,
Gan for to laughe, and scorned him ful faste;
'No dreem', quod he, 'may so myn herte agaste,
That I wolle lette for to do my thynges;
I sette not a straw by thy dremynges,

For swevenes been but vanytees and japes;
Men dreme al day of owles or of apes,
And eke of many a maze therwithal;
Men dreme of thyng that never was ne shal;
But sith I see that thou wolt heere abyde,
And thus forslewthen wilfully thy tyde,
God woot it reweth me – and have good day!'
    And thus he took his leve, and wente his way;
But er that he hadde half his cours y-seyled,
Noot I nat why, ne what myschaunce it eyled,
But casuelly the shippes botme rente,
And shipe and man under the water wente
In sight of othere shippes it bisyde,
That with hem seyled at the same tyde.

GEOFFREY CHAUCER: Nun's Priest's Tale

Spouter

As soon as her anchor was down we went aboard, and found
her to be the whale-ship *Wilmington and Liverpool Packet*, of
New Bedford, last from the 'off-shore ground' with nineteen
hundred barrels of oil. A 'spouter' we knew her to be as soon
as we saw her, by her cranes and boats, and by her stump topgallant masts, and a certain slovenly look to the sails, rigging,
spars and hull, and when we got on board we found everything
to correspond – spouter fashion. She had a false deck which
was rough and oily, and cut up in every direction by the
chines of oil-casks; her rigging was slack and turning white; no
paint on the spars or blocks; clumsy seizings and straps without
covers, and homeward-bound splices in every direction. Her
crews, too, were not in much better order. Her captain was a
slab-sided, shamble-legged Quaker, in a suit of brown, with a
broad-brimmed hat, and sneaking about decks, like a sheep,
with his head down, and the men looked more like fishermen
and farmers than they did like sailors.

Though it was by no means cold weather (we having on only our red shirts and duck trousers), they had on woollen trousers – not blue and ship-shape, but of all colours – brown, drab, grey, ay and *green*, with suspenders over their shoulders, and pockets to put their hands in. This, added to Guernsey frocks, striped comforters about the necks, thick cowhide boots, woollen caps, a strong oily smell and a decidedly green look, will complete the description.

Eight or ten were on the foretopsail yard, and as many more in the main, furling the topsails, while eight or ten were hanging about the forecastle doing nothing. This was a strange sight for a ship coming to anchor, so we went up to them to see what was the matter. One of them, a stout, hearty-looking fellow, held out his leg and said he had the scurvy; another had cut his hand, and others had got nearly well but said that there were plenty aloft to furl the sails, so they were sogering on the forecastle. There was only one 'splicer' on board, a fine-looking old tar, who was in the bunt of the fore-topsail. He was, probably, the only sailor in the ship, before the mast. The mates, of course, and the boat-steerers, and also two or three of the crew, had been to sea before, but only whaling voyages, and the greater part of the crew were raw hands, just from the bush, as green as cabbages, and had not yet got the hayseed out of their heads. The mizen topsail hung in the buntlines until everything was furled forward. Thus a crew of thirty men were half an hour in doing what would have been done in the *Alert*, with eighteen hands to go aloft, in fifteen or twenty minutes.

R. H. DANA: *Two Years Before the Mast*

Sailor on Horseback

A shipman was ther, wonynge fer by weste;
For aught I woot he was of Dertemouthe.
He rood upon a rouncy as he kouthe,

In a gown of falding to the knee.
A daggere hangynge on a lass hadde he
About his nekke under his arm adown.
The hoote somer hadde maad his hewe al broun;
And certeinly he was a good felawe.
Ful many a draught of wyn hadde he y-drawe
Fro Burdeuxward whil that the Chapman sleepe.
Of nyce conscience took he no keepe.
If that he fought, and hadde the hyer hond,
By water he sente hem hoom to every lond.
But of his craft to rekene wel his tydes,
His stremes and his daungers him bisides,
His herberwe and his moone, his lode-menage,
Ther nas noon swich from Hulle to Cartage.
Hardy he was, and wys to undertake:
With many a tempest hadde his berd been shake;
He knew well al the havenes, as they were,
From Gootlond to the Cape of Fynystere,
And every cryke in Britaigne and in Spayne.
His barge y-cleped was the Maudelayne.

GEOFFREY CHAUCER: *Prologue to the Canterbury Tales* (xix)

Sailing Ships

Lying on Downs above the wrinkling bay
I with the kestrels shared the cleanly day,
The candid day; wind-shaven, brindled turf;
Tall cliffs; and long sea-line of marbled surf
From Cornish Lizard to the Kentish Nore
Lipping the bulwarks of the English shore,
While many a lovely ship below sailed by
On unknown errand, kempt and leisurely;
And after each, oh, after each, my heart
Fled forth, as, watching from the Downs apart,

I shared with ships good joys and fortunes wide
That might befall their beauty and their pride;

Shared first with them the blessed void repose
Of oily days at sea, when only rose
The porpoise's slow wheel to break the sheen
Of satin water indolently green,
When for'ard the crew, caps tilted over eyes,
Lay heaped on deck; slept; murmured; smoked; threw dice;
The sleepy summer days; the summer nights
(The coast pricked out with rings of harbour-lights);
The motionless nights, the vaulted nights of June
When high in the cordage drifts the entangled moon,
And blocks go knocking, and the sheets go slapping,
And lazy swells against the sides come lapping;
And summer mornings off red Devon rocks,
Faint inland bells at dawn and crowing cocks.
Shared swifter days, when headlands into ken
Trod grandly; threatened; and were lost again,
Old fangs along the battlemented coast;
And followed still my ship, when winds were most
Night-purified, and, lying steeply over,
She fled the wind as flees a girl her lover,
Quickened by that pursuit for which she fretted,
Her temper by the contest proved and whetted;
While stars swept overhead; her lofty spars
Reared to a ragged heaven sown with stars
As leaping out from narrow English ease
She faced the roll of long Atlantic seas;
Her captain then was I, I was her crew,
The mind that laid her course, the wake she drew,
The waves that rose against her bows, the gales, –
Nay, I was more: I was her very sails
Rounded before the wind, her eager keel,
Her straining mast-heads, her responsive wheel,
Her pennon stiffened like a swallow's wing;
Yes, I was all her slope and speed and swing,

Whether by yellow lemons and blue sea
She dawdled through the isles off Thessaly,
Or saw the palms like sheaves of scimitars
On desert's verge below the sunset's bars,
Or passed the girdle of the planet where
The Southern Cross looks over to the Bear,
And strayed, cool Northerner beneath strange skies,
Flouting the lure of tropic estuaries,
Down that long coast, and saw Magellan's clouds arise.

And some that beat up Channel homeward-bound
I watched, and wondered what they might have found,
What alien ports enriched their teeming hold
With crates of fruit or bars of unwrought gold?
And thought how London clerks with paper-clips
Had filed the bills of loading of those ships,
Clerks that had never seen the embattled sea,
But wrote down jettison and barratry,
Perils, Adventures, and the Act of God,
Having no vision of such wrath flung broad;
Wrote down with weary and accustomed pen
The classic dangers of sea-faring men;
And wrote 'Restraint of Princes,' and 'the acts
Of the King's Enemies,' as vacant facts,
Blind to the ambushed seas, the encircling roar
Of angry nations foaming into war.

                                    V. SACKVILLE-WEST

Seascape

Over that morn hung heaviness, until,
Near sunless noon, we heard the ship's bell beating
A melancholy staccato on dead metal;
Saw the bare-footed watch come running aft;
Felt, far below, the sudden telegraph jangle

Its harsh metallic challenge, thrice repeated;
Stand by. Half-speed ahead. Slow. Stop her. They stopped.
The plunging pistons sank like a stopped heart:
She held, she swayed, a bulk, a hollow carcass
Of blistered iron that the grey-green, waveless,
Unruffled tropic waters slapped languidly.
Burial at sea! A Portuguese official. . . .
Poor fever-broken devil from Mozambique.
Came on half-tight: the doctor calls it heat-stroke.
Why do they travel steerage? It's the exchange:
So many million reis to the pound.
What did he look like? No-one ever saw him:
Took to his bunk, and drank and drank and died.
They're ready! Silence!

    We clustered to the rail,
Curious and half-ashamed. The well-deck spread
A comfortable gulf of segregation
Between ourselves and Death. *Burial at sea.* . . .
The master holds a black book at arm's length;
His droning voice comes for'ard: *This our brother.* . . .
We therefore commit his body to the deep
To be turned into corruption. . . .

    The bo's'n whispers
Hoarsely behind his hand: *Now, all together!*
The hatch cover is tilted; a mummy of sailcloth
Well ballasted with iron shoots clear of the poop;
Falls, like a diving gannet. The green sea closes
Its burnished skin; the snaky swell smooths over. . . .
While he, the man of the steerage, goes down, down,
Feet-foremost, sliding swiftly down the dim water:
Swift to escape
Those plunging shapes with pale, empurpled bellies
That swirl and veer about him. He goes down
Unerringly, as though he knew the way

Through green, through gloom, to absolute watery
        darkness,
Where no weed sways nor curious fin quivers:
To the sad, sunless deeps, where, endlessly,
A downward drift of death spreads its wan mantle
In the wave-moulded valleys that shall enfold him
Till the sea give up its dead.
There shall he lie dispersed amid great riches:
Such gold, such arrogance, so many bold hearts!
All the sunken armadas pressed to powder
By weight of incredible seas! That mingled wrack
No livening sun shall visit till the crust
Of earth be riven, or this rolling planet
Reel on its axis; till the moon-chained tides,
Unloosed, deliver up that white Atlantis,
Whose naked peaks shall bleach above the slaked
Thirst of Sahara, fringed by weedy tangles
Of Atlas's drowned cedars, frowning Eastward
To where the sands of India lie cold,
And heaped Himalaya's a rib of coral
Slowly uplifted, grain on grain. . . .

        We dream
Too long! Another jangle of alarum
Stabs at the engines: *Slow. Half-speed. Full speed.*
The great bearings rumble; the screw churns, frothing
Opaque water to downward swelling plumes
Milky as woodsmoke. A shoal of flying-fish
Spurts out like animate spray. The warm breeze wakens,
And we pass on, forgetting,
Toward the solemn horizon of bronzed cumulus
That bounds our brooding sea, gathering gloom
That, when night falls, will dissipate in flaws
Of watery lightning, washing the hot sky,
Cleansing all hearts of heat and restlessness.
Until, with day, another blue be born.

FRANCIS BRETT YOUNG

Laid-Up

There she lies, stranger. Hark now, and let her tell you
How she would show her heels to every craft afloat –
Leave them all standing – a flyer, under sail or oar.
The squally Adriatic knew how she could go,
The Aegean isles and the wild Thracian coast,
The waters of Rhodes, famed in story, and Propontis;
Yes, and the stormy Pontic gulf, where long ago
Her hull was a dream in the trees of a leafy forest.
There on Cytorus her leaves whispered in the wind –
Ah, Cytorus and Amastris! how well you knew
And remember yet that on your slopes she stood,
And in your waters for the first time dipped her oars
To bring her owner safe over wild, wide seas,
Steady on either tack, or running cleanly before the wind.
No need was hers to pay wreck-rites to the gods
For rescue after stranding, when, her last voyage over,
She came to this calm, inland lake.
　　But this was long ago;
She's an old ship now, laid up for good, and dedicate
To Castor and Pollux, the Twin Brethren of the sea.

CATULLUS (xx)

As some grave Tyrian trader, from the sea,
Descried at sunrise an emerging prow
Lifting the cool-haired creepers stealthily,
The fringes of a southward-facing brow
　　Among the Aegean Isles;
And saw the merry Grecian coaster come,
　　Freighted with amber grapes and Chian wine,
　　Green, bursting figs, and tunnies steep'd in brine –
And knew the intruders on his ancient home,

The young, light-hearted masters of the waves –
　　And snatch'd his rudder, and shook out more sail;

And day and night held on indignantly
O'er the blue Midland waters with the gale,
  Betwixt the Syrtes and soft Sicily,
  To where the Atlantic raves
Outside the western straits; and unbent sails
  There, where down cloudy cliffs, through sheets of
    foam,
  Shy traffickers, the dark Iberians come;
And on the beach undid his corded bales.

MATTHEW ARNOLD: *The Scholar Gypsy* (xxi)

Encounter

A lovely sunrise, sunny morning, mild;
Calm, the ship still. Soper reported land
Which proved to be a fogbank. He was ril'd!
Cape Pigeons put a turn on, a brisk band
Of thirty birds or forty, as we mann'd
The break o' the poop with scraps. Tonight a green
Light on the starboard bow: so close at hand
A full-rigged ship crept by, that men were seen
And voices heard across the smooth dark strait between.

H. G. DIXEY: *A Passage in Square Rig*

Home-Coming

Forenoon: a downpour and the weather thick
And several smacks close-to like phantoms pass'd.
Then it fined up. We set the royals quick,
Which the port watch had overnight made fast.
At sunset, lo! the Bishop Light at last,

And next the Lizard; and the breeze blew fair
As sail by sail came in, till each pale mast,
Save for its upper tops'l, glimmered bare
Like a new Venus born into the Cornish air.

And so we crept, the zephyr soft abeam,
Off Helford River, on through Falmouth Bay,
And unassisted by the proffered steam
Right into harbour made our silent way.
Then crash! and crash! we shook 'em where they lay
To hear us sweetly chant the capstan round;
Who, when they woke again to light of day,
A stately barque before their windows found
From Sydney New South Wales arrived home safe and
    sound.

H. G. DIXEY: *Ibid.*

Hard Facts

At sea there is no advocacy. We are free from that most
noisome form of falsehood, which corrupts the very inward
of the soul. Truth is one of the great gifts of the sea. You
cannot persuade yourself nor listen to the persuasion of another
that the wind is not blowing when it is, or that a cabin with half
a foot of water in it is dry, or that a dragging anchor holds.
Everywhere the sea is a teacher of truth. I am not sure that the
best thing I find in sailing is not this salt of reality.

HILAIRE BELLOC: *The Cruise of the Nona*

Hove-To

A full-rigged ship never looks more majestic I think than when
she is hove to under all plain sail, that is, when all canvas but
stun'sails is piled upon her and her main topsail is to the mast,

with the great main course hauled up to the yard and windily swaying in festoons. She is then like a noble mare reined in; her very hawse pipes seem to grow large like the nostrils of some nervous creature impatiently sniffing the air; she bows the sea as though informed with a spirit of fire that maddens her to leap the surge, and to rush forward once more in music and in thunder, in giddy shearing and in long floating plunges on the wings of the wind. Never does a ship show so much as a thing of life as when she is thus restrained.

CLARK RUSSELL: *A Marriage at Sea*

The decks were dark with wet; as the vessel rolled to windward the froth of the green seas rushing at us from out the haze of the near horizon glanced ghastly and melancholy above the tall rail of the bulwark; there was a dreary shrill whistling of the wet wind in the iron-taut weather shrouds, and in the slack damp-blackened rigging curved to leeward by the rush of the blast. Yet the ship under comparatively small canvas was sailing nobly, shouldering off the blows of the olive-coloured surge with volcanic shocks of her bow as she plunged, and flinging the sea into boiling froth to right and left of her as she went, so that from aloft the path of her keel must have resembled the sweeping career of the foaming foot of the water-spout.

CLARK RUSSELL: *A Strange Elopement*

I went on deck in the twilight, when the remains of the sunset lay in a rusty, dirty, stain like old gore amongst the scud that swept into it, and found the ship clothed again almost to her topmost yards. She was a gallant picture in that weak light. The darkness of the night was descending upon the froth of the sea and the spirit of desolation lay cold in that vast breast of waters. The ship seemed alive whilst she floated with proud fearlessness into the mystery of the night. I had never admired

247

her so much before. You went below and sat in the radiant saloon; you played at cards, read, talked, did as you would in a hotel drawing-room ashore, and, seasoned to the movement of the fabric, forgot for a long hour or two where you were; then returning on deck, lo! the bleakness of the night suddenly encompassed you, dimly on high soar the spectral wings of the ship, the roar of the bow-wave slants off on the wind, and the sound of rushing waters strikes a chill to the very marrow; but the gallant fabric has been heroically doing her work whilst you were gone; she does it whilst you watch – in your sleep she will be faithful to you. I could not but think of her as one thinks of a beautiful horse, as something to love, something full of spirit, that knows what is expected of it, but whose patient dutifulness makes her more wonderful and touching as a creation than had she owed her life to nature.

CLARK RUSSELL: *The Good Ship Mohock*

The Revenge

The Spanish fleet having shrouded their approach by reason of the Island were now so soon at hand, as our ships had scarce time to way their anchors, but some of them were driven to let slippe their Cables and set saile. Sir Richard Grinvile was the last that wayed, to recover the men that were upon the Island, which otherwise had bene lost. The Lord Thomas with the rest very hardly recovered the winde, which Sir Richard Grinvile not being able to doe, was perswaded by the Master and others to cut his maine sayle, and cast about, and to trust to the sayling of the ship; for the squadron of Sivil were on his weather bow. But Sir Richard utterly refused to turne from the enemie, alleaging that hee would rather choose to die, than to dishonour himself, his countrey, and her Majesties shippe, perswading his companie that hee would passe through the two squadrons, in dispight of them, and enforce those of Sivil to give him way. Which he performed upon divers of the formost, who, as the Mariners terme it, sprang their luffe, and fell under the lee of the *Revenge*. But the other course had beene the better, and might right well have bene answered in so great an impossibility of prevaling. Notwithstanding out of the greatnesse of his minde, he could not be perswaded.

In the meane while as hee attended those which were nearest him, the great *San Philip* being in the winde of him, and comming towards him, becalmed his sailes in such sort, as the shippe could neither make way nor feele the helme: so huge and high charged was the Spanish ship, being of a thousand and five hundreth tuns. Who after layd the *Revenge* aboord.

When he was thus bereft of his sailes, the ships that were under his lee luffing up, also layd him aboord: of which the next was the *Admiral of the Biscaines*, a very mighty and puissant shippe commanded by Brittandona. The sayd *Philip* carried three tier of ordinance on a side, and eleven pieces in every tier. She shot eight forth right out of her chase, besides those of her sterne ports.

After the *Revenge* was entangled with this *Philip*, foure other boorded her; two on her larboard, two on her starboord. The fight thus beginning at three of the clock in the afternoone, continued very terrible all that evening. But the great *San Philip* having received the lower tier of the *Revenge*, discharged with crossbar shot, shifted herselfe with all diligence from her sides, utterly misliking her first entertainement. Some say that the shippe foundred, but we cannot report it for truth, unlesse we were assured. The Spanish ships were filled with companies of souldiers, in some two hundred besides the mariners; in some five, in others eight hundreth. In ours there were none at all beside the mariners, but the servants of the commanders and some few voluntary gentlemen onely.

After many enterchanged volies of great ordinance and small shot, the Spaniards deliberated to enter the *Revenge*, and made divers attempts, hoping to force her by the multitudes of their armed souldiers and Musketters, but were still repulsed againe and againe, and at all times beaten backe into their owne ships, or into the seas. In the beginning of the fight, the *George Noble* of London having received some shot thorow her by the Armadas, fell under the lee of the *Revenge*, and asked Sir Richard what he would command him, being but one of the victuallers and of small force: Sir Richard bid him save himselfe, and leave him to his fortune.

After the fight had thus, without intermission, continued while the day lasted and some houres of the night, many of our men were slaine and hurte, and one of the great Gallions of the Armada and the *Admirall of the Hulkes* both sunke, and in many other of the Spanish shippes great slaughter was made. Some write that Sir Richard was very dangerously hurte almost in the beginning of the fight, and lay speechlesse for a time ere he recovered. But two of the *Revenge*'s owne company, brought home in a ship of Lime from the Ilandes, examined by some of the Lordes, and others, affirmed that hee was never so wounded as that he forsooke the upper deck, till an houre before midnight; and then being shot into the bodie with a Musket as hee was a dressing, was againe shot into the head, and with all his Chirwigion wounded to death.

But to return to the fight, the Spanish ships which attempted to bord the *Revenge*, as they were wounded and beaten off, so alwayes others came in their places, she having never lesse then two mighty Gallions by her sides, and aboord her. So that ere morning, from three of the clock the day before, there had fifteen several Armadas assayled her; and all so ill approved their entertainement, as they were by the breake of day far more willing to harken to a composition than hastily to make any more assaults or entries. But as the day encreased, so our men decreased: and as the light grew more and more, by so much more grewe our discomforts. For none appeared in sight but enemies, saving one small ship called the *Pilgrim*, commaunded by Jacob Whiddon, who hovered all night to see the successe; but in the morning bearing with the *Revenge*, was hunted like a hare amongst many ravenous houndes, but escaped.

All the powder of the *Revenge* to the last barrell was now

spent, all her pikes broken, fortie of her best men slaine, and the most part of the rest hurte. In the beginning of the fight she had but one hundreth free from sickness, and fourescore and ten sicke, laid in hold upon the Ballast. A small troup to man such a ship, and a weake garrison to resist so mighty an army. By those hundred all was susteined, the voleis, boordings, and entrings of fifteen ships of warre, besides those which beat her at large. On the contrary, the Spanish were always supplied with souldiers brought from every squadron: all maner of Armes and powder at will. Unto ours there remained no comfort at all, no hope, no supply either of ships, men, or weapons; the Mastes all beaten over boord, all her tackle cut asunder, her upper worke altogether rased, and in effect evened shee was with the water, but the very foundation or bottome of a ship, nothing being left overhead either for flight or defence. Sir Richard finding himselfe in this distresse, and unable any longer to make resistance, having endured in this fifteene houres fight the assault of fifteene severall Armadas, all by turnes aboord him, and by estimation eight hundred shotte of great Artillerie, besides many assaults and entries; and that himself and the shippe must needes be possessed by the enemy, who were now all cast in a ring about him (the *Revenge* not able to moove one way or another, but as she was moved with the waves and billows of the sea) commaunded the Master gunner, whom hee knew to be a most resolute man, to split and sinke the shippe; that thereby nothing might remaine of glory or victory to the Spaniards: seeing in so many houres fight, and with so great a Navie they were not able to take her, having had fifteene houres time, above ten thousand men, and fiftie and three saile of men of warre to performe it withall: and perswaded the company, or as many as he could induce, to yeelde themselves unto God, and to the mercie of none else; but as they had, like valiant resolute men, repulsed so many enemies, they should not nowe shorten the honour of their Nation, by prolonging their owne lives for a few houres, or a fewe dayes.

The Master gunner readily condescended and divers others;

but the Captaine and the Master were of another opinion, and besought Sir Richard to have care of them: alleaging that the Spaniard would be as ready to entertaine a composition, as they were willing to offer the same: and that there being divers sufficient and valiant men yet living, and whose wounds were not mortal, they migh doe their Countrey and prince acceptable service hereafter. And whereas Sir Richard had alleaged that the Spaniards should never glory to have taken one shippe of her Majestie, seeing that they had so long and so notably defended themselves; they answered that the shippe had six foote water in holde, three shot under water, which were so weakely stopped as with the first working of the sea she must needs sinke, and was besides so crusht and brused, as shee could never be removed out of the place.

And as the matter was thus in dispute, and Sir Richard refusing to hearken to any of those reasons: the Master of the *Revenge* (while the Captaine wanne unto him the greater party) was convoyd aboord the *Generall Don Alfonso Bacan*. Who (finding none over hastie to enter the *Revenge* againe, doubting least Sir Richard would have blowne them up and himselfe, and perceiving by the report of the Master of the *Revenge* his dangerous disposition) yeelded that all their lives should be saved, the company sent for England, and the better sorte to pay such reasonable ransome as their estate would beare, and in the meane season to be free from Gally or imprisonment. To this he so much the rather condescended as wel, as I have said, for feare of further losse and mischiefe to themselves, as also for the desire he had to recover Sir Richard Greenvil; whom for his notable valure he seemed greatly to honour and admire.

When this answere was returned, and that safetie of life was promised, the common sort being now at the ende of their perill, the most drew backe from Sir Richard and the Master gunner, being no hard matter to diswade men from death to life. The Master gunner finding himselfe and Sir Richard thus prevented and mastered by the greater number, would have slaine himself with a sword, had he not bene by force with-held and locked into his Cabben. Then the Generall sent many boates aboord the *Revenge*, and divers of our men fearing Sir Richard's disposition, stole away aboord the *Generall* and other shippes. Sir Richard thus overmatched, was sent unto by *Alfonso Bacan* to remoove out of the *Revenge*, the shippe being marveilous unsavourie, filled with blood and bodies of dead, and wounded men like a slaughter house. Sir Richard answered that hee might doe with his body what he list, for hee esteemed it not, and as he was carried out of the ship hee swounded, and reviving againe desired the company to pray for him. The *Generall* used Sir Richard with all humanitie, and left nothing unattempted that tended to his recoverie, highly commending his valour and worthinesse, and greatly bewailing the danger wherein he was, being unto them a rare spectacle, and a resolution sildome approoved, to see one shippe turne toward so many enemies, to endure the charge and boording of so many huge Armadas, and to resist and repell the assaults and entries of so many souldiers. All which and more is confirmed by a Spanish Captaine of the same Armada, and a present actor in the fight, who being severed from the rest in a storme, was by the *Lion of London* a small ship taken, and is now prisoner in London.

Sir Richard died as it is sayd, the second or third daye aboord the *Generall*, and was by them greatly bewailed. What became of his body, whether it were buried in the sea or on the land we know not: the comfort that remayneth to his friends is, that hee hath ended his life honourably in respect of the reputation wonne to his nation and countrey, and of the same to his posteritie, and that being dead, he hath not outlived his owne honour.

SIR WALTER RALEIGH:

from Hakluyt's *The English Voyages* (xxii)

253

Sail If You Must

Spring and summer are the time: the sea then will not wreck ships or drown men – unless earth-shaking Poseidon has a grudge against them, or Zeus the King of Heaven doesn't like their looks. They, after all, have the last word. At any rate, that is the season for kindly winds and calm seas; without anxiety then you can trust your vessel to the breezes, get her afloat and load her up. But mind you come home again at the first possible moment: don't wait for the new wine and the autumn rains, the bad weather which is sure to come – with southerly gales, constant companions of the autumn rain, making the sea an unwholesome place to be in.

But to sail in spring and summer is another matter. When on the tips of the branches the new leaves have grown to the length of a crow's footprint, then is the sea fit to sail on. Then you'll have a summer passage – not that I recommend it myself; for I do not care for such things. Even then you may hardly escape disaster. Ah well! men do these things, poor fools! For money is life to miserable mortals. Yet it's a dreadful fate to drown.

However, if sail you must, take my advice: never trust all you possess on board of a ship. Leave the greater part at home, and freight your vessels with the lesser part only. For I say again it's a terrible thing to perish at sea.

HESIOD: *Works and Days*

The Fisherman

There were two old fishermen lodged together; in their wattled hut they had spread dry sea-moss for a bed, and there they lay, against the wall of leaves. Beside them were the tools of their trade – creels, rods, hooks, buckets of bait and weed, lines, baskets, lobster-pots, seine-nets, a pair of oars and an elderly boat on legs. Under their heads was a bit of matting, with their jackets and caps. Such was all their wealth, all their resources. The hut had no door, no watch-dog. What need of such super-fluity, when Poverty kept watch for them?

THEOCRITUS: *Idylls*

The Faeroes

To the stranger's eye, approaching from the sea, they are a geographical menace. Among overfalls and the anger of the tide their tall peaks rise from an iron-grey sea to iron-grey clouds that conceal their upper parts, and the slope of the land is so precipitous and dark that nothing, one fears, can grow on it and no man subsist. But on shore the view improves, it becomes cheerful in the stir of human endeavour, and with the colours of spring it is even gay. At Torshavn the quay is crowded, and in little boats like miniatures of Viking longships the red-capped fishermen coming ashore have added to their catch of ling and haddock a feathery bundle of razor-bills, puffins, and guillemots; for they have hearty appetites, and their table delicacies – a brace of puffins stewed in milk, the kidney of a bottle-nosed whale – are stronger than ours.

The great cliffs, populous with innumerable birds, give the Faeroese more food than their fields, and their staple harvest must still be reaped on the sea. Under sail, in old wooden fishing-boats bought in Lowestoft and Brixham and patched with a cabinet-maker's skill, they use the North Atlantic as far from home as the southern coasts of Greenland. They have all the domestic virtues, a passion for cleanliness and orderly bright homes that they fill with lint-haired children; but the men are seafarers.

Between the islands – Kalso the Man Island, Kuno the Woman, and Svino the Swine, Big Demon and Little Demon – run tidal streams of the utmost turbulence; the Atlantic pours through submarine chasms, and our soldiers who thinly guarded the outlying parts grew accustomed to the wildest tossing as they went to and fro in a little motor-drifter that had escaped, like so many others, from the German occupation of Norway. More certainly or clearly than in Iceland or Shetland or Orkney it was the estranging sea that challenged our garrison in the Faeroes, and in its strictest meaning isolation was the reality of life. In response to the challenge men discovered in themselves resources they had not suspected, and never before had used. This, of course, was a common discovery of the war, but it showed itself most strikingly when only a few men were stationed on a small island; and one realised that in the huge overcrowded areas of our civilisation there is, for lack of opportunity, an extravagant waste of native ability.

ERIC LINKLATER: *The Art of Adventure*

SONG

The Night of Trafalgar

In the wild October night-time, when the wind raved round the land,
And the Back-sea met the Front-sea, and our doors were blocked with sand,
And we heard the drub of Dead-man's Bay, where bones of thousands are,
We knew not what the day had done for us at Trafalgar.
      Had done,
      Had done,
   For us at Trafalgar.

'Pull hard and make the Nothe, or down we go!' one says, says he;
We pulled; and bedtime brought the storm; but snug at home slept we.

Yet all the while our gallants after fighting through the day,
Were beating up and down the dark, sou'-west of Cadiz Bay.
      The dark,
      The dark,
   Sou'-west of Cadiz Bay.

The victors and the vanquished then the storm it tossed and
   tore,
As hard they strove, those worn-out men, upon that surly
   shore;
Dead Nelson and his half-dead crew, his foes from near and far,
Were rolled together on the deep that night at Trafalgar.
      The deep,
      The deep,
   That night at Trafalgar!

THOMAS HARDY: The Dynasts

Nelson at Trafalgar

He wore that day, as usual, his admiral's frock-coat, bearing
on the left breast four stars of the different orders with which
he was invested. Ornaments which rendered him so conspicuous a mark for the enemy were beheld with ominous
apprehensions by his officers. It was known that there were
riflemen on board the French ships; and it could not be doubted
but that his life would be particularly aimed at. They com-
municated their fears to each other; and the surgeon, Mr Beatty,
spoke to the chaplain, Dr Scott, and to Mr Scott the public
secretary, desiring that some person should entreat him to
change his dress, or cover the stars; but they knew that such a
request would highly displease him. 'In honour I gained them,'
he had said when such a thing had been hinted to him formerly,
'and in honour I will die with them.' Mr Beatty, however,
would not have been deterred by any fear of exciting dis-
pleasure from speaking to him himself upon a subject in which

the weal of England, as well as the life of Nelson, was concerned, but he was ordered from the deck before he could find an opportunity. This was a point upon which Nelson's officers knew that it was hopeless to remonstrate or reason with him; but both Blackwood and his own captain, Hardy, represented to him how advantageous to the fleet it would be for him to keep out of action as long as possible; and he consented at last to let the *Leviathan* and the *Temeraire*, which were sailing abreast of the *Victory*, be ordered to pass ahead. Yet even here the last infirmity of this noble mind was indulged; for these ships could not pass ahead if the *Victory* continued to carry all her sail; and so far was Nelson from shortening sail, that it was evident he took pleasure in pressing on, and rendering it impossible for them to obey his own orders.

A long swell was setting into the bay of Cadiz; our ships, crowding all sail, moved majestically before it, with light winds from the south-west. The sun shone on the sails of the enemy; and their well-formed line, with their numerous three-deckers made an appearance which any other assailants would have thought formidable; but the British sailors only admired the beauty and the splendour of the spectacle, and in full confidence of winning what they saw, remarked to each other what a fine sight yonder ships would make at Spithead.

The French admiral, from the *Bucentaure*, beheld the new manner in which his enemy was advancing, Nelson and Collingwood each leading his line; and pointing them out to his officers, he is said to have exclaimed that such conduct could not fail to be successful. Yet Villeneuve had made his own dispositions with the utmost skill, and the fleets under his command waited for the attack with perfect coolness. Ten minutes before twelve they opened their fire. Eight or nine of the ships immediately ahead of the *Victory*, and across her bows, fired single guns at her, to ascertain whether she was yet within their range. As soon as Nelson perceived that their shot passed over him, he desired Blackwood, and Captain Prowse of the *Sirius*, to repair to their respective frigates, and on their way to tell all the captains of the line-of-battle ships that he depended on their exertions, and that if by the prescribed mode of attack they found it impracticable to get into action immediately, they might adopt whatever they thought best, provided it led them quickly and closely alongside an enemy. As they were standing on the front poop, Blackwood took him by the hand, saying he hoped soon to return and find him in possession of twenty prizes. He replied, 'God bless you, Blackwood; I shall never see you again.'

Nelson's column was steered about two points more to the north than Collingwood's, in order to cut off the enemy's escape into Cadiz; the lee line, therefore, was first engaged. 'See,' cried Nelson, pointing to the *Royal Sovereign* as she steered right for the centre of the enemy's line, cut through it astern of the *Santa Anna*, three-decker, and engaged her at the muzzle of her guns on the starboard side; 'see how that noble fellow Collingwood carries his ship into action!' Collingwood, delighted at being first in the heat of the fire, and knowing the feelings of his commander and old friend, turned to his captain and exclaimed, 'Rotherham, what would Nelson give to be here!' Both these brave officers, perhaps, at this moment thought of Nelson with gratitude, for a circumstance which had occurred on the preceding day. Admiral Collingwood, with some of the captains, having gone on board the *Victory* to receive instructions, Nelson inquired of him where his captain was, and was told in reply that they were not upon good terms with each other. 'Terms!' said Nelson, 'good terms with each other!' Immediately he sent a boat for Captain Rotherham, led him as soon as he arrived to Collingwood, and saying, 'Look; yonder are the enemy!' bade them shake hands like Englishmen.

The enemy continued to fire one gun at a time at the *Victory*, till they saw that a shot had passed through her main-top-gallant sail; then they opened their broadsides, aiming chiefly at her rigging, in the hope of disabling her before she could close with them. Nelson as usual had hoisted several flags, lest one should be shot away. The enemy showed no colours till late in the action, when they began to feel the necessity of having them to strike. For this reason the *Santissima Trinidad*, Nelson's old acquaintance, as he used to call her, was distinguishable only by her four decks; and to the bow of this opponent he ordered the *Victory* to be steered. Meantime, an incessant raking fire was kept up upon the *Victory*. The admiral's secretary was one of the first who fell; he was killed by a cannon shot while conversing with Hardy. Captain Adair of the marines, with the help of a sailor, endeavoured to remove the body from Nelson's sight, who had a great regard for Mr Scott; but he anxiously asked, 'is that poor Scott that's gone?' and being informed that it was indeed so, exclaimed, 'Poor fellow!' Presently a double-headed shot struck a party of marines, who were drawn up on the poop, and killed eight of them; upon which Nelson immediately desired Captain Adair to disperse his men round the ship, that they might not suffer so much from being together. A few minutes afterwards a shot struck the fore-brace bitts on the quarter-deck, and passed between Nelson and Hardy, a splinter from the bitt tearing off Hardy's buckle, and bruising his foot. Both stopped and looked anxiously at each other; each supposed the other to be wounded. Nelson then smiled, and said, 'This is too warm work, Hardy, to last long.'

The *Victory* had not yet returned a single gun; fifty of her men had been by this time killed or wounded, and her main-top-mast with all her studding-sails and their booms shot away. Nelson declared that in all his battles he had seen nothing which surpassed the cool courage of his crew on this occasion. At four minutes after twelve, she opened her fire from both sides of her deck. It was not possible to break the enemy's line without running on board one of their ships; Hardy informed him of this, and asked him which he would prefer. Nelson replied, 'Take your choice, Hardy; it does not signify much.' The master was ordered to put the helm to port, and the *Victory* ran on board the *Redoubtable*, just as her tiller-ropes were shot away. The French ship received her with a broadside, then instantly let down her lower-deck ports, for fear of being boarded through them, and never afterwards fired a great gun during the action. Her tops, like those of all the enemy's ships, were filled with riflemen. Nelson never placed musketry in his tops; he had a strong dislike to the practice, not merely because it endangers setting fire to the sails, but also because it is a murderous sort of warfare, by which individuals may suffer, and a commander now and then be picked off, but which never can decide the fate of a general engagement.

. . . It had been part of Nelson's prayer that the British fleet might be distinguished by humanity in the victory he expected. Setting an example himself, he twice gave orders to cease firing upon the *Redoubtable*, supposing that she had struck, because her great guns were silent; for, as she carried no flag, there was no means of instantly ascertaining the fact. From this ship, which he had thus twice spared, he received his death. A ball fired from her mizen-top, which, in the then situation of the two vessels, was not more than fifteen yards from that part of the deck where he was standing, struck the epaulette on his left shoulder about a quarter after one, just in the heat of action. He fell upon his face, on the spot which was covered with his poor secretary's blood. Hardy, who was a few steps from him, turning round, saw three men raising him up. 'They have done for me at last, Hardy,' he said. 'I hope not,' cried Hardy. 'Yes,' he replied, 'my backbone is shot through.' Yet even now, not for a moment losing his presence of mind, he observed, as they were carrying him down the ladder, that the tiller-ropes, which had been shot away, were not yet replaced, and ordered that new ones should be rove immediately. Then, that he might not be seen by the crew, he took out his handkerchief and covered his face and stars. Had he but concealed these badges of honour from the enemy, England perhaps would not have had cause to receive with sorrow the news of the battle of Trafalgar.

ROBERT SOUTHEY: *Life of Nelson*

Endeavour in Danger

As no accident of any moment had befallen our adventurers during a navigation of more than 1,300 miles, upon a coast everywhere abounding with the most dangerous rocks and shoals, no name expressive of distress had hitherto been given to any cape or point of land which they had seen. But now they gave the name of Cape Tribulation to a point which they had just discovered, as they here became acquainted with misfortune. This cape is in 16°8′ south latitude, and 214°39′ west longitude.

To avoid the danger of some rocks, they shortened sail, and kept standing off from six o'clock in the evening till near nine, with a fine breeze and bright moon. They had got from fourteen into twenty-one fathoms water, when suddenly they fell into twelve, ten, and eight fathoms, in a few minutes. Every man was instantly ordered to his station, and they were on the point of anchoring, when, on a sudden, they had again deep water, so that they thought all danger was at an end, concluding that they had sailed over the tail of some shoals which they had seen in the evening. In less than an hour, however, the water shallowed at once from twenty to seventeen fathoms, and, before soundings could be again taken, the ship struck against a rock, and remained fixed but from the motion given her from the beating of the surge. Everyone was instantly on deck, with countenances fully expressive of the agitation of their minds. As they knew they were not near the shore, they concluded that they had struck against a rock of coral, the points of which being sharp, and the surface so rough, as to grind away whatever is rubbed against it, though with a gentle motion, they had reason to dread the horror of their situation.

The sails being taken in, and boats hoisted out to examine the depth of water, they found that the ship had been carried over a ledge of the rock, and lay in a hollow within it. She beat so violently that the crew could scarcely keep on their legs. The moon now shone bright, by the light of which they could see the sheathing boards float from the bottom of the vessel, till at length the false keel followed, so that they expected instant destruction. Their best chance of escaping seemed to be now by lightening her. They therefore instantly started the water in the hold, and pumped it up. The decayed stores, oil-jars, casks, ballast, six of their guns, and other things, were thrown overboard, in order to get at the heavier articles; and in this business they were employed till daybreak, during all which time it was observed that not an oath was sworn, so much were the minds of the sailors impressed with a sense of their danger.

At daylight they saw the land at eight leagues distance, but not a single island between them and the main; so that the destruction of the greater part of them would have been inevitable, had the ship gone to pieces. It happened, however, that the wind died away to a dead calm before noon. As they expected high water at eleven o'clock, everything was prepared to make another effort to free the ship; but the tide fell so much short of that in the night, that she did not float by eighteen inches, though they had thrown overboard near fifty tons weight, they now, therefore, renewed their toil, and threw overboard everything that could be possibly spared. As the tide fell, the water poured in so rapidly that they could scarcely keep her free by the constant working of two pumps. Their only hope now depended on the midnight tide, and preparations were accordingly made for another effort to get the ship off. The tide began to rise at five o'clock, when the leak likewise increased to such a degree, that three pumps were kept going till nine o'clock, at which time the ship righted; but so much water had been admitted by the leak, that they expected that she would sink as soon as the water should bear her off the rock.

Their situation was now deplorable beyond description, and the imagination must paint what would baffle the powers of language to describe. They knew that when the fatal moment should arrive, all authority would be at an end. The boats were incapable of conveying them all on shore, and they dreaded a contest for the preference as more shocking than the shipwreck itself; yet, it was considered, that those who might be left on board would eventually meet with a milder fate than those who, by gaining the shore, would have no chance but to linger the remains of life among the rudest savages in the universe, and in a country where firearms would barely enable them to support a wretched existence.

At twenty minutes after ten the ship floated, and was heaved into deep water; when they were happy to find that she did not admit more water than she had done before; yet, as the leak had for a considerable time gained on the pumps, there was now three feet nine inches water in the hold. By this time the men were so worn by fatigue of mind and body that none of them could pump more than five or six minutes at a time, and then threw themselves, quite spent, on the deck. The succeeding man being fatigued in his turn, threw himself down in the same manner, while the former jumped up and renewed his labour; thus mutually struggling for life, till the following accident had like to have given them up a prey to absolute despair.

Between the inside lining of the ship's bottom and the outside planking, there is a space of about seventeen or eighteen inches. The man who had hitherto taken the depth of water at the well, had taken it no farther than the ceiling; but being now relieved by another person, who took the depth to the outside planking, it appeared by this mistake that the leak had suddenly gained upon the pumps the whole difference between the two plankings. This circumstance deprived them of all hopes, and scarce anyone thought it worth while to labour for the longer preservation of a life which must so soon have a period. But the mistake was soon discovered; and the joy arising from such unexpected good news inspired the men with so much vigour, that before eight o'clock in the morning they had pumped out considerably more water than they had shipped. They now talked confidently of getting the ship into some harbour, and set heartily to work to get in their anchors;

264

one of which, and the cable of another, they lost. Having a good breeze from the sea, they got under sail at eleven o'clock, and stood for the land.

As they could not discover the exact situation of the leak, they had no prospect of stopping it within side of the vessel; but the following expedient, which one of the midshipmen had formerly seen tried with success, was adopted. They took an old studding-sail, and having mixed a large quantity of oakum and wool, chopped small, it was stitched down in handfuls on the sail, as light as possible, the dung of their sheep, and other filth, being spread over it. Thus prepared, the sail was hauled under the ship by ropes, which kept it extended till it came under the leak, when the suction carried in the oakum and wool from the surface of the sail. This experiment succeeded so well, that instead of three pumps, the water was easily kept under by one.

CAPTAIN JAMES COOK'S *Narrative of his First Voyage,*
edited by John Barrow

The Dover Patrol

The great sailor-like qualities of the Dover Patrol, the consummate seamanship displayed in the planning and execution of its incessant operations, its steady manner of meeting deadly emergencies, its cool vigilance in the presence of an ever-menacing situation, may well compel the admiration of any man who knows something, however little, of the demands of sea service. To the risks of actual warfare the crews of the drifters watching over the barrage nets were often helplessly exposed. But nothing could dismay either the naval or the auxiliary branches of the Dover Patrol. These men were concerned about the perfection of their work, but the sudden flash of German guns in the night troubled them not at all. As, indeed, why should it? In their early days some of them had but a single rifle on board to meet the three four-inch guns of German destroyers. Unable to put up a fight and without speed to get away, they made a sacrifice of their lives every time they went out for a turn of duty; they concentrated their valour on the calm, seamanlike execution of their work amongst the exploding mines and bursting shells. It was their conception of their honour, and they carried it out of this war unblemished by a single display of weakness, by the slightest moment of hesitation in the long tale of dangerous service.

In this simple way these seamen, professional and unprofessional, naval and civilian, have earned for themselves the memorial erected to their faithful labours. The record of the Dover Patrol's work contains a great moral and a good many professional lessons for their children and their successors; the incalculable value of a steady front, the perfecting of nets, the exact process of laying barrages in a tideway, the evolving of an ingenious method for night bombardments, and of a system of long-range firing – a whole great store of new ideas and new practice laid up for future use. But in truth that which in the last instance kept the German forces from breaking disastrously on any dark night into the Channel, and jeopardising the very foundations of our resisting power, was not the wonderfully planned and executed defences of nets and mines, but the indomitable hearts of the men of the Dover Patrol.

JOSEPH CONRAD: *Last Essays*

Endeavour *penetrates the Great Barrier Reef*

Having anchored on the 14th, they steered a westerly course on the following day, to get sight of the land, that a passage between that land and New Guinea might not be missed, if there was any such passage. They stood northward till midnight. When daylight came on, they saw a dreadful surf break at a vast height, within a mile of the ship, towards which the rolling waves carried her with great rapidity. Thus distressed the boats were sent ahead to tow, and the head of the vessel was brought about, but not till she was within one hundred yards of the rock, between which and her there was nothing left but the chasm made by the last wave that had washed her side. In the moment they expected instant destruction, a breeze, hardly discernible, aided the boats in getting the vessel in an oblique direction from the rock.

At this time a small opening was seen in the reef, and a young officer being sent to examine it, found that there was smooth water on the other side of the rocks. Animated by the hope of preserving life, they now attempted to pass the opening, but this was impossible; for it having become high water in the interim, the ebb tide rushed through it with amazing impetuosity, carrying the ship to a considerable distance from the reef. When the ebb tide was spent, the tide of flood again drove the vessel very near the rocks; so that their prospect of destruction was renewed, when they discovered another opening, and a light breeze springing up, they entered it, and were driven through it with a rapidity that prevented the ship from striking against either side of the channel.

The name Providential Channel was given to the opening through which the ship had thus escaped the most imminent dangers.

CAPTAIN JAMES COOK'S *Narrative of his First Voyage*,
edited by John Barrow

Fog on the Thames

Our skipper thought he saw a lane along the river, and up-anchored. The noise of our cable awoke a tumult of startled bells.

Ours was a perishable cargo. We were much overdue. Our skipper was willing to take any risk – what a good master mariner would call a reasonable risk – to get home; and so, when a deck hand, on the third morning, with the thawing fog dripping from his moustache, appeared in the saloon with the news that it was clearing a little, the master decided he would go.

I then saw, from the deck of the *Windhover*, so strange a vision that it could not be related to this world of ours. It was possible to believe that dawn's bluish beginning radiated from the *Windhover*. We were the luminary, and our faint aura revealed, through the melting veil, an outer world that had no sky, no plane, no bounds. It was void. There was no River, except that small oval of glass on which rested our ship, like a model.

The universe, which that morning had only begun to form in the void, was grouped about us. This was the original of mornings. We were its gravitational point. It was inert and voiceless. It was pregnant with unawakened shapes, dim surprising shadows, and suggestions of form. Those near to us more nearly approached the shapes we knew in another life. Those beyond, diminishing and fainting in the opacity of the dawn, were beyond remembrance and recognition. The *Windhover* alone was substantial and definite. But placid about us, suspended in a night that was growing translucent, were the shadows of what once might have been ships, perhaps were ships to be, but were then steamers and sailers without substance, waiting some creative word, shrouded spectres that had left the wrecks of their old hulls below, their voyages finished, and were waiting to begin a new existence, having been raised to our level in a new world boundless and serene, with unplumbed deeps beneath them. There, on our level, we maintained them in their poise with our superior gravity and our certain body, giving them light, being what sun there was in this new system in another day. Above them there was nothing, and around them was blind distance, and below them the abyss of space. Their lights gathered to our centre, an incoming of delicate and shining mooring lines.

It was all so silent, too. But our incoming cable shattered the spell, and when our siren warned them that we were moving, a wild pealing commenced which accompanied us on the long drift up to Gravesend. There were eight miles of ships: barges, colliers, liners, clippers, cargo steamers, ghost after ghost took form ahead, and then went astern. More than once the fog thickened again, but the skipper never took way off her while he could make out a ship ahead of us. We drifted stern first on the flood, with half-turns of the propeller for steering purchase, till a boatman, whom we hailed, cried that we were off Gravesend. And was there anyone for the shore? There was. I took no more risks. . . .

H. M. TOMLINSON: London River

West and South of Magellan

Among these Ilands making our abode with some quietnesse for a very little while (viz. two days), and finding divers good and wholesome herbs, together with fresh water, our men, which before were weak, and much empaired in their health, began to receive good comfort. . . . But the winds returning to their old wont, and the seas raging after their former manner, yea everything as it were setting itselfe against our peace and desired rest, here was no stay permitted us, neither any safety to be looked for.

For such was the present danger by forcing and continuall flaws, that we were rather to look for present death then hope for any delivery, if God Almightie should not make the way for us. The winds were such as if the bowels of the earth had set all at libertie, or as if the clouds under heaven had been called together to lay their force upon that one place. The seas, which by nature and of themselves are heavy, and of a weightie substance, were rowled up from the depths, even from the roots of the rocks, as if it had been a scroll of parchment, which by the extremity of heate runneth together; and being aloft were carried in most strange manner and abundance, as feathers or drifts of snow, by the violence of the winds, to water the exceeding tops of high and loftie mountains. Our anchors, false friends in such a danger, gave over their holdfast, and as if it had beene with horror of the thing, did shrink down to hide themselves in this miserable storm, committing the distressed ship and helplesse men to the uncertaine and rowling seas, which tossed them like a ball in a racket. In this case, to let fall more anchors would availe us nothing; for being driven from our first place of anchoring, so unmeasurable was the depth, that 500 fathome would fetch no ground. So that the violent storm without intermission, the impossibility to come to anchor; the want of opportunitie to spread any sayle; the most mad seas; the lee shores; the dangerous rocks; the contrary and most intollerable winds; the impossible passage out; the desperate tarrying there; and inevitable perils on every side, did lay before us so small likelihood to escape present destruction, that if the speciall providence of God himself had not supported us, we could never have endured that wofull state: as being invironed with most terrible and most fearfull judgements round about. For truly, it was more likely that the mountaines should have been rent in sunder from the top to the bottome, and cast headlong into the sea, by these unnaturall winds, then that we, by any helpe or cunning of man, should free the life of any one amongst us.

SIR FRANCIS DRAKE (the Admiral's nephew):
from his account of the Circumnavigation

The Ferry

I too saw the reflection of the summer sky in the water,
Had my eyes dazzled by the shimmering track of beams,
Looked at the fine centrifugal spokes of light round the shape
of my head in the sun-lit water,
Looked on the haze of the hills southward and south-westward,

Looked on the vapour as it flew in fleeces tinged with violet,
Looked toward the lower bay to notice the arriving ships,
Saw their approach, saw aboard those that were near me,
Saw the white sails of schooners and sloops, saw the ships at
    anchor,
The sailors at work in the rigging, or out astride the spars,
The round masts, the swinging motion of the hulls, the slender,
    serpentine pennants,
The large and small steamers in motion, the pilots in their
    pilot-houses,
The white wake left by the passage, the quick tremulous whirl
    of the wheels,
The flags of all nations, the falling of them at sunset,
The scallop-edged waves in the twilight, the ladled cups, the
    frolicsome crests and glistening,
The stretch afar growing dimmer and dimmer, the grey walls
    of the granite store-houses by the docks,
On the river the shadowy group, the big steam-tug closely
    flanked on each side by the barges – the hay-boat, the
    belated lighter,
On the neighbouring shore, the fires from the foundry
    chimneys burning high and glaringly into the night,
Casting their flicker of black, contrasted with wild red and
    yellow light, over the tops of houses and down into the
    clefts of streets.
These, and all else, were to me the same as they are to you;
I project myself a moment to tell you. . . .

WALT WHITMAN: *Crossing Brooklyn Ferry*

How the Action at Salamis Began

The Greek commanders at Salamis were still at loggerheads.
They did not yet know that the enemy ships had blocked their
escape at both ends of the channel, but supposed them to

occupy the same position as they had seen them in during the day. However, while the dispute was still at its height, Aristides came over in a boat from Aegina. This man, an Athenian and the son of Lysimachus, had been banished from Athens by popular vote, but the more I have learned of his character, the more I have come to believe that he was the best and most honourable man that Athens ever produced. Arrived at Salamis, Aristides went to where the conference was being held and, standing outside, called for Themistocles. Themistocles was no friend of his; indeed he was his most determined enemy; but Aristides was willing, in view of the magnitude of the danger which threatened them, to forget old quarrels in his desire to communicate with him. He was already aware of the anxiety of the Peloponnesian commanders to withdraw to the Isthmus; as soon therefore as Themistocles came out of the conference in answer to his call, he said: 'At this moment, more than ever before, you and I should be rivals; and the object of our rivalry should be to see which of us can do most good to our country. First, let me tell you that the Peloponnesians may talk as much or as little as they please about withdrawing from Salamis – it will make not the least difference. What I tell you, I have seen with my own eyes: they *cannot* get out of here, however much the Corinthians or Eurybiades himself may wish to do so, because our fleet is surrounded. Go back to the conference, and tell them.'

'Good news, and good advice,' Themistocles answered, 'what I most wanted has happened – and you bring me the evidence of your own eyes that it is true. It was I who was responsible for this move of the enemy; for as our men would not fight here of their own free will, it was necessary to make them, whether they wanted to do so or not. But take them the good news yourself; if I tell them, they will think I have invented it and will not believe me. Please, then, go in and make the report yourself. If they believe you, well and good; if they do not, it's no odds; for if we are surrounded, as you say we are, escape is no longer possible.'

Aristides accordingly went in and made his report, saying he had come from Aegina and had been hard put to it to slip through the blockading enemy fleet, as the entire Greek force was surrounded. He advised them, therefore, to prepare at once to repel an attack. That said, he left the conference; whereupon another dispute broke out, because most of the Greek commanders refused to believe in the truth of Aristides' report. Nor were their doubts settled until a Tenian warship, commanded by Panaetius, the son of Sosimenes, deserted from the Persian navy and came in with a full account of what had occurred.

Forced to accept the Tenians' report, the Greeks now at last prepared for action. At dawn the fighting men were assembled and Themistocles was chosen to address them. The whole burden of what he said was a comparison of the nobler and baser parts of human nature, and an exhortation to the men to follow the former in the coming ordeal. Then, having rounded off his speech, he gave the order for embarkation. The order was obeyed and, just as the men were going aboard, the ship which had been sent to Aegina to fetch the 'Sons of Aeacus', rejoined the fleet.

The whole fleet now got under way, and in a moment the Persians were upon them. The Greeks checked their way and began to back astern, and they were on the point of running aground when Ameinias of Pallene, in command of an Athenian ship, drove ahead and rammed an enemy vessel. Seeing the two ships foul of one another and locked together, the rest of the Greek fleet hurried to Ameinias' assistance, and the general action began.

HERODOTUS: *Histories*

Nelson at Cape St Vincent

'Well Mr Simple, as I was head signalman, I was perched on the poop and didn't serve at a gun. I had to report all I could see, which was not much, as the smoke was so thick; but now and then I could get a peep, as it were through the holes in the blanket. Of course I was obliged to keep my eye as much as possible upon the admiral, not to make out his signals, for Commodore Nelson wouldn't thank me for that; I knew he hated a signal when in action, so I never took no notice of the bunting, but just watched to see what he was about. . . . As soon as old Jervis had done for the Spanish admiral, he hauled his wind on the larboard tack, and followed by four or five other ships, weathered the Spanish line and joined Collingwood in the *Excellent*. Then they all dashed through the line; the *Excellent* was the leading ship, and she first took the shine out of the *Salvadore del Mondo*, and then left her to be picked up by the other ships, while she attacked a two-decker, who hauled down her colours. . . . And now, Mr Simple, the old *Captain* comes into play again. Having parted company with the four-decker, we had recommenced action with the *San Nicolas*, a Spanish eighty, and while we were hard at it, old Collingwood comes up in the *Excellent*. The *San Nicolas*, knowing that the *Excellent*'s broadsides would send her to old Nick, put her helm up to avoid being raked; in so doing, she fell foul of the *San Josef*, a Spanish three-decker, and we being all cut to pieces and unmanageable – all of us indeed reeling about like drunken men – Nelson ordered his helm a-starboard, and in a jiffy there we were, all three hugging each other, running in one another's guns, smashing our chainplates, and poking our yard-arms through each other's canvas.

' "All hands to board!" roared Nelson, leaping on the hammocks and waving his sword.

' "Hurrah! Hurrah!" echoed through the decks, and up flew the men, like as many angry bees out of a bee-hive. In a moment pikes, tomahawks, cutlasses and pistols were seized, and our men poured into the eighty-gun ship, and in two minutes the decks were cleared and all the dons pitched below. I joined the boarders and was on the main deck when Captain Miller came down, and cried out "On deck again immediately!" Up we went, and what do you think it was for, Mr Simple? Why, to board a second time, for Nelson having taken the two-decker, swore

274

that he'd have the three-decker as well. So away we went again, clambering up her lofty sides how we could, and dropping down on her decks like hailstones. We all made for the quarter-deck, beat down every Spanish beggar that showed fight, and in five minutes more we had hauled down the colours of two of the finest ships in the Spanish navy. If that wasn't taking the shine out of the Dons, I should like to know what is. And didn't the old captains cheer and shake hands, as Commodore Nelson stood on the deck of the *San Josef*, and received the swords of the Spanish officers! There was enough of them to go right round the capstan, and plenty to spare. Now, Mr Simple, what do you think of that for a spree?'

CAPTAIN MARRYAT: *Peter Simple*

They that go down to the sea . . .

They that go down to the sea in ships, that do business in great waters, these see the works of the Lord and his wonders in the deep. For he commandeth and raiseth the stormy wind, which lifteth up the waves thereof. They mount up to the heaven, they go down again to the depths; their soul is melted because of trouble. They reel to and fro and stagger like a drunken man, and are at their wits end. Then they cry unto the Lord in their trouble, and he bringeth them out of their distresses. He maketh the storm a calm, so that the waves thereof are still. Then are they glad because they be quiet; so he bringeth them unto their desired haven.

Oh that men would praise the Lord for his goodness, and for his wonderful works to the children of men!

PSALM 107

A Black Day

This was a black day in our calendar. At seven o'clock in the morning, it being our watch below, we were aroused from a sound sleep by the cry of 'All hands ahoy! A man overboard!' This unwonted cry sent a thrill through the heart of everyone, and hurrying on deck we found the vessel flat aback, with all her studding-sails set; for the boy who was at the helm left it to throw something overboard, and the carpenter, who was an old sailor, knowing that the wind was light, put the helm down and hove her aback. The watch on deck were lowering away the quarter-boat, and I got on deck just in time to heave myself into her as she was leaving the side; but it was not until out upon the wide Pacific, in our little boat, that I knew whom we had lost. It was George Bolemer, a young English sailor, who was prized by the officers as an active and willing seaman, and by the crew as a lively, hearty fellow, and a good shipmate. He was going aloft to fit a strap round the main topmast head, for ringtail halyards, and had the strap and block, a coil of halyards and a marline-spike about his neck. He fell from the starboard futtock shrouds, and not knowing how to swim, and being heavily dressed, with all those things round his neck, he probably sank immediately. We pulled astern, in the direction in which he fell, and though we knew that there was no hope of saving him, yet no-one wished to speak of returning, and we rowed about for nearly an hour, without the hope of doing anything, but unwilling to acknowledge to ourselves that we must give him up. At length we turned the boat's head and made towards the vessel.

Death is at all times solemn, but never so much so as at sea. . . . A man dies on shore; his body remains with his friends, and 'the mourners go about the streets'; but when a man falls overboard at sea and is lost, there is a suddenness in the event, and a difficulty in realizing it, which give to it an air of awful mystery. A man dies on shore – you follow his body to the grave, and a stone marks the spot. You are often prepared for the event. There is always something which helps you realize it when it happens, and to recall it when it has passed. A man is shot down by your side in battle, and the mangled body remains an *object*, and a *real evidence*; but at sea the man is near you – at your side – you hear his voice, and in an instant he is gone, and nothing but a *vacancy* shows his loss. Then, too, at sea, to use a homely but expressive phrase, you *miss* a man so much. A dozen men are shut up together in a little bark, upon the wide, wide sea, and for months and months see no forms and hear no voices but their own, and one is taken suddenly from among them and they miss him at every turn. It is like losing a limb. There are no new faces or new scenes to fill the gap. There is always an empty berth in the forecastle, and one man wanting when the small night watch is mustered. There is one less to take the wheel, and one less to lay out with you upon the yard. You miss his form, and the sound of his voice, for habit had made them almost necessary to you, and each of your senses feels the loss.

All these things make such a death peculiarly solemn, and the effect of it remains upon the crew for some time. There is more kindness shown by the officers to the crew, and by the crew to one another. There is more quietness and seriousness. The oath and the loud laugh are gone. The officers are more watchful, and the crew go more carefully aloft. The lost man is seldom mentioned, or is dismissed with a sailor's rude eulogy.

'Well, poor George is gone. His cruise is up soon. He knew his work and did his duty, and was a good shipmate.' Then usually follows some allusion to another world, for sailors are almost all believers; but their notions and opinions are unfixed and at loose ends. They say – 'God won't be hard upon the poor fellow'; and seldom get beyond the common phrase which seems to imply that their sufferings and hard treatment here will excuse them hereafter – 'To work hard, live hard, die hard, and go to Hell after all, would be hard indeed!' Our cook, a simple-hearted old African, who had been through a good deal in his day, and was rather seriously inclined, always going to church twice a day when on shore, and reading his Bible on a Sunday in the galley, talked to the crew about spending their Sabbaths badly, and told them that they might go as suddenly as George had, and be as little prepared.

R. H. DANA: *Two Years Before the Mast*

Ancient Cargo Coracles on the Euphrates

I will next describe the thing which surprised me most of all in this country, after Babylon itself: I mean the boats which ply down the Euphrates to the city. These boats are circular in shape and made of hide; they build them in Armenia to the northward of Assyria, where they cut the withies to make the frames, and then stretch skins taut on the under-side for the body of the craft; they are not fined-off or tapered in any way at bow or stern, but quite round like a shield. The men fill them with straw, put the cargo on board – mostly wine in palm-wood casks – and let the current take them downstream. They are controlled by two men; each has a paddle which he works standing up, one in front drawing his paddle towards him, the other behind giving it a backward thrust. The boats vary a great deal in size, some are very big, the biggest of all having a capacity of some fourteen tons. Every boat carries a live donkey – the larger ones several – and when they reach Babylon and the cargoes have been offered for sale, the boats are broken up, the frames and straw disposed of and the hides loaded on the donkeys' backs for the return journey overland to Armenia. It is quite impossible to paddle the boats upstream because of the strength of the current, and that is why they are constructed of hide instead of wood. Back in Armenia with their donkeys, the men build another lot of boats to the same design.

HERODOTUS: *Histories*

Shipbuilding on the Nile in the Fifth Century B.C.

The Nile boats used for carrying freight are built of acantha wood – the acantha resembles in form the lotus of Cyrene, and exudes gum. They cut short planks, about three feet long, from this tree, and the method of construction is to lay them together like bricks and through-fasten them with long spikes set close together, and then, when the hull is complete, to lay the deck-beams across the top. The boats have no ribs and are caulked from inside with papyrus. They are given a single steering-oar, which is driven down through the keel; the masts are of acantha wood, the sails of papyrus. These vessels cannot sail up the river without a good leading wind, but have to be towed from the banks; and for dropping downstream with the current they are handled as follows: each vessel is equipped with a raft made of tamarisk wood, with a rush mat fastened on top of it, and a stone with a hole through it weighing some four hundredweight; the raft and the stone are made fast to the vessel with ropes, fore and aft respectively, so that the raft is carried rapidly forward with the current and pulls the 'baris' (as these boats are called) after it, while the stone, dragging along the bottom astern, acts as a check and gives her steerage-way. There are a great many of these vessels on the Nile, some of them of enormous carrying capacity.

HERODOTUS: *Histories* (xxiv)

'Sogering'

The next day being Sunday, which is the liberty day among merchantmen, when it is usual to let a part of the crew go ashore, the sailors had depended upon a day on land, and were already disputing who should ask to go, when, upon being called in the morning, we were turned-to upon the rigging, and found that the topmast, which had been sprung, was to come down, and a new one to go up, and topgallant and royal masts, and the rigging, to be set up. This was too bad. If there is anything that irritates sailors and makes them feel hardly used, it is being deprived of their Sabbath. Not that they would always, or indeed generally, spend it religiously, but it is their only day of rest. Then, too, they are so often necessarily deprived of it by storms, and unavoidable duties of all kinds, that to take it from them when lying quietly and safely in port, without any urgent reason, bears the more hardly. The only reason in this case was that the captain had determined to have the custom-house officer on board on Monday, and wished to have his brig in order. Jack is a slave aboard ship; but still he has many opportunities of thwarting and balking his master. When there is danger, or necessity, or when he is well used, no-one can work faster than he; but the instant he feels that he is kept at work for nothing, no sloth could make less headway. He must not refuse his duty, or be in any way disobedient, but all the work an officer gets out of him he may be welcome to. Every man who has been three months at sea knows how 'to work Tom Cox's traverse' – 'three turns round the long-boat, and a pull at the scuttle-butt.' This morning everything went in this way. *Sogering* was the order of the day. Send a man below to get a block, and he would capsize everything before finding it, then not bring it up until an officer had called twice, and take as much time to put things in order again. Marline-spikes were not to be found, knives wanted a deal of sharpening, and, generally, three or four men were waiting round the grindstone at a time. When a man got to the masthead, he would come slowly down again to get something he had forgotten, and after the tackles were got up, six men would pull less than one who pulled 'with a will'. When the mate was out of sight, nothing was done. It was all up-hill work; and at eight o' clock, when we went to breakfast, things were nearly where they were when we began.

R. H. DANA: *Two Years Before the Mast*

How to Join the Navy

As for my own part, I saw no resource but the army or navy, between which I hesitated so long that I found myself reduced to a starving condition. My spirit began to accommodate itself to my beggarly fate, and I became so mean as to go down towards Wapping, with an intention to enquire for an old schoolfellow, who, I understood, had got the command of a small coasting vessel, then in the river, and implore his assistance. But my destiny prevented this abject piece of behaviour; for as I crossed Tower Wharf, a squat tawny fellow with a hanger by his side, and a cudgel in his hand, came up to me, calling, 'Yo, ho! brother, you must come along with me.' As I did not like his appearance, instead of answering his salutation, I quickened my pace, in hope of ridding myself of his company; upon which he whistled aloud, and immediately another sailor appeared before me, who laid hold of me by the collar, and began to drag me along. Not being of a humour to relish such treatment, I disengaged myself of the assailant, and with one blow of my cudgel laid him motionless on the ground: and perceiving myself surrounded in a trice by ten or a dozen more, exerted myself with such dexterity and success, that some of my opponents were fain to attack me with drawn cutlasses; and after an obstinate engagement, in which I received a large wound on my head and another on my left cheek, I was disarmed, taken prisoner, and carried on board a pressing tender, where, after being pinioned like a malefactor, I was thrust down into the hold, among a parcel of miserable wretches, the sight of whom well nigh distracted me. As the commanding officer had not humanity enough to order my wounds to be dressed, and I could not use my own hands, I desired one of my fellow captives who was unfettered, to take a handkerchief out of my pocket and tie it round my head to stop the bleeding. He pulled out my handkerchief, 'tis true, but instead of applying it to the use for which I designed it, went to the grating of the hatchway, and with astonishing composure sold it before my face to a bum-boat woman then on board for a quart of gin, with which he treated his companions, regardless of my circumstances and intreaties.

I complained bitterly of this robbery to the midshipman on deck, telling him, at the same time, that unless my hurts were dressed, I should bleed to death. . . . But compassion was a weakness of which no man could justly accuse this person, who squirting a mouthful of dissolved tobacco upon me through the gratings, told me, 'I was a mutinous dog, and that I might die and be damned.' Finding there was no other remedy, I appealed to patience, and laid up this usage in my memory, to be recalled at a fitter season. In the mean time loss of blood, vexation and want of food, contributed, with the noisome stench of the place, to throw me into a swoon; out of which I was recovered by a tweak of the nose, administered by the tar who stood sentinel over us, who at the same time regaled me with a draught of flip, and comforted me with the hopes of being put on board of the *Thunder* next day where I should be freed from handcuffs, and cured of my wounds by the doctor.

TOBIAS SMOLLETT: *Roderick Random*

The Surgeon's Mate Joins the Ship Thunder *of His Majesty's Navy*

While he entertained us with reflections suitable to this event, we heard the boatswain pipe to dinner, and immediately the boy belonging to our mess, ran to the locker, from whence he carried off a large wooden platter, and in a few minutes returned with it full of boiling pease, crying 'Scaldings', all the way as he came. The cloth, consisting of a piece of old sail, was instantly laid, covered with three plates, which by the colour I could with difficulty discern to be metal, and as many spoons of the same composition, two of which were curtailed in the handles, and the other abridged in the lip. Mr Morgan himself enriched this mess with a lump of salt butter, scooped from an old gallipot, and a handful of onions shorn, with some pounded pepper. I was not very much tempted with the appearance of this dish, of which, nevertheless, my messmates ate heartily, advising me to follow their example, as it was banyan day, and we could have no meat till next noon. But I had already laid in sufficient for the occasion, and therefore desired to be excused, expressing a curiosity to know the meaning of banyan day. They told me, that on Mondays, Wednesdays and Fridays the ship's company had no allowance of meat, and that these meagre days were called banyan days, the reason of which they did not know, but I have since learned they take their denomination from a sect of devotees in some parts of the East Indies, who never taste flesh.

After dinner, Thomson led me round the ship, shewed me the different parts, described their uses, and as far as he could, made me acquainted with the particulars of the discipline and economy practised on board. He then demanded of the boat-swain an hammock for me, which was slung in a very neat manner by my friend Jack Rattlin; and as I had no bed-cloaths, procured credit for me with the purser for a matrass and two blankets. At seven o'clock in the evening Morgan visited the sick, and having ordered what was proper for each, I assisted Thomson in making up his prescriptions; but when I followed him with the medicines into the sick-berth or hospital, and observed the situation of the patients, I was much less surprised that people should die on board, than that any sick person should recover. Here I saw about fifty miserable distempered wretches, suspended in rows, so huddled upon one another that not more than fourteen inches space was allotted for each with his bed and bedding; and deprived of the light of the day, as well as of fresh air, breathing nothing but a noisome atmosphere of the morbid steams exhaling from their own excrements and diseased bodies, devoured with vermin hatched in the filth that surrounded them, and destitute of every convenience necessary for people in that helpless condition.

TOBIAS SMOLLETT: *Roderick Random* (xxv)

Fleet Orders

Orders agreed upon by the Captaines and Masters to be observed by the fleet of Sir Humfrey Gilbert.

First: the Admirall to cary his flag by day, and his light by night.

2. Item, if the Admirall shall shorten his saile by night, then to show two lights untill he be answered again by every ship shewing one light for a short time.

3. Item, if the Admirall after his shortening of saile, as aforesayd, shall make more saile againe: then he to shew three lights one above another.

4. Item, if the Admirall shall happen to hull in the night, then to make a wavering light over his other light, wavering the light upon a pole.

5. Item, if the fleet should happen to be scattered by weather, or other mishap, then so soon as one shall descry another, to hoise both toppe sailes twise, if the weather will serve, and to strike them twise againe; but if the weather serve not, then to hoise the maine top saile twise, and forthwith to strike it twise again.

6. Item, if it shall happen a great fogge to fall, then presently every shippe to beare up with the Admirall, if there be winde; but if it be a calme, then every ship to hull, and so to lie at hull till it be cleere. And if the fogge do continue long, then the Admirall to shoot off two pieces every evening, and every ship to answer it with one shot: and every man bearing to the ship that is to leeward so neere as he may.

7. Item, every master to give charge unto the watch to looke out well, for laying aboord of one another in the night, and in fogges.

8. Item, every evening every ship to haile the Admirall, and so to fall asterne him, sailing thorow the Ocean: and being on the coast, every ship to haile him both morning and evening.

9. Item, if any ship be in danger any way, by leake or other-

wise, then she to shoot off a piece, and presently to hang out one light, whereupon every man to beare towards her, answering her with one light for a short time, and so to put it out again; thereby to give knowledge that they have seen her token.

10. Item, whensoever the Admirall shall hang out her ensigne in the maine shrouds, then every man to come aboord her, as a token of counsell.

11. Item, if there happen any storm or contrary winde to the fleete after the discovery, whereby they are separated: then every ship to repaire unto their last good port, there to meet again.

HAKLUYT: The English Voyages

Under Way

They brought the gear and stores and stowed them in the well-built ship, as Telemachus bade them; and Telemachus embarked, following Athene who took her seat by the vessel's stern. He sat beside her, and the crew cast off the ropes, came aboard and took their places on the thwarts. Then Athene, the goddess, sent them a fresh fair wind from the West, sighing over the wine-dark sea; Telemachus sang out to his men to lay hold on the tackle, and they obeyed the command. They raised the mast of pine and dropped it into the hollow mast-step, stayed it well, and hauling on the ox-hide halliards set the white sail. The wind filled it, and under the vessel's stem a dark wave sang aloud as she ran swiftly on her course.

Then when all had been made secure in the black ship, they brought the mixing-bowls on deck, filled them to the brim with wine and poured libations to the deathless gods, to the daughter of Zeus first of all, the Maiden Goddess with the grey eyes. And all through the night and the following dawn the ship ran on.

HOMER: The Odyssey

The Fisherman

I was never one for work. Give me the lightest of breezes on the grey-green sea, or, still better, a calm, and perhaps I may forget the charms of the shore. The sea is no place for me when the dark water begins to murmur, and long angry waves get up, with curling crests on top of them; dry land and trees are what I look for then – thick woods where the pines sing, however much it blows.

It's a hard life, the fisherman's: his work the sea, his home his boat, his prey the elusive fish. *My* pleasure is a snooze deep under the leaves of a plane, and the plashing of a spring not far away – lovely music for the poor countryman, lulling him to rest.

MOSCHUS: *An Idyll*

Odysseus Sails

Odysseus, full of joy, spread his sail to the breeze and sitting at the helm used all his seaman's cunning to hold the vessel to her course. He never closed his eyes in sleep but kept them on the Pleiads, or watched the slow setting of Boötes, or the Bear, called by some men the Wain, which wheels round in the sky and alone never bathes in the streams of Ocean but keeps constant watch upon Orion the Hunter. The Bear it was that the goddess Calypso had bidden him keep on his left hand as he sailed over the sea.

For seventeen days he held his course, and on the eighteenth he made out some shadowy hills, which were the nearest point of the Phaeacians' isle. The land lay like a shield on the misty sea.

But now the Lord Poseidon, the Earth Shaker, as he returned from Ethiopia saw Odysseus and his ship from the distant mountains of the Solymi, and was angry at the sight. He shook his head, and murmured, 'So the gods changed their minds about this man, once I was out of the way amongst the Ethiops! And now he is near Phaeacia, where he is destined to escape at last from all his troubles. But I mean to give him plenty yet before he gets there!'

So he gathered the clouds together and with his trident stirred the sea. He roused the blast of all winds that blow; in lowering cloud he hid land and sea alike, and darkness rushed down from the sky. East wind and South fell upon Odysseus, and the wild West wind too, and the sky-born Norther rolling a great wave before it. Odysseus' knees were loosened, his heart quailed, and for all his gallantry he cried out in anguish and fear: 'What will become of me now, unhappy man that I am? I fear the goddess spoke all too truly when she said that before I reached my home I should have my fill of misery upon the sea. The prophecy is indeed being fulfilled – for see how Zeus has covered the wide sky with murk, and roused up the breaking seas, while fierce squalls from every quarter rush down upon me! My utter destruction is now sure. Thrice and four times lucky were the Greeks who died on the broad plains of Troy, fighting for Menelaus and Agamennon; and would that I too had fallen there, when the Trojan armies hurled their brazen spears at me over the corpse of Achilles. Then should I have been buried with honour, and the Greeks would have spread my fame; but now it is my fate to die a dishonourable death.'

At that very instant a great comber curled and broke, rushing down upon him with dreadful speed and weight, and his vessel broached-to. The steering-oar was torn from his grasp; the warring winds snapped the mast in two and flung both sail and yard far out into the sea. Swept overboard, Odysseus for a long time was kept under, and could not struggle to the surface beneath the downrush of that wave, weighted as he was by the clothes Calypso had given him. At last he rose again, spitting out the bitter brine as the water streamed down his face; but for all the punishment he had taken, he did not forget his boat, but made after her through the seas, caught her, scrambled in and sat amidships – safe for the moment. . . .

Now Odysseus was not utterly alone, for Cadmus' daughter saw him – Ino of the slender ankles, who was once a woman speaking human words, but now dwells in the sea-depths and is honoured by the gods under the name of Leucothoe. She took pity on his misery, and, rising from the waves like a gull, settled on the boat. 'Poor man,' she said, 'why is Poseidon, Shaker of Earth, so angry with you that he plans nothing but trouble wherever you go? But he shall not kill you, however much he would like to. Come now, do as I bid you: strip off those clothes, leave the boat for the winds to do their will with, and swim for your life to the coast of Phaeacia, where it is your destiny to be saved. Take this scarf and twist it round your body, and you need fear neither death nor hurt; and when you touch dry land, unwind it again and fling it far out upon the wine-dark sea, turning your eyes away.'

Then the sea-nymph gave Odysseus the scarf, and plunged back like a sea-bird into the turbulent waves, vanishing into their dark depths; Odysseus was left wondering and, in his distress, took counsel thus with his own brave heart: 'Can it be my luck that some god, in urging me to abandon my boat, is but making a fresh net to trap me in? I shall not yet obey, for indeed the land is in sight where she promised me safety. No – this rather is my wisest course: so long as the planks hold together, I shall stay aboard and endure what I must; and when a wave breaks her up, then will I swim for it. I can think of no better plan.'

Even as Odysseus was making up his mind, the Earth Shaker, Lord of the Sea, sent another wave, steep and terrible, with a hollow crest that hung above him. Down it came, and smashed and scattered the planks of the boat as a sudden gust will scatter a heap of chaff. Odysseus seized a floating timber and bestrode it as a rider his horse, and stripped off the clothes Calypso had given him; then he wound the scarf around him, under his breast, and spreading out his arms plunged headlong into the sea, and with eager strokes struck out for land.

Poseidon saw him and with a shake of his immortal head, 'Thus then,' he murmured, 'make your way, poor wretch, across the sea, till you come to a people whom the gods respect. Even then you will hardly, I fancy, make light of your sufferings.' With this Poseidon touched his fair-maned horses with the whip and drove to his palace at Aegae.

And now Athene, daughter of Zeus, had a different thought; she checked the other winds and bade them fall into the calm of sleep, and called up a brisk breeze from the North to flatten the seas in Odysseus' path and help him to reach in safety the country of the Phaeacians, those far-famed mariners.

For two days and nights he was all but lost in the wild sea, and again and again he felt death close upon him. But when Dawn, that goddess with beautiful tresses, brought in the third day, the wind fell and there was calm. Eagerly straining his eyes as a great roller lifted him, Odysseus saw land close ahead. His joy was like the joy of children who see life returning to their father who has long been wasting with disease – no less glad was he at that glimpse of land and trees, and with all his strength he swam, longing to set foot on solid ground again. But as soon as he was within call of the shore, he heard the roar of surf on rocks, for on that inhospitable coast the rollers were breaking in thunder and all was veiled in a mist of spume. Harbours or landing-beaches there were none, but only jagged headlands and cruel reefs. Odysseus' knees were loosened; his brave heart quailed and he cried out in misery: 'Against all hope Zeus let me see land – and I have swum to it across all these miles of sea; now there is no way to get out of the water, and the grey sea must hold me yet. Off-shore are reefs, sharp as knives, and a surge of breakers; behind them a cliff sheer and smooth, with deep water at its base, and no chance to get a foothold and escape. If I try, a wave will get me and dash me against the rocks, – a sorry end to my attempt. If I swim further along the coast in the hope of finding some sheltered beach or cove, it is odds but another squall of wind will sweep me out again to the fish-haunted deeps, or else ill-luck will send a sea-monster to snap me up – one of the many fearsome creatures in Amphitrite's flock – and well I know how bitterly the great Earth Shaker hates me.'

But poor Odysseus had no more time to think what was best to do, for a huge roller picked him up and swept him on to the jagged shore, where his skin might have been stripped off and all his bones broken, had not grey-eyed Atheme made him lay hold with a mighty effort with both hands on a rock, to which he clung, gasping, till the roller had passed. For an instant he was safe; but then the backwash caught him and flung him into deep water again, while fragments of skin torn from his hands stuck to the rock like the pebbles on the suckers of an octopus which has been dragged from its lair. Submerged by the wave, he would indeed have met a miserable end, had not Athene once again put a thought into his mind: coming to the surface, he struggled clear of the broken water and swam coastwise in the smooth, keeping an eye on the shore in the hope of finding an inlet where the force of the seas would be broken. At last he reached the mouth of a fair-flowing river free from rocks and sheltered from the wind, and 'This,' he cried, 'is the place for me.'

Then he uttered a silent prayer to the God of that river: 'Hear me, though I know not thy name. I come to thee as to the answer to all my prayers for deliverance from the sea and Poseidon's anger. Even the immortal gods will hearken to a poor wanderer like me, who turn now to thee for help and seek sanctuary within thy stream after all my sufferings; Lord, pity me and receive me as thy suppliant.'

At once the river checked its current, calmed the waves and smoothed the windless water in Odysseus' path, bringing him safe to land at its mouth. Worn out with his struggle, he could hardly stand; his sturdy arms were weak, his flesh swollen, and salt water streamed from his mouth and nostrils. Speechless and breathless he lay, half dead and overwhelmed with a dreadful exhaustion. But soon his breath returned and his spirit revived; he unwound the goddess' scarf from his body and flung it into the seaward-moving stream. Down it went on the tide, and soon Ino had it in her hands again, while Odysseus turned away from the river, threw himself down amongst the reeds and kissed the life-giving earth. 'And what,' he thought, 'will become of me now? How will these things end? If I stay here by the river all through the night, frost and dew together may well make an end of one as exhausted as I am, for the river winds blow cold at dawn; but should I climb the hill yonder and find a bed in the undergrowth of the woods, I might indeed sleep sweetly and be warm and rested – but wild beasts might find and devour me, even as I slept.'

At last he decided to make for the woods. Quite near the river he came to a copse with clear ground all round it, and crawled under a pair of bushes growing from a single stem. Their branches were so thick that no breath of the moist wind could penetrate them, nor yet the sun's heat nor the rain. Into this shelter Odysseus crept, and scraped together a broad bed of leaves to lie on – for they lay there thick enough to keep two or three men warm and snug through the hardest winter weather, a pleasant sight for the weary wanderer. So down he lay, piling the leaves on top of him, covering himself as carefully as a lonely cottager hides his burning brand in black ashes, lest he lose the seed of fire. And Athene poured sleep upon his eyes and closed their lids – the best medicine for a weary man.

HOMER: *The Odyssey*

Keep then the Sea

Keep then the sea abought in specialle,
Whiche of England is the towne walle;
As thoughe England were lykened to a cite
And the walle enviroun were the see.
Kepe then the see, that is the walle of England,
And than is England kepte by Goddes hande.

Libelle of Englysshe Policie. Anon. (xxix)

Argo Sets Sail for the Golden Fleece

Wet was the Old Man's eye as he turned it away from his
    homeland;
Solemn the chant of the crew to the twang of the cither, their
    oarblades
Chunking the surge, whose ravening tongues came sluicing
    aboard, while
Overside slavered and bubbled the black brine darkly resentful.
Lit by the sun, tho', her gear flashed flame as she marched, and
    astern shone
Ever her long double wake like a far road crossing a prairie.

*   *   *

Soon the great mast they stepped in the partner, and setting
    up backstays
Poured their cascade of canvas from maintop out to the
    yardarms.
Shrill piped the breeze from aloft as they hove down the sheets
    and belayed aft
Each round its polished pin. She ran without fuss with the
    fair wind
On past the far-thrust foreland, while, up from the deep, little
    fishes
Bounded – big ones as well – and arrowing over the surface
Tagged along wetly astern. As flock full-fed to the sheepfold
Sheep at the shepherd's heels, who leads them, pastoral-piping
Shrill sweet country tunes, at the ship's heel followed the
    fishes . . .
Airs fell light with the dawn; so they took to their oars, and
    around them
Windless the puffs died down, and the sea lay asleep, and a flat
    calm
Gave them heart for a long day's pull.

APOLLONIUS RHODIUS: Argonautica, tr. H. G. Dixey

Alexander the Great on the Hydaspes

The final preparations made, the embarkation began at dawn, and Alexander offered his customary sacrifice, not omitting a special offering to the river Hydaspes, according to the soothsayer's instructions. Stepping aboard, he stood in the bows of his vessel and from a golden bowl poured a libation into the water, solemnly invoking the river . . . then, after a libation to Heracles his ancestor and to Ammon and the other gods it was his custom to honour, he ordered the trumpets to sound the signal for departure, and the whole fleet, each vessel in her proper station, began to move down-river. To avoid the danger of running foul of each other, all craft – carriers, horse-transports, and warships – had instructions to keep their exact distances, the faster vessels being ordered to check their speed so as not to break formation.

One may imagine the noise of this great fleet getting away under oars all together: it was like nothing ever heard before, what with the coxswains calling the *in . . . out, in . . . out* for every stroke and the rowers' triumphant cries as, like one man, they flung themselves upon the swirling water. The lofty banks, often towering above the ships, caught the clamour, and held it, and intensified it, tossing it to and fro across the stream, echoing and re-echoing, while silent and deserted glens on one side or other of the river reverberated with the din and helped to swell it. The natives had never before seen horses on ship-board, and the sight of them crowding the barges filled them with so much amazement that all who witnessed the departure of the fleet followed it along the banks for miles, and other friendly tribesmen who were near enough to hear the cries of the rowers and the dash and clatter of the oars came running to the river-bank and joined in the procession, singing their barbaric songs.

ARRIAN: *Life of Alexander* (xxvi)

Cleopatra's Barge

The barge she sat in like a burnish'd throne
Burned on the water; the poop was beaten gold;
Purple the sails, and so perfumed that
The winds were love-sick with them; the oars were silver,
Which to the tune of flutes kept stroke, and made
The water which they beat to follow faster,
As amorous of their strokes. For her own person
It beggar'd all description: she did lie
In her pavilion – cloth-of-gold of tissue –
O'erpicturing that Venus where we see
The fancy outwork nature. On each side her
Stood pretty dimpled boys, like smiling Cupids,
With divers-colour'd fans, whose wind did seem
To glow the delicate cheeks which they did cool,
And what they undid did.

　　　　　　　　O, rare for Antony!
　Her gentlewomen, like the Nereides,
So many mermaids, tended her i' the eyes,
And made their bends adornings; at the helm
A seeming mermaid steers; the silken tackle
Swells with the touches of those flower-soft hands
That yarely frame the office. From the barge
A strange invisible perfume hits the sense
Of the adjacent wharfs. The city cast
Her people out upon her; and Antony,
Enthron'd i' the market-place, did sit alone,
Whistling to the air, which, but for vacancy,
Had gone to gaze on Cleopatra too
And made a gap in nature.

WILLIAM SHAKESPEARE: *Antony and Cleopatra*

Odysseus' Homecoming

When they came down to the waterside where the ship lay, the gallant young men who formed Odysseus' escort got all the stores aboard, both food and drink, and on the after deck of the hollow ship spread for him a bed of rugs, with a linen sheet, that he might sleep soundly. Then Odysseus himself embarked, and lay down without a word; and the crew took their places in due order on the thwarts, cast off the mooring-rope from the pierced stone, and bending to the oars flung back the water with the blades, while on Odysseus' eyes deep sleep fell – sweet sleep, as deep as death. And the ship bounded on, swift as a chariot when four yoked stallions gallop under the lash, seeming almost to leave the ground in their speed: even so her stern lifted to the seas, while a great dark wave rushed roaring close in her wake. The wheeling falcon, swiftest of birds, could never have flown so fast; and thus the good ship ran lightly on, cutting her path through the waves, and carrying a man as resourceful as the very gods, a man who, after much suffering in war and upon the deep, now at last slept quietly, all pain forgotten.

And when arose that brightest of all stars which heralds the dawn, the sea-wandering bark drew near the island of Ithaca. There is a harbour there, sacred to Phorcys, the Old Man of the Sea. On either side of the haven two cliffy promontories rise sheer, and run down into the water, half-enclosing it and protecting it from the surge of the open sea when the storm-wind blows; and within it benched ships need not even a hawser to ride in safety, once they are within mooring distance of the beach. The seamen knew this spot of old, and thither they now came; and the ship, such was her speed under the vigour of the rowers' hands, ran half her length upon the shore. They leaped out and, as their first care, lifted Odysseus as he lay in the smooth soft rugs and set him down upon the sand, still fast asleep.

HOMER: *The Odyssey*

Ulysses

There lies the port; the vessel puffs her sail:
There gloom the dark, broad seas. My mariners,
Souls that have toil'd, and wrought and fought with me –
That ever with a frolic welcome took
The thunder and the sunshine, and opposed
Free hearts, free foreheads – you and I are old;
Old age hath yet his honour and his toil;
Death closes all: but something ere the end,
Some work of noble note, may yet be done,
Not unbecoming men that strove with Gods.
The lights begin to twinkle from the rocks;
The long day wanes; the slow moon climbs; the deep
Moans round with many voices. Come, my friends,
'Tis not too late to seek a newer world.
Push off, and sitting well in order smite
The sounding furrows; for my purpose holds
To sail beyond the sunset, and the baths
Of all the western stars, until I die . . .

ALFRED LORD TENNYSON: *Ulysses* (xxvii)

Argo Sets Sail for the Golden Fleece

And when her crew, so beautiful, came down to Iolcos,
Jason numbered them, thanking each one, and the Seer
Foretelling success from God's omens and the flight of birds
With willing heart bade them embark. Then they hung the
    anchors at the prow,
And Lord Jason on the poop took in his hands a golden cup
And called in prayer upon Zeus the Thunderer, Father of the
    Heavenly Ones,
And on the swinging winds and waves to give them swift
    passage,

The nights, and the sea-ways, and days of calm, and the
    happiness of safe return.
In answer to his prayer came a voice from the clouds in thunder,
Lightning burst from them brilliant, and the heroic company
Accepted the sign and were eased at heart.
Then the Seer bade them pull at the oars, giving them sweet
    hopes,
And stroke followed stroke under the strong, swift hands.
The south wind blew, and they came to the entrance of the
    Unfriendly Sea,
Where they made a shrine for Poseidon the Sea-god,
Having ready to their hands the dark Thracian bulls for
    sacrifice
And an altar of stones, new-built.
But peril lay ahead, and they prayed Poseidon, the Lord of
    Ships,
To escape the dreadful inrush of the Clashing Rocks –
Twin rocks they were, both alive, and would rush over the
    waters
Swiftlier than the marching ranks of winds, but now their
    days of life were over,
For the passage of Argo was to root them for ever.
So they came to Phasis. . . .

PINDAR: *Odes* (xxviii)

Strange Adventures

The Cavern

Just when the delightful days were beginning to pall upon us, a real adventure befel us, which, had we been attending strictly to business, we should not have encountered. For a week previous we had been cruising constantly without ever seeing a spout, except those belonging to whales out at sea, whither we knew it was folly to follow them. We tried all sorts of games to while away the time, which certainly did hang heavy, the most popular of which was for the whole crew of the boat to strip, and, getting overboard, be towed along at the ends of short warps, while I sailed her. It was quite mythological – a sort of rude reproduction of Neptune and his attendant Tritons.

At last, one afternoon as we were listlessly lolling (half asleep, except the look-out man) across the thwarts, we suddenly came upon a gorge between two cliffs that we must have passed before several times unnoticed. At a certain angle it opened, disclosing a wide sheet of water, extending a long distance ahead. I put the helm up, and we ran through the passage, finding it about a boat's length in width and several fathoms deep, though overhead the cliffs nearly came together in places. Within, the scene was very beautiful, but not more so than many similar ones we had previously witnessed. Still, as the place was new to us, our languor was temporarily dispelled, and we paddled along, taking in every feature of the shores with keen eyes that let nothing escape.

After we had gone on in this placid manner for nearly an hour, we suddenly came to a stupendous cliff – that is, for those parts – rising almost sheer from the water for about a thousand feet. Of itself it would not have arrested our attention, but at its base was a semicircular opening, like the mouth of a small tunnel. This looked alluring, so I headed the boat for it, passing through a deep channel between two reefs which led straight to the opening. There was ample room for us to enter, as we had lowered the mast; but just as we were passing through, a heave of the unnoticed swell lifted us unpleasantly near the crown of this natural arch. Beneath us, at a great depth, the bottom could be dimly discerned, the water being of the richest blue conceivable, which the sun, striking down through, resolved into some most marvellous colour-schemes in the path of its rays. A delicious sense of coolness, after the fierce heat outside, saluted us as we entered a vast hall, whose roof rose to a minimum height of forty feet, but in places could not be seen at all. A sort of diffused light, weak, but sufficient to reveal the general contour of the place, existed, let in, I supposed, through some unseen crevices in the roof or walls. At first, of course, to our eyes fresh from the fierce glare outside, the place seemed wrapped in impenetrable gloom, and we dared not stir lest we should run into some hidden danger. Before many minutes, however, the gloom lightened as our pupils enlarged, so that, although the light was faint, we could find our way about with ease. We spoke in low tones, for the echoes were so numerous and resonant that even a whisper gave back from those massy walls in a series of recurring hisses, as if a colony of snakes had been disturbed.

We paddled on into the interior of this vast cave, finding everywhere the walls rising sheer from the silent, dark waters, not a ledge or a crevice where one might gain foothold. Indeed, in some places there was a considerable overhang from above, as if a great dome whose top was invisible sprang from some level below the water. We pushed ahead until the tiny semicircle of light through which we had entered was only faintly visible; and then, finding there was nothing to be seen except what we were already witnessing, unless we cared to go on into the thick darkness, which extended apparently into the bowels of the mountain, we turned and started to go back.

Do what we would, we could not venture to break the solemn hush that surrounded us as if we were shut within the dome of some vast cathedral in the twilight. So we paddled noiselessly along for the exit, till suddenly an awful, inexplicable roar set all our hearts thumping fit to break our bosoms. Really, the sensation was most painful, especially as we had not the faintest idea whence the noise came or what had produced it. Again it filled that immense cave with its thunderous reverberations; but this time all the sting was taken out of it, as we caught sight of its author. A goodly bull-humpback had found his way in after us, and the sound of his spout, exaggerated a thousand times in the confinement of that mighty cavern, had frightened us all so that we nearly lost our breath. So far, so good; but, unlike the old nigger, though we were 'doin' blame well,' we did not 'let blame well alone.' The next spout that intruder gave, he was right alongside of us. This was too much for the semi-savage instincts of my gallant harpooner, and before I had time to shout a caution he had plunged his weapon deep into old Blowhard's broad back.

I should like to describe what followed, but, in the first place, I hardly know; and, in the next, even had I been cool and collected, my recollections would sound like the ravings of a fevered dream. For of all the hideous uproars conceivable, that was, I should think, about the worst. The big mammal seemed to have gone frantic with the pain of his wound, the surprise of the attack, and the hampering confinement in which he found himself. His tremendous struggles caused such a commotion that our position could only be compared to that of men shooting Niagara in a cylinder at night. How we kept afloat I do not know. Someone had the gumption to cut the line, so that by the radiation of the disturbance we presently found ourselves close to the wall, and trying to hold the boat in to it with our fingertips. Would he never be quiet? we thought, as the thrashing, banging and splashing still went on with unfailing vigour. At last, in, I suppose, one supreme effort to escape, he leaped clear of the water like a salmon. There was a perceptible hush, during which we shrank together like unfledged chickens on a frosty night; then, in a never-to-be-forgotten crash that ought to have brought down the massy roof, that mountainous carcass fell. The consequent violent upheaval of the water should have smashed the boat against the rocky walls, but that final catastrophe was mercifully spared us. I suppose the rebound was sufficient to keep us a safe distance off.

A perfect silence succeeded, during which we sat speechless, awaiting a resumption of the clamour. At last Abner broke the heavy silence by saying, 'I doan' see the do'way any mo' at all, sir.' He was right. The tide had risen, and that half-moon of light had disappeared, so that we were now prisoners for many hours, it not being at all probable that we should be able to find our way out during the night ebb. Well, we were not exactly children, to be afraid of the dark, although there is a considerable difference between the velvety darkness of a dungeon and the clear, fresh night of the open air. Still, as long as that beggar of a whale would only keep quiet or leave the premises, we should be fairly comfortable. We waited and waited until an hour had passed, and then came to the conclusion that our friend was either dead or gone out, as he gave no sign of his presence.

That being settled, we anchored the boat, and lit pipes, preparatory to passing as comfortable a night as might be under the circumstances, the only thing troubling me being the anxiety of the skipper on our behalf. Presently the blackness beneath was lit up by a wide band of phosphoric light, shed in the wake of no ordinary-sized fish, probably an immense shark. Another and another followed in rapid succession, until the depths beneath were all ablaze with brilliant foot-wide ribands of green glare, dazzling to the eye and bewildering to the brain. Occasionally a gentle splash or ripple alongside, or a smart tap on the bottom of the boat, warned us how thick the concourse was that had gathered below. Until that weariness which no terror is proof against set in, sleep was impossible, nor could we keep our anxious gaze from that glowing inferno beneath, where one would have thought all the population of Tartarus were holding high revel. Mercifully, at last we sank into a fitful slumber, though fully aware of the great danger of our position. One upward rush of any of those ravening monsters, happening to strike the frail shell of our boat, and a few fleeting seconds would have sufficed for our obliteration as if we had never been.

But the terrible night passed away, and once more we saw the tender, iridescent light stream into that abode of dread. As the day strengthened, we were able to see what was going on below, and a grim vision it presented. The water was literally alive with sharks of enormous size, tearing with never-ceasing energy at the huge carcass of the whale lying on the bottom, who had met his fate in a singular but not unheard-of way. At that last titanic effort of his he had rushed downward with such terrific force that, striking his head on the bottom, he had broken his neck. I felt very grieved that we had lost the chance of securing him, but it was perfectly certain that before we could get help to raise him, all that would be left on his skeleton would be quite valueless to us. So with such patience as we could command we waited near the entrance until the receding ebb made it possible for us to emerge once more into the blessed light of day. I was horrified at the haggard, careworn appearance of my crew, who had all, excepting the two Kanakas, aged perceptibly during that night of torment. But we lost no time in getting back to the ship, where I fully expected a severe wigging for the scrape my luckless curiosity had led me into. The captain, however, was very kind, expressing his pleasure at seeing us all safe back again, although he warned me solemnly against similar investigations in future.

A hearty meal and a good rest did wonders in removing the severe effects of our adventure, so that by next morning we were all fit and ready for the day's work again.

FRANK BULLEN: *The Cruise of the Cachalot*

Squid

At about eleven p.m. I was leaning over the lee rail, gazing steadily at the bright surface of the sea, where the intense radiance of the tropical moon made a broad path like a pavement of burnished silver. Eyes that saw not, mind only confusedly conscious of my surroundings, were mine; but suddenly I started to my feet with an exclamation, and stared with all my might at the strangest sight I ever saw. There was a violent commotion in the sea right where the moon's rays were concentrated, so great that, remembering our position, I was at first inclined to alarm all hands; for I had often heard of volcanic islands suddenly lifting their heads from the depths below, or disappearing in a moment, and, with Sumatra's chain of active volcanoes so near, I felt doubtful indeed of what was now happening. Getting the night glasses out of the cabin scuttle, where they were always hung in readiness, I focused them on the troubled spot, perfectly satisfied by a short examination that neither volcano nor earthquake had anything to do with what was going on; yet so vast were the forces engaged that I might well have been excused for my first supposition. A very large sperm whale was locked in deadly conflict with a cuttle-fish, or squid, almost as large as himself, whose interminable tentacles seemed to enlace the whole of his great body. The head of the whale especially seemed a perfect network of writhing arms – naturally, I suppose, for it appeared as if the whale had the tail part of the mollusc in his jaws, and, in a businesslike, methodical way, was sawing through it.

By the side of the black columnar head of the whale appeared the head of the great squid, as awful an object as one could well imagine even in a fevered dream. Judging as carefully as possible, I estimated it to be at least as large as one of our pipes, which contained three hundred and fifty gallons; but it may have been, and probably was, a good deal larger. The eyes were very remarkable from their size and blackness, which, contrasted with the livid whiteness of the head, made their appearance all the more striking. They were at least a foot in diameter, and, seen under such conditions, looked decidedly eerie and hobgoblin-like. All around the combatants were numerous sharks, like jackals round a lion, ready to share the feast, and apparently assisting in the destruction of the huge cephalopod. So the titanic struggle went on, in perfect silence as far as we were concerned, because, even had there been any noise, our distance from the scene of conflict would not have permitted us to hear it.

Thinking that such a sight ought not to be missed by the captain, I overcame my dread of him sufficiently to call him, and tell him of what was taking place. He met my remarks with such a furious burst of anger at my daring to disturb him for such a cause, that I fled precipitately on deck again, having the remainder of the vision to myself, for none of the others cared sufficiently for such things to lose five minutes sleep in witnessing them.

The conflict ceased, the sea resumed its placid calm, and nothing remained to tell of the fight but a strong odour of fish, as of a bank of seaweed left by the tide in the blazing sun. Eight bells struck, and I went below to a troubled sleep, wherein all the awful monsters that an over-excited brain could conjure up pursued me through the gloomy caves of ocean, or mocked my pigmy efforts to escape.

FRANK BULLEN: *The Cruise of the Cachalot*

The Pilot of the Pinta

Since reaching the islands I had lived most luxuriously on fresh bread, butter, vegetables and fruits of all kinds. Plums seemed the most plentiful on the *Spray*, and these I ate without stint. I had also a Pico white cheese that General Manning, the American consul-general, had given me, which I supposed was to be eaten, and of this I partook with the plums. Alas! by night time I was doubled up with cramps. The wind, which was already a smart breeze, was increasing somewhat, with a heavy sky to the sou'west. Reefs had been turned out, and I must turn them in again somehow. Between cramps I got the mainsail down, hauled out the earings as best I could and tied away point by point, in the double reef. There being sea-room, I should, in strict prudence, have made all snug and gone down at once to my cabin. I am a careful man at sea, but this night, in the coming storm, I swayed up my sails, which, reefed though they were, were still too much in such heavy weather; and I saw to it that the sheets were securely belayed. In a word, I should have laid to, but did not. I gave her the double-reefed mainsail and whole job instead, and set her on her course. Then I went below, and threw myself upon the cabin floor in great pain. How long I lay there I could not tell, for I became delirious. When I came to, as I thought, from my swoon, I realised that the sloop was plunging into a heavy sea, and look-ing out of the companionway, to my amazement, I saw a tall man at the helm. His rigid hand, grasping the spokes of the wheel, held them as in a vice. One may imagine my astonish-ment. His rig was that of a foreign sailor, and the large red cap he wore was cockbilled over his left ear, and all was set off with shaggy black whiskers. He would have been taken for a pirate in any part of the world. While I gazed upon his threaten-ing aspect I forgot the storm, and wondered if he had come to cut my throat. This he seemed to divine. 'Senor,' said he, doffing his cap, 'I have come to do you no harm.' And a smile, the faintest in the world, but still a smile, played on his face, which seemed not unkind when he spoke. 'I have come to do you no harm. I have sailed free,' he said, 'but was never worse than a *contrabandista*. I am one of Columbus' crew,' he con-tinued, 'I am the pilot of the *Pinta* come to aid you. Lie quiet, senor captain,' he added, 'and I will guide your ship tonight. You have a *calentura*, but you will be all right tomorrow.' I thought what a very devil he was to carry sail. Again, as if he read my mind, he exclaimed: 'Yonder is the *Pinta* ahead; we must overtake her. Give her sail! Give her sail! *Vale, vale, muy vale.*' Biting off a large quid of black twist, he said: 'You did wrong, captain, to mix cheese with plums. White cheese is never safe unless you know whence it comes. *Quien sabe*, it may have been taken from *leche de Capra*, and becoming capricious . . . '

'Avast, there!' I cried. 'I have no mind for moralising.'

I made shift to spread a mattress and lie on that instead of the hard floor, my eyes all the while fastened on my strange guest, who, remarking again that I would have 'only pains and calentura,' chuckled as he chanted a wild song:

> *High are the waves, fierce, gleaming,*
> *High is the tempest roar!*
> *High the sea-bird screaming,*
> *High the Azore!*

I suppose I was now on the mend, for I was peevish, and complained: 'I detest your jingle. Your Azore should be at roost, and would have been were it a respectable bird.' I begged that he would tie a rope-yarn on the rest of the song, if there was any more of it. I was still in agony. Great seas were boarding the *Spray*, but in my fevered brain I thought they were boats falling on deck, that careless draymen were throwing from wagons on the pier to which I imagined the *Spray* was now moored and without fenders to breast her off. 'You'll smash your boats,' I called out again and again, as the seas crashed on the cabin over my head. 'You'll smash your boats, but you can't hurt the *Spray*. She is strong!' I cried.

I found, when my pains and calentura had gone, that the deck, now as white as a shark's tooth from seas washing over it, had been swept of everything movable. To my astonishment, I saw now at broad day that the *Spray* was still heading as I had left her, and was going like a race-horse. Columbus himself could not have held her more exactly on her course. The sloop had made ninety miles in the night through a rough sea. I felt grateful to the old pilot, but I marvelled some that he had not taken in the jib. The gale was moderating, and by noon the sun was shining. A meridian altitude and the distance on the patent log, which I always kept towing, told me that she had made a true course throughout the twenty-four hours. I was getting much better now, but was very weak, and did not turn out reefs that day or the night following, although the wind fell light; but I just put my wet clothes out in the sun when it was shining, and, lying down there by myself, fell asleep. Then who should visit me again but my old friend of the night before, this time, of course, in a dream. 'You did well last night to take my advice,' said he, 'and if you would, I should like to be with you often on the voyage, for the love of adventure alone.' Finishing what he had to say, he again doffed his cap and disappeared as mysteriously as he came, returning, I suppose, to the phantom *Pinta*. I awoke much refreshed, and with the feeling that I had been in the presence of a friend and a seaman of vast experience. I gathered up my clothes, which by this time were dry, then, by inspiration, I threw overboard all the plums in the vessel.

JOSHUA SLOCUM: *Sailing Alone Around the World*

A Memory

. . . The most amazing wonder of the deep is its unfathomable cruelty.

I felt its dread for the first time in mid-Atlantic one day, many years ago, when we took off the crew of a Danish brig homeward bound from the West Indies. A thin, silvery mist softened the calm and majestic splendour of light without shadows – seemed to render the sky less remote and the ocean less immense. It was one of the days when the might of the sea appears indeed lovable, like the nature of a strong man in moments of quiet intimacy. At sunrise we had made out a black speck to the westward, apparently suspended high up in the void behind a stirring, shimmering veil of silvery blue gauze that seemed at times to stir and float in the breeze that fanned us slowly along. The peace of that enchanting forenoon was so profound, so untroubled, that it seemed that every word pronounced loudly on our deck would penetrate to the very heart of that infinite mystery born from the conjunction of water and sky. We did not raise our voices. 'A water-logged derelict, I think, Sir,' said the second officer quietly, coming down from aloft with the binoculars in their case slung across his shoulders; and our captain, without a word, signed to the helmsman to steer for the black speck. Presently we made out a low, jagged stump sticking up forward – all that remained of her departed masts.

The captain was expatiating in a low conversational tone to the chief mate upon the danger of these derelicts, and upon his dread of coming upon them at night, when suddenly a man forward screamed out, 'There's people on board of her, sir! I see them!' in a most extraordinary voice – a voice never heard before in our ship; the amazing voice of a stranger. It gave the signal for a sudden tumult of shouts. The watch below ran up the forecastle head in a body, the cook dashed out of the galley. Everybody saw the poor fellows now. They were there! And all at once our ship, which had the well-earned name of being without a rival for speed in light winds, seemed to us to have lost the power of motion, as if the sea, becoming viscous, had clung to her sides. And yet she moved. Immensity, the inseparable companion of a ship's life, chose that day to breathe upon her as gently as a sleeping child. The clamour of our excitement had died out, and our living ship, famous for never losing steerage way as long as there was air enough to float a feather, stole, without a ripple, silent and white as a ghost, towards her mutilated and wounded sister, come upon at the point of death in the sunlit haze of a calm day at sea.

With the binoculars glued to his eyes, the captain said in a quavering tone: 'They are waving to us with something aft there.' He put down the glasses on the skylight brusquely, and began to walk about the poop. 'A shirt or a flag,' he ejaculated irritably. 'Can't make it out ... some damn rag or other!'

He took a few more turns on the poop, glancing down over the rail now and then to see how fast we were moving. His nervous footsteps rang sharply in the quiet of the ship, where the other men, all looking the same way, had forgotten themselves in a staring immobility. 'This will never do!' he cried out suddenly; 'Lower the boats at once! Down with them!'

Before I jumped into mine he took me aside, as being an inexperienced junior, for a word of warning:

'You look out as you come alongside that she doesn't take you down with her. You understand?'

He murmured this confidentially, so that none of the men at the falls should overhear, and I was shocked. 'Heavens! as if in such an emergency one stopped to think of danger!' I exclaimed to myself mentally, in scorn of such cold-blooded caution.

It takes many lessons to make a real seaman, and I got my rebuke at once. My experienced commander seemed in one searching glance to read my thoughts on my ingenuous face.

'What you're going for is to save life, not to drown your boat's crew for nothing,' he growled severely in my ear. But as we shoved off he leaned over and cried out: 'It all rests on the power of your arms, men. Give way for life!'

We made a race of it, and I would never have believed that a common boat's crew of a merchantman could keep up so much determined fierceness in the regular swing of their stroke. What our captain had clearly perceived before we left had become plain to all of us since. The issue of our enterprise hung on a hair above that abyss of waters which will not give up its dead till the Day of Judgement. It was a race of two ship's boats matched against Death for a prize of nine men's lives, and Death had a long start. We saw the crew of the brig from afar working at the pumps – still pumping on that wreck, which already had settled so far down that the gentle, low swell, over which our boats rose and fell easily without a check to their speed, welling up almost level with her head-rails, plucked at the ends of broken gear swinging desolately under her naked bowsprit.

We could not, in all conscience, have picked out a better day for our regatta had we had the free choice of all the days that ever dawned upon the lonely struggles and solitary agonies of ships since the Norse rovers first steered to the westward against the run of Atlantic waves. It was a very good race. At the finish there was not an oar's length between the first and second boat, with Death coming in a good third on the top of the very next smooth swell, for all one knew to the contrary. The scuppers of the brig gurgled softly all together when the water rising against her sides subsided sleepily with a low wash, as if playing about an immovable rock. Her bulwarks were gone fore and aft, and one saw her bare deck low-lying like a raft and swept clean of boats, spars, houses – of everything except the ringbolts and the heads of the pumps. I had one dismal glimpse of it as I braced myself up to receive upon my breast the last man to leave her, the captain, who literally let himself fall into my arms.

It had been a weirdly silent rescue – a rescue without a hail, without a single uttered word, without a gesture or a sign, without a conscious exchange of glances. Up to the very last moment those on board stuck to their pumps, which spouted two clear streams of water upon their bare feet. Their brown skin showed through the rents of their shirts; and the two small bunches of half-naked, tattered men went on bowing from the waist to each other in their back-breaking labour, up and down, absorbed, with no time for a glance over the shoulder at the help that was coming to them. As we dashed, unregarded, alongside a voice let out one, only one hoarse howl of command, and then, just as they stood, without caps, with the salt drying grey in the wrinkles and folds of their hairy, haggard faces, blinking stupidly at us their red eyelids, they made a bolt away from the handles, tottering and jostling against each other, and positively flung themselves over upon our very heads. The clatter they made tumbling into the boats had an extraordinarily destructive effect upon the illusion of tragic dignity our self-esteem had thrown over the contests of mankind with the sea. On that exquisite day of gently breathing peace and veiled sunshine perished my romantic love of what men's imagination had proclaimed the most august aspect of Nature. The cynical indifference of the sea to the merits of human suffering and courage, laid bare in this ridiculous, panic-tainted performance extorted from the dire extremity of nine good and honourable seamen, revolted me. I saw the duplicity of the sea's most tender mood. It was so because it could not help itself, but the awed respect of the early days was gone. I felt ready to smile bitterly at its enchanting charm and glare viciously at its furies. In a moment, before we shoved off, I had looked coolly at the life of my choice. Its illusions were gone, but its fascination remained. I had become a seaman at last.

We pulled hard for a quarter of an hour, then laid on our oars waiting for our ship. She was coming down on us with swelling sails, looking delicately tall and exquisitely noble through the mist. The captain of the brig, who sat in the stern sheets by my side with his face in his hands, raised his head and began to speak with a sort of sombre volubility. They had lost their masts and sprung a leak in a hurricane; drifted for weeks, always at the pumps, met more bad weather; the ships they sighted failed to make them out, the leak gained upon them slowly, and the seas had left them nothing to make a raft of. It was very hard to see ship after ship pass by at a distance, 'as if everybody had agreed that we must be left to drown,' he added. But they went on trying to keep the brig afloat as long as possible, and working the pumps constantly on insufficient food, mostly raw, till 'yesterday evening,' he continued monotonously, 'just as the sun went down, the men's hearts broke.'

He made an almost imperceptible pause here, and went on again with exactly the same intonation:

'They told me the brig could not be saved, and they thought they had done enough for themselves. I said nothing to that. It was true. It was no mutiny. I had nothing to say to them. They lay about aft all night, as still as so many dead men. I did not lie down. I kept a look out. When the first light came I saw

314

your ship at once. I waited for more light; the breeze began to fail on my face. Then I shouted out as loud as I was able, "Look at that ship!" but only two men got up very slowly and came to me. At first only we three stood alone, for a long time, watching you coming down to us, and feeling the breeze drop to a calm almost; but afterwards others, too, rose, one after another, and by and by I had all my crew behind me. I turned round and said to them that they could see the ship was coming our way, but in this small breeze she might come too late after all, unless we turned to and tried to keep the brig afloat long enough to give you time to save us all. I spoke like that to them, and then I gave the command to man the pumps.'

He gave the command, and gave the example, too, by going himself to the handles, but it seems that these men did actually hang back for a moment, looking at each other dubiously before they followed him. 'He! he! he!' he broke out into a most unexpected, imbecile, pathetic, nervous little giggle. 'Their hearts were broken so! They had been played with too long,' he explained apologetically, lowering his eyes, and became silent.   JOSEPH CONRAD: *The Mirror of the Sea*

The Voluntary Castaway

During the afternoon, Jack surrendered to my insistence and began to drink sea-water in small amounts. I had just explained that if he did not make up his mind to do so, his system would become so dehydrated that to drink it would be useless and even dangerous. To my great relief, he accepted my reasoning, and the next morning all the incipient signs of dehydration had disappeared. Even his thirst had gone. We laughed a good deal about his conversion to heresy and our spirits became excellent.

*   *   *

On Saturday 25th, after half-catching and indeed wounding a number of fish and then seeing them wriggle off the end of my make-shift harpoon, I managed to catch my first dolphin (or, to be correct, dorado. This is a fish, not a mammal, but I shall use its more common name). I was saved, not only did I have food and drink, but bait and hook as well. Behind the gill cover, there is a perfect natural bone hook, such as has been found in the tombs of prehistoric men, and which I think I can claim to have adapted to modern use. My first fishing line was at hand. From then on I had all the food and liquid I needed every day, and was never in danger of starving. That was probably the most heretical aspect of my self-imposed role of castaway.

DR ALAIN BOMBARD: *The Bombard Story*
(English edition)

And straightway he constrained his disciples to get into the ship, and to go to the other side before unto Bethsaida, while he sent away the people. And when he had sent them away, he departed into a mountain to pray. And when even was come, the ship was in the midst of the sea, and he alone on the land. And he saw them toiling in rowing; for the wind was contrary unto them; and about the fourth watch of the night he cometh unto them, walking upon the sea, and would have passed by them. But when they saw him walking upon the sea, they supposed it had been a spirit, and cried out; for they all saw him and were troubled. And immediately he talked with them, and saith unto them, 'Be of good cheer; it is I. Be not afraid.'

And he went up unto them into the ship, and the wind ceased; and they were sore amazed in themselves beyond measure, and wondered.

ST MARK'S GOSPEL

Phantom Ship

With throats unslaked, with black lips baked,
Agape they heard me call:
Gramercy, they for joy did grin,
And all at once their breath drew in,
As they were drinking all.

A flash of joy;

See! See! I cried, she tacks no more
Hither to work us weal –
Without a breeze, without a tide,
She steadies with upright keel!

And horror
follows. For can
it be a ship that
comes onward
without wind or
tide?

The western wave was all aflame,
The day was wellnigh done;
Almost upon the western wave
Rested the broad, bright Sun;
When that strange shape drove suddenly
Betwixt us and the Sun.

And straight the Sun was fleck'd with bars
(Heaven's Mother send us grace!),
As if through a dungeon-grate he peer'd
With broad and burning face.

It seemeth him
but the skeleton
of a ship.

Alas! (thought I, and my heart beat loud)
How fast she nears and nears!
Are those her sails that glance in the Sun
Like restless gossameres?

Are those her ribs through which the Sun
Did peer, as through a grate?
And is that Woman all her crew?
Is that a Death? and are there two?
Is Death that Woman's mate?

And its ribs are
seen as bars on
the face of the
setting sun. The
Spectre-Woman
and her Death-
mate, and no
other, on board
the skeleton
ship. Like
vessel, like
crew!

317

Her lips were red, her looks were free,
Her locks were yellow as gold;
Her skin was as white as leprosy,
The nightmare Life-in-Death was she,
Who thicks man's blood with cold.

Death and Life-
in-Death have
diced for the
ship's crew, and
she (the latter)
winneth the
ancient Mariner.
The naked hulk alongside came,
And the twain were casting dice;
'The game is done! I've won, I've won!'
Quoth she, and whistles thrice.

No twilight
within the
Courts of the
Sun.
The Sun's rim dips; the stars rush out;
At one stride comes the dark;
With far-heard whisper o'er the sea
Off shot the spectre bark.

We listened and look'd sideways up;
Fear at my heart, as at a cup,
My life-blood seem'd to sip.
The stars were dim, and thick the night,
At the rising of
the Moon,
The steersman's face by his lamp gleam'd white;
From the sails the dew did drip –
Till clomb above the Eastern bar
The horned Moon, with one bright star
Within the nether tip.

One after one by the star-dogg'd Moon,
Too quick for groan or sigh,
Each turn'd his face with a ghastly pang,
And cursed me with his eye.

Four times fifty living men
His shipmates
drop down dead.
(And I heard nor sigh nor groan),
With heavy thump, a lifeless lump,
They dropp'd down one by one.

318

The souls did from their bodies fly –
They fled to bliss or woe;
And every soul it pass'd me by
Like the whizz of my crossbow.

S. T. COLERIDGE: *The Ancient Mariner*

Jonah

Now the word of the Lord came unto Jonah the son of Amittai, saying, 'Arise, go to Nineveh, that great city, and cry against it; for their wickedness is come up before me.'

But Jonah rose up to flee unto Tarshish from the presence of the Lord, and went down to Joppa; and he found a ship going to Tarshish; so he paid the fare thereof, and went down into it, to go with them unto Tarshish from the presence of the Lord. But the Lord sent out a great wind into the sea, and there was a mighty tempest in the sea, so that the ship was like to be broken. Then the mariners were afraid, and cried every man unto his god, and cast forth the wares that were in the ship into the sea, to lighten it of them.

But Jonah was gone down into the sides of the ship, and he lay, and was fast asleep. So the ship-master came to him and said unto him: 'What meanest thou, O sleeper? Arise, call upon thy God, if so be that God will think upon us, that we perish not.' And they said every one to his fellow: 'Come, and let us cast lots, that we may know for whose cause this evil is upon us.' So they cast lots, and the lot fell upon Jonah.

Then they said unto him: 'Tell us, we pray thee, for whose cause this evil is upon us? What is thine occupation? And whence comest thou? What is thy country? And of what people art thou?'

And he said unto them: 'I am an Hebrew, and I fear the Lord, the God of heaven, which hath made the sea and the dry land.' Then were the men exceedingly afraid and said unto him: 'Why hast thou done this?' For the men knew that he fled from the presence of the Lord, because he had told them.

Then they said unto him: 'What shall we do unto thee, that the sea may be calm unto us?' For the sea wrought and was tempestuous. And he said unto them: 'Take me up, and cast me forth into the sea. So shall the sea be calm unto you; for I know that for my sake this great tempest is upon you.' Nevertheless the men rowed hard to bring it to the land, but they could not, for the sea wrought and was tempestuous against them. Wherefore they cried unto the Lord and said: 'We beseech thee, O Lord, we beseech thee, let us not perish for this man's life, and lay not upon us innocent blood. For thou, O Lord, hast done as it pleased thee.' So they took up Jonah and cast him forth into the sea, and the sea ceased from her raging.

Then the men feared the Lord exceedingly, and offered a sacrifice unto the Lord and made vows.

Now the Lord had prepared a great fish to swallow up Jonah; and Jonah was in the belly of the fish three days and three nights. Then Jonah prayed unto the Lord his God out of the fish's belly, and said: 'I cried by reason of mine affliction unto the Lord, and he heard me; out of the belly of hell cried I, and thou heardest my voice; for thou hadst cast me into the deep, in the midst of the seas; and the floods compassed me about: all thy billows and thy waves passed over me. Then I said, "I am cast out of thy sight, yet I will look again toward thy holy temple." The waters compassed me about, even to the soul; the depth closed me round about, the weeds were wrapped about my head. I went down to the bottoms of the mountains; the earth with her bars was about me for ever; yet hast thou brought up my life from corruption, O Lord my God. When my soul fainted within me I remembered the Lord, and my prayer came in unto thee, into thine holy temple. I will sacrifice unto thee with the voice of thanksgiving; I will pay that that I have vowed. Salvation is of the Lord.'

And the Lord spake unto the fish, and it vomited out Jonah upon the dry land.

And the word of the Lord came unto Jonah the second time, saying: 'Arise, go unto Nineveh, that great city, and preach unto it the preaching that I bid thee.' So Jonah arose and went unto Nineveh, according to the word of the Lord.

THE BOOK OF JONAH

Ariel's Song

Full fathom five thy father lies;
   Of his bones are coral made;
Those are pearls that were his eyes;
   Nothing of him that doth fade
But doth suffer a sea change
Into something rich and strange.
Sea-nymphs hourly ring his knell:
   Ding-dong.
  Hark! Now I hear them –
   Ding-dong bell.

WILLIAM SHAKESPEARE: *The Tempest*

Sailors' Yarns

  that sea-beast
Leviathan, whom God of all his works
Created hugest that swim th' Ocean stream:
Him haply slumbring on the Norway foam
The pilot of some small, night-founder'd skiff,
Deeming some island, oft, as seamen tell,
With anchor fixed in his scaly rind
Moors by his side, under the lee, while night
Invests the sea, and wished morn delays.

JOHN MILTON: *Paradise Lost* (xxx)

321

The Coming of the King

                        . . . on the night
When Uther in Tintagel past away
Moaning and wailing for an heir, the two
Left the still king, and passing forth to breathe,
Then from the castle gateway by the chasm
Descending through the dismal night – a night
In which the bounds of heaven and earth were lost –
Beheld, so high upon the dreary deeps
It seem'd in heaven, a ship, the shape thereof
A dragon wing'd, and all from stem to stern
Bright with a shining people on the decks,
And gone as soon as seen. And then the two
Dropt to the cove, and watch'd the great sea fall,
Wave after wave, each mightier than the last,
Till last, a ninth one, gathering half the deep
And full of voices, slowly rose and plunged
Roaring, and all the wave was in a flame:
And down the wave and in the flame was borne
A naked babe, and rode to Merlin's feet,
Who stoopt and caught the babe, and cried, 'The King!'

ALFRED LORD TENNYSON: *The Coming of Arthur*

The Emperor Nero turns Naval Architect

This plan (i.e. to make his mother's bedroom ceiling fall in on top of her while she was in bed) unfortunately got abroad, so Nero was obliged to think of something else. This time, he invented a boat so constructed that, if it did not sink of itself, the cabin-roof could be made to fall in and kill her. He then pretended to be once again on the best of terms with her and wrote an affectionate letter inviting her to come to Baiae to celebrate the feast of Minerva with him. When she arrived, he told his sea-captains to wreck the galley which had brought her by 'accidentally' running it down, and then, when she asked, after a deliberately protracted evening meal, to sail back to Bauli, he offered her his own contraption in place of the damaged galley. She accepted perforce, and he escorted her on board in the best of spirits, kissing her breasts by way of goodbye. The remainder of the night was an anxious time for him; he could not sleep a wink, until he should know whether or not his plan had succeeded. Unfortunately, everything went wrong, and news came next morning that she had swum ashore in safety.

SUETONIUS: *Lives of the Caesars*

The Ship and the Man

Sailing from Baltic Port, one of a crew of four in another man's ship, I came to the far end of the Dagorort Peninsula, and there had an experience which I cannot refrain from putting into this book, so full it was of the romance of those rarely visited waters.

We had anchored half a mile from the shore off the place that is called Ermuiste, which means 'the terrible', for it is a place of many wrecks, a rocky point open to the widest sweep of the winds across the Baltic Sea. We had not dared to go nearer, and I was glad we had not, for, as I rowed ashore in the little boat, I passed many rocks awash and saw others a foot or two under water. There were dark purple clouds rising over the sea to the N.W., wind was coming, and we were impatient to be off again, to find shelter, or at least to put some miles of sea between us and that notorious coast. But there was still sunlight on the rocky shore and on the dark pinewoods that ran down almost to the water's edge and on the little wooden pierheads, unmarked on the chart, which, seen through binoculars, had tempted us to run in and look for information and supplies. Beyond the pierhead was a little stretch of beach where I meant to land. But, looking over my shoulder as I pulled in, bobbing over the waves in my little boat, I could see none of the things that a pierhead usually promises. There was no watchman's hut on the pier, no smoke above the trees, no cottage, no loaders, no fishermen, no sign of any kind of life. And then, coming nearer, I saw that the pier was in ruins. Much of its planking had gone, great beams were leaning perilously over from it, and here and there masses of it had actually fallen into the water. I wished to waste no time, and was on the point of turning and pulling back to the ship, when I saw something else more promising than the pier. Just within the forest that stretched down to the beach, almost hidden by the tall pines, was the great golden body of an unfinished ship. Where a ship was building, there, surely, must be men, and I rowed in confidently past the ruined pier, slipped off my shoes, rolled up my trousers and, jumping overboard, pulled the little boat through the shallow water and up on a narrow strip of small pebbles.

Then, walking up in the shadow of the trees, I came to the ship, the upper part of which, far above my head, was glowing in the splashes of sunshine that came through the tops of the pines which brushed the sides of the ship as they waved in the gathering wind. There was not a man to be seen, or a hut for men, nor was there sound of hammers or any of the usual accompaniments of shipbuilding. But for the ruined pier and the golden hull in the shadows among those tall trees, the coast might have been that of an undiscovered island. And then I began to notice one or two things about the ship herself which seemed a little odd. She was a very large ship to be building on that bit of coast, where there is no real harbour and the most ambitious launches are those of the twenty-foot fishing-boats which a man builds during the winter to earn his living in the summer months. She seemed even larger than she was, as ships do on land, shut in there among the trees that pressed about her as if they had grown up round her. And her lines were not those of a new ship. There was something a little old-fashioned about them, as though she were an unfinished masterpiece of an older period. A few schooners of her type survive today among those 'laibas' that carry timber and potatoes round the Esthonian coast, and they outsail those modern ships in which an obstreperous motor, tucked away in the stern, makes up for the want of the love and thought that went into the lines of the older vessels. And then I saw that I was wrong in thinking that she had been newly planked. The upper planking was new, certainly, ruddy gold where the sun caught it, but lower down her hull was weathered. Only the topmost planks had been freshly put on, and as the eye descended from them it passed imperceptibly from a new to an old piece of shipbuilding. The keel, laid on great stones, was joined to them by moss. There was lichen upon it, and on the foot of the stern-post was a large bright cluster of scarlet toadstools.

Just then I found a narrow, lightly worn track running from the ship farther into the forest. I walked along it, and only a few score yards away, but quite invisible from the shore, I came out of the silence and the trees into a small clearing and a loud noise of grasshoppers. There was a tiny hayfield, not bigger than a small suburban garden, a cornfield, perhaps three times the size, and an old log cabin with a deep thatched roof, an outhouse or two, a dovecot and pigeons fluttering about it.

The pigeons fluttered and murmured, but no dog barked and no-one answered when I knocked at the low door of the hut. I knocked again, and then, doubtfully, tried the wooden latch, opened it and walked in. A very little light came through the small windows, heavily overhung by the deep thatch. The hut was divided into two rooms. In the first were a couple of spinning-wheels, one very old, black with age, the other quite new, a precise copy of it, the two contrasting like the upper planking and keel of that still unfinished ship. There was also a narrow wooden bed, a great oak chest and a wooden stool, all made as if to last for ever. A few very clean cooking things were on the stove, and fishing lines and nets were hanging from wooden pegs on the walls. The second room held no furniture but a bench and a big handloom for weaving. There was some grand strong canvas being made upon it, and, as I looked at it, I guessed suddenly that here were being made the sails for the ship.

Without knowing why, I hurried out of the cabin into the sunshine. Leaning on the gate into the cornfield, as if he had been there all the time, an old man stood watching me. He had steely-grey curly hair and very dark-blue eyes. The skin of his face was clear walnut. He might have been any age from fifty to a hundred. His clothes were of some strong homespun cloth, probably made on the loom where he was making the sails. The shoes on his bare brown feet were of woven string with soles of thick rope. With his arrival the whole place seemed to have sprung to life. He was accompanied by three sheep, and two pigs snuffled in the ground close by. A dog, impassive as his master, lay beside the gate, half opening his eyes, as if he had been waked from sleep.

Somehow I could make no apology for having gone into his cottage. I asked him where to land eastwards along the coast and for the nearest anchorage sheltered from the north-west. He told me what I wanted gravely, and with a curious air of taking his words one by one out of a lumber room and dusting them before use. I tried to get eggs and butter from him, but he said he had no eggs and never made more butter than he needed. I should get some from the forester at Palli or at Luidja, near the anchorage. I asked him about the pier. Once upon a time there had been people here and timber traffic?

'Yes, but that was a long time ago, and the people have all gone away.'

'Was it then that you began building the ship?'

'Yes: that was when I began building the ship.'

His dark-blue eyes, watching me, but indifferent as the sea itself, invited no more questions. I turned back by the path under the great ship so many times larger than his cottage, and found myself oddly hurried as I pushed our little boat into the water and rowed away. I could just catch the sunlight splashes on the body of the ship among the trees. Would she ever be finished? And what then? What had he planned as he worked at her year after year? Would he die before his dream came true, or before he knew that the dreaming was the better part of it?

But the sunlight faded and the wind had freshened, and for a time I thought no more about him, for we had enough to do with our own ship.

ARTHUR RANSOME: Racundra's First Cruise

ℯ𝒜 Nightmare

I was now trying to get the better of the stupor which had come over me, and to collect my senses so as to see what was to be done, when I felt somebody grasp my arm. It was my elder brother, and my heart leaped for joy, for I had made sure that he was overboard – but the next moment all this joy was turned to horror – for he put his mouth close to my ear, and screamed out the word '*Moskoe-strom!*'

No-one will ever know what my feelings were at that moment. I shook from head to foot as if I had had the most violent fit of the ague. I knew what he meant by that one word well enough – I knew what he wished to make me understand. With the wind that now drove us on, we were bound for the whirl of the Strom, and nothing could save us.

You perceive that in crossing the Strom *channel*, we always went a long way up above the whirl, even in the calmest weather, and then had to wait and watch carefully for the slack, but now we were driving right upon the pool itself, and in such a hurricane as this! 'To be sure,' I thought, 'we shall get there just about the slack – there is some little hope in that' – but in the next moment I cursed myself for being so great a fool as to dream of hope at all. I knew very well that we were doomed, had we been ten times a ninety-gun ship.

By this time the fury of the tempest had spent itself; or perhaps we did not feel it so much, as we scudded before it, but at all events the seas, which had at first been kept down by the wind and lay flat and frothing, now got up into absolute mountains. A singular change, too, had come over the heavens. Around in every direction it was as black as pitch, but nearly overhead there burst out, all at once, a circular rift of clear sky – as clear as I ever saw – and of a deep, bright blue – and through it there blazed forth the full moon with a lustre that I never before knew her to wear. She lit up everything about us with the greatest distinctness – but, oh God, what a scene it was to light up!

I now made one or two attempts to speak to my brother – but in some manner which I could not understand, the din had so increased that I could not make him hear a single word, although I screamed at the top of my voice in his ear. Presently he shook his head, looking as pale as death, and held up one of his fingers as if to say '*listen!*'

At first I could not make out what he meant – but soon a hideous thought flashed upon me. I dragged my watch from its fob. It was not going. I glanced at its face by the moonlight, and then burst into tears as I flung it far away into the ocean. *It had run down at seven o'clock! We were behind the time of the slack, and the whirl of the Strom was in full fury!*

Well, so far we had ridden the swells very cleverly, but presently a gigantic sea happened to take us right under the counter, and bore us with it as it rose – up – up – as if into the sky. I would not have believed that any wave could rise so high. And then down we came with a sweep, a slide and a plunge that made me feel sick and dizzy, as if I was falling from some lofty mountain-top in a dream. But while we were up I had thrown a quick glance around – and that one glance was all-sufficient. I saw our exact position in an instant. The Moskoe-strom whirlpool was about a quarter of a mile dead ahead – but no more like the every-day Moskoe-strom than the whirl, as you now see it, is like a mill-race. If I had not known where we were, and what we had to expect, I should not have recognised the place at all. As it was I involuntarily closed my eyes in horror. The lids clenched themselves together as if in a spasm.

It could not have been more than two minutes afterwards

when we suddenly felt the waves subside, and were enveloped in foam. The boat made a sharp half-turn to larboard, and then shot off in its new direction like a thunderbolt. At the same moment the roaring noise of the water was completely drowned in a kind of shrill shriek – such a sound as you might imagine given out by the water-pipes of many thousand steam-vessels letting off their steam all together. We were now in the belt of surf that always surrounds the whirl, and I thought, of course, that another moment would plunge us into the abyss, down which we could only see indistinctly on account of the amazing velocity with which we were borne along. The boat did not seem to sink into the water at all, but to skim like an air-bubble upon the surface of the surge. Her starboard side was next the whirl, and on the larboard arose the world of ocean we had left. It stood like a huge writhing wall between us and the horizon. . . . Scarcely had I secured myself in my new position, when we gave a wild lurch to starboard, and rushed headlong into the abyss. As I felt the sickening sweep of the descent, I had instinctively tightened my hold upon the barrel, and closed my eyes. For some seconds I dared not open them – while I expected instant destruction. But moment after moment elapsed. I still lived. I took courage and looked once again upon the scene.

Never shall I forget the sensation of awe, horror and admiration with which I gazed about me. The boat appeared to be hanging, as if by magic, midway down, upon the interior surface of a funnel vast in circumference, prodigious in depth, and whose perfectly smooth sides might have been mistaken for ebony, but for the bewildering rapidity with which they spun around, and for the gleaming and ghastly radiance they shot forth, as the rays of the full moon, from that circular rift amid the clouds which I have already described, streamed in a flood of golden glory along the black walls, and far away down into the inmost recesses of the abyss.

EDGAR ALLAN POE: *A Descent into the Maelstrom*

Clarence's Dream

Methought that I had broken from the Tower,
And was embarked to cross to Burgundy;
And, in my company, my brother Gloucester,
Who from my cabin tempted me to walk
Upon the hatches. Thence we looked toward England,
And cited up a thousand fearful times,
During the wars of York and Lancaster
That had befall'n us. As we paced along
Upon the giddy footing of the hatches,
Methought that Gloucester stumbled; and, in falling,
Struck me, that thought to stay him, overboard
Into the tumbling billows of the main.
Lord! Lord! methought, what pain it was to drown!
What dreadful noise of waters in mine ears!
What ugly sights of death within mine eyes!
Methought I saw a thousand fearful wrecks,
Ten thousand men, that fishes gnawed upon;
Wedges of gold, great anchors, heaps of pearl,
Inestimable stones, unvalued jewels,
All scattered in the bottom of the sea.
Some lay in dead men's skulls; and, in those holes
Where eyes did once inhabit, there were crept,
As 'twere in scorn of eyes, reflecting gems,
Which woo'd the slimy bottom of the deep,
And mocked the dead bones that lay scattered by.

Had you such leisure in the time of death
To gaze upon the secrets of the deep?

Methought I had, and often did I strive
To yield the ghost, but still the envious flood
Kept in my soul, and would not let it forth
To seek the empty, vast and wandering air,
But smothered it within my panting bulk,
Which almost burst to belch it in the sea.

WILLIAM SHAKESPEARE: *Richard III*

Danae and the Baby Perseus

When in the well-wrought chest she lay,
And the wind blew, driving it
Over the wild sea,
Fear stole upon her heart, and with tear-wet cheeks
She took Perseus in her arms, and said: 'My baby
All is grief for me,
But you are sleeping; so young, so tender,
You lie at rest in the grim
Nail-studded chest,
Though the murk thickens and the night is starless.
The surge of the passing wave, towering high,
You heed not, nor the wind's voice, as you lie wrapped
In your cloak, your face close to mine.
If to you terror were terrible,
You might have listened to my words.
Sleep on, my baby; and may the sea sleep too,
And our own distress.'

SIMONIDES

The Ship Argo in Narrow Waters

As when a school of dolphins at play round a free-running
ship's hull
Jumps, to the joy of the crew, now ahead, now astern, now
alongside,
So the Nymphs frolicked athrong, out-darting, up-leaping,
on-diving,
Skipped on the top of the reef or danced in the smash of the
breakers,
Here, there, facing each other across the strong stream of the
tide which
Caught the ship broadside-asprawl, while about her a boisterous
wave came

Bursting with laughter over the rocks. The Nymphs like a
    fog-puff
One minute soared to the cliff, the next shot down through the
    water
Right to the roots of the sea where the wild swell gathers, and
    crouched there,
Then (like girls on the sands who, doubling their skirts to the
    waistline
Sport with a round ball, catching, high flinging it one to
    another,
Never to fall to the floor) so tossed up the ship as she drifted
One to another in turn, ballooning her over the billows
Further and further away from the reef, foam belching about
    them.
Long as an hour of the sweet spring day their convoy con-
    tinued
Fending the ship from the shore, till she picked up a slant for
    herself and
They like the seamew sank into the deep, having done the
    Queen's bidding.

APOLLONIUS RHODIUS:

Argonautica. tr. by H. G. Dixey (xxxi)

The Pieuvre

Only the sight of the pieuvre can persuade us of its reality.
Compared with it, the legendary hydra makes one smile. God,
when he wills it, is the supreme artist in the abominable. The
reason for such willing is the most terrifying problem of
religion. All ends being admitted, then, if the horrible is one
of them, the pieuvre is a masterpiece.

The pieuvre has none of the strength of mere size; it utters
no menacing cry; it has neither armour, nor horns, nor sting;
no powerful tail to seize or bruise its prey; no fins to cut or

332

tear; no electric discharge, no poison, no claws, beak, or teeth. Yet of all creatures it is the most formidably armed. You ask then what it is? It is a Sucker.

Amongst the off-shore reefs, the secret places where the sea exhibits all its splendours, in rocky caverns seldom seen by the eye of man or unknown caves rich with shells and shell-fish and marine vegetation, under the deep portals of the sea – in such places as these a swimmer, lured on by their beauty, runs the risk of an encounter. . . .

Swaying there in the water is a greyish Something, like a piece of rag, about as thick as one's arm and a couple of feet long. In shape it resembles a closed umbrella without a handle. It moves stealthily towards you. Suddenly it opens; with a swift movement, eight arms spread out, like the spokes of a wheel, round a face which has two eyes. The spokes are alive; as they sway they flicker like flame. The thing is four or five feet in diameter – frightful in its sudden expansion. It darts upon you.

* * *

A bite is bad enough; suction is worse. Claws are nothing compared with suckers. With claws, it is the creature which enters your flesh; with suckers, it is you who enter the creature. Your muscles swell, every fibre in your body is wrung. Your skin bursts under a revolting pressure, your blood spurts out and mingles horribly with the mollusc's lymph. It superposes itself upon you by innumerable vile mouths; the monster and the man become incorporate, a single, dreadful entity. The nightmare has got you. Tigers can but eat their prey, but the octopus – God help you – breathes you in. It draws you to, and into, itself, till, bound and helpless, you are slowly emptied into a horrible bag which is yet a living creature. Beyond the terror of being eaten alive is the inexpressible horror of being *drunk* alive. . . .

Such was the creature to which, for the last few moments, Gilliatt had belonged. It lived in that cavern, the evil genius

333

of the spot, the dark demon of the water. All the splendour and beauty of the place was but the frame to horror.

A month before, when Gilliatt first found his way into the cavern, he had glimpsed a shape, dimly outlined, in the secret enfoldings of the water. It was the pieuvre – at home. Now, entering the cave for the second time in pursuit of the crab, he had observed the crevice in the rock where he supposed that it had hidden – and the pieuvre was there, watching him.

Imagine the horror of this watch. No bird would dare to sit, or egg to hatch; no flower could open or breast give suck; no heart would have courage to love, or mind to soar, if thought once dwelt upon the sinister shapes of Patience, watching and waiting in the abyss.

Gilliatt had thrust his arm into the crevice, and the pieuvre had seized it, and was holding it fast. He was the fly, and the spider had got him.

He was in water up to his waist. His toes clung as they could to the smooth and slippery stones; his right arm was firmly held by the coils of the monster's flat, thong-like tentacles, and the upper part of his body was almost covered under their intricate and horrible criss-cross swathings. Three of the monster's eight arms still clung to the rock; the other five held Gilliatt. Two hundred and fifty suckers were fastened upon his flesh.

No strength can tear a man from the pieuvre's grip. Let him try, and he is the more surely held. Gilliatt had but one resource, his knife. Only his left arm was free, but the reader knows he could use it well, having, as one might put it, two right hands. In his grasp was his open knife.

An octopus' tentacles cannot be cut. Tough as leather, they are impervious to steel, and slip beneath the blade. Moreover they are laid so closely upon the body of the prey that an attempt to cut them would penetrate as soon the victim's own flesh. Yet, formidable though the monster is, there is a way he can be dealt with. The Serk fishermen know it well, as anyone will remember who has seen them execute certain rapid movements when they are at sea; porpoises know it too, in that they attack it in such a manner as to decapitate it – which is why one so often finds the headless bodies of octopus, squid and cognate creatures floating off-shore. In short, the pieuvre's one vulnerable point is its head. Gilliatt was aware of this. Never before had he seen an octopus of such size. Any man but he would have been troubled.

Like the bull-fighter, the man who contends with an octopus must await his moment. For the former, it is the instant when the bull bows its neck; for the latter, the swift moment when the octopus advances its head. Miss it, and you are lost.

All this had taken only a few minutes; but Gilliatt was already feeling the power of the two hundred and fifty suckers growing more intense. The pieuvre is treacherous; it endeavours to benumb its prey; having seized it, it waits while it can.

Gilliat's knife was in his hand. The suction on his body increased. He and the monster looked at one another. Suddenly it detached its sixth antenna from the rock, and flung it towards Gilliatt in an attempt to take hold of his left arm; at the same instant its head was thrust swiftly forward. A second more, and its anus-mouth would have fastened on his chest; his flesh pierced, and both arms bound, he would have been a dead man. But he was on his guard – watching his chance, as the octopus watched its own. He avoided the antenna and, just as the creature was about to fasten upon his chest, his left hand, holding the knife, came down upon it. The point of the knife sank into the flat and viscous head, and with a movement like the twist of a whip-lash, making a circle around its two eyes, Gilliatt tore its head out as one might pull a tooth. It was over.

The whole creature fell away to nothing, like a piece of stuff coming unwound. The pump destroyed, the vacuum was filled, and the four hundred suckers loosed their hold at the same instant upon rock and man. The pieuvre sank, like an old rag, to the bottom of the water.

Gilliatt, breathless from the struggle, saw on the stones at his feet two shapeless lumps of gelatinous matter – the pieuvre's head on one side of him, the rest of it on the other. The rest, I say, for it could not be called the body. Nonetheless, he stepped back out of reach of those tentacles, lest the death-agony should produce some reflex, or convulsive, movement. But the monster was dead indeed, and Gilliatt closed his knife.

VICTOR HUGO: tr. from Les Travailleurs de la Mer

Forty Singing Seamen

'In our lands be Beeres and Lyons of dyvers colours as ye redd, grene, black and white. And in our land be also unicornes and these Unicornes slee many Lyons. . . . Also there dare no man make a lye in our lande, for if he dyde he sholde in-continent be sleyn.'

Medieval Epistle of Pope Prester John

I

Across the seas of Wonderland to Mogadore we plodded,
   Forty singing seamen in an old, black barque,
And we landed in the twilight where a Polyphemus nodded
    With his battered moon-eye winking red and yellow through
      the dark.
    For his eye was growing mellow,
    Rich and ripe and red and yellow,
As was time, since old Ulysses made him bellow in the dark.
Cho.—Since Ulysses bunged his eye up with a pine-torch in
    the dark!

II

Were they mountains in the gloaming or the giant's ugly
   shoulders
   Just beneath the rolling eyeball, with its bleared and vinous
    glow,
Red and yellow o'er the purple of the pines among the boulders

336

And the shaggy horror brooding on the sullen slopes below,
Were they pines among the boulders
Or the hair upon his shoulders?
We were only simple seamen, so of course we didn't know.
Cho.—We were simple singing seamen, so of course we couldn't know.

III

But we crossed a plain of poppies, and we came upon a fountain
Not of water, but of jewels, like a spray of leaping fire;
And behind it, in an emerald glade, beneath a golden mountain
There stood a crystal palace, for a sailor to admire;
For a troop of ghosts came round us,
Which with leaves of bay they crowned us,
Then with grog they wellnigh drowned us, to the depth of our desire!
Cho.—And 'twas very friendly of them, as a sailor can admire!

IV

There was music all about us, we were growing quite forgetful
We were only singing seamen from the dirt of London-town,
Though the nectar that we swallowed seemed to vanish half regretful
As if it wasn't good enough to take such vittles down,
When we saw a sudden figure,
Tall and black as any nigger,
Like the devil – only bigger – drawing near us with a frown!
Cho.—Like the devil – but much bigger – and he wore a golden crown!

V

And 'What's all this?' he growls at us. With dignity we chaunted,
'Forty singing seamen, sir, as won't be put upon!'

'What? Englishmen?' he cries; 'Well, if ye don't mind being
    haunted,
    Faith, you're welcome to my palace; I'm the famous Prester
    John!
    Will ye walk into my palace?
    I don't bear 'ee any malice.
One and all ye shall be welcome in the halls of Prester John.'
Cho.—So we walked into the palace and the halls of Prester
    John.

VI

Now the door was one great diamond and the hall a hollow
    ruby –
    Big as Beachy Head, my lads, nay bigger by a half!
And I sees the mate with mouth agape, a-staring like a booby,
    And the skipper close behind him, with his tongue out like
    a calf.
    Now the way to take it rightly
    Was to walk along politely
Just as if you didn't notice – so I couldn't help but laugh!
Cho.—For they both forgot their manners and the crew was
    bound to laugh.

VII

But he took us through his palace, and, my lads, as I'm a sinner,
    We walked into an opal like a sunset-coloured cloud –
'My dining-room,' he says, and, quick as light we saw a dinner
    Spread before us by the fingers of a hidden fairy crowd;
    And the skipper, swaying gently
    After dinner, murmurs faintly,
'I looks to-wards you, Prester John, you've done us very
    proud!'
Cho.—And we drank his health with honours, for he *done* us
    very proud.

VIII

Then he walks us to his garden where we sees a feathered
    demon

Very splendid and important on a sort of spicy tree.
'That's the Phoenix,' whispers Prester, 'which all eddicated
    seamen
    Knows the only one existent, and *he's* waiting for to flee!
    When his hundred years expire
    Then he'll set hisself afire
And another from his ashes rise most beautiful to see!'
Cho.—With wings of rose and emerald most beautiful to see!

IX

Then he says, 'In yonder forest there's a little silver river,
    And whosoever drinks of it, his youth shall never die.
The centuries go by, but Prester John endures for ever
    With his music in the mountains and his magic on the sky.
    While *your* hearts are growing colder,
    While your world is growing older,
There's a magic in the distance, where the sea-line meets the
    sky.'
Cho.—It shall call to singing seamen till the fount o' song is
    dry!

X

So we thought we'd up and seek it, but that forest fair defied
    us, –
    First a crimson leopard laughs at us most horrible to see,
Then a sea-green lion came and sniffed and licked his chops
    and eyed us,
    While a red and yellow unicorn was dancing round a tree.
    We was trying to look thinner,
    Which was hard, because our dinner
Must ha' made us very tempting to a cat o' high degree.
Cho.—Must ha' made us very tempting to the whole menarjeree!

XI

So we scuttled from that forest and across the poppy meadows
    Where the awful shaggy horror brooded o'er us in the dark.

And we pushes out from shore again a-jumping at our shadows,
  And pulls away most joyful to the old black barque!
  And home again we plodded
  While the Polyphemus nodded
With his battered moon-eye winking red and yellow through
  the dark.
Cho.—Oh, the moon above the mountains, red and yellow
  through the dark!

XII

Across the seas of Wonderland to London-town we blundered,
  Forty singing seamen as was puzzled for to know
If the visions that we saw was caused by – here again we
    pondered –
  A tipple in a vision forty thousand years ago.
  Could the grog we *dreamt* we swallowed
  Make us *dream* of all that followed?
We were only simple seamen, so of course we didn't know.
Cho.—We were simple singing seamen, so of course we could
  not know!

ALFRED NOYES

Small Stuff

In Magellan Straits

Of all the little haps and mishaps to the *Spray* at Port Angosto, of the many attempts to put to sea, and of each return for shelter, it is not my purpose to speak. Of hindrances there were many to keep her back, but on the thirteenth day of April, and for the seventh and last time, she weighed anchor from that port. Difficulties, however, multiplied all about in so strange a manner that had I been given to superstitious fears I should not have persisted in sailing on a thirteenth day, notwithstanding that a fair wind blew in the offing. Many of the incidents were ludicrous. When I found myself, for instance, disentangling the sloop's mast from the branches of a tree after she had drifted three times around a small island, against my will, it seemed more than one's nerves could bear, and I had to speak about it, so I thought, or die of lockjaw, and I apostrophised the *Spray* as an impatient farmer might his horse or his ox. 'Didn't you know,' cried I – 'didn't you know that you couldn't climb a tree?' But the poor old *Spray* had essayed, and successfully too, nearly everything else in the strait of Magellan, and my heart softened toward her when I thought of what she had gone through. Moreover, she had discovered an island. On the charts this one that she had sailed round was traced as a point of land. I named it Alan Erric Island, after a worthy literary friend whom I had met in strange by-places, and I put up a sign, 'Keep off the grass,' which, as discoverer, was within my rights.

JOSHUA SLOCUM: *Sailing Alone Around the World*

Navigation

(i)

. . . the greatest science was in reckoning the longitude. My tin clock and only timepiece had by this time lost its minute-hand, but after I boiled her she told the hours, and that was near enough on a long stretch.

Etiquette

(ii)

When we arrived at Hong-Kong there was a letter in the ship's mail for me. I was in the boat with the captain some hours while he had it. But do you suppose he could hand a letter to a seaman? No, indeed; not even to an ordinary seaman. When we got to the ship he gave it to the first mate; the first mate gave it to the second mate, and he laid it, michingly, on the capstan-head, where I could get it.

Obiter Dicta

(iii)

Any weather that one's craft can live in, after escaping a lee shore, is pleasant weather – though some may be pleasanter than other.

(iv)

I once knew a writer who, after saying beautiful things about the sea, passed through a Pacific hurricane, and he became a changed man.

JOSHUA SLOCUM: *Sailing Alone Around the World*

Yesterday

. . . he kept eye on the elegant vessel as she glided swan-like to her moorings off Mount Laurels park through dusky merchant craft, colliers and trawlers, loosely shaking her towering snow-white sails, unchallenged in her scornful supremacy; an image of a refinement of beauty, and of a beautiful servicelessness.

GEORGE MEREDITH: *Beauchamp's Career*

Pockets

I recollect his (Captain Sir Lewis Tobias Jones) running foul of me only on one occasion; and no doubt I deserved it. It was a bitterly cold day, and (as is the custom when a ship is under canvas) the wretched middy of the watch had to walk the lee side of the deck. Unfortunately, the main topsail was set – the most draughty sail in the world, sending all its winds bang down your neck from one end of the quarter-deck to the other. I felt perished with cold, and in a moment of inadvertence put my poor little fingers into my pocket, to keep them warm. Now, the weather side is the sheltered side (it sounds illogical, but so it is); and no doubt Captain Jones did not realise my benumbed state, he being on the more sheltered side of the deck. Seeing my hands in my pockets on the sacred precincts of Her Majesty's quarter-deck was beyond what he could bear. He called me up, therefore, and said, in rather a stentorian voice, 'Pray, sir, who allowed you to keep your hands in your pockets on the quarter-deck? Go down immediately to the tailor on the half-deck (a worthy who was always seen squatting with his mate between two guns at the after end of the main deck, sewing clothes) 'and tell him from me to sew your pockets up instantly; and report to me, sir, when he has done so.' I fled, feeling disgraced, and knowing that the only chance of retrieving my character was to urge the tailor to 'bear a hand', as the sooner I appeared on deck sewn up, the better. It was but the work of an instant. The tailor twigged the situation, dropped all his work, and sewed me up in no time. When I reached the deck, trembling almost, with my report ready, the stentorian voice had disappeared, and I was accosted in the most fatherly manner. 'Now, my boy, this is a lesson to you. Do not do it again. Go below to the tailor, and tell him to unsew your pockets.'

REAR ADML. V. A. MONTAGUE: *A Middy's Recollections*

Good Morning

Talking of a friendly Good-morning puts me in mind of what occurred between a young lieutenant just joined and an officer I knew very well, who, though a most pleasant man off duty, had very strong opinions as to the sanctity of being on duty: he carried them to such an extent that he would not even shake hands with any Captain of his own standing who might happen to call on board his ship. The young lieutenant was keeping the morning watch for the first time, and at about 7.30 a.m. the Commander of the ship came up on the poop before the morning evolution of crossing yards and so on. As he approached the lieutenant, the latter said, 'Good-morning, sir.' To that no answer was given. Thinking that the Commander had not heard his salutation, the lieutenant repeated it. Thereupon the Commander turned round and asked, 'What is that you say?' The lieutenant answered, 'Oh! I was only saying Good-morning to you, sir.' 'Oh! were you? I will tell you, once for all, there is no Good-morning here, sir. It's all work.'

REAR ADML. V. A. MONTAGUE: *A Middy's Recollections*

An Unlucky Purchase

Near the *Chico* (lightship) we passed the new Argentine man-of-war, the *Admirante Brown*. This vessel was constructed in England, and recently steamed over the Atlantic with the intention of reaching some port of the Argentine Republic. This she has not done, and never will do, for it is found that this white elephant draws too much water to enter Argentine waters at all, so here she remains at anchor in the high seas, disconsolately rolling about, a constant butt for the caricaturists and comic papers of Montevideo.

E. F. KNIGHT: *The Cruise of the Falcon*

Wash-Down

It is a fine morning. The ship is only rolling very slightly and lazily, just enough to dull the vibration of the screw. The port-hole is open, and the fresh sea breeze is blowing on my face.

At this point the steward enters with my tea, or what is supposed to be tea, and I decide to have my bath at once before the rush, so as to avoid having to wait. My decision is partly due to the fact that further sleep is out of the question, owing to the noise which is now going on on deck just over my head.

It is said to be caused by cleaning the decks, but this is hard to believe. Judging by one's hearing, one man is beating the deck hard with something like a glorified wet towel, another is doing a step dance of a complicated character to express his satisfaction, whilst others pump on them with the hose. Periodically the rest of the crew get tired of this and drag the two men away on their backs. Then somebody suggests that a race round the ship would be fun, and starts the competitors with a singularly harsh whistle.

LORD EDWARD CECIL: *The Leisure of an Eygptian Official*

347

Channel Passage

The damned ship lurched and slithered. Quiet and quick
  My cold gorge rose; the long sea rolled; I knew
I must think hard of something, or be sick;
  And could think hard of only one thing – you!
You, you alone could hold my fancy ever!
  And with you memories come, sharp pain, and dole.
Now there's a choice – heartache or tortured liver!
  A sea-sick body, or a you-sick soul.

Do I forget you? Retchings hoist and tie me,
  Old meat, good meals, brown gobbets, up I throw.
Do I remember? Acrid return and slimy,
  The sobs and slobber of a last year's woe.
And still the sick ship rolls. 'Tis hard, I tell ye,
To choose 'twixt love and nausea, heart and belly.

RUPERT BROOKE

A Grave by the Sea

Lie where the light foam of the sea may beat
Thy grave-stone daily. . . .

WILLIAM SHAKESPEARE: Timon

The unplumbed, salt, estranging sea.

MATTHEW ARNOLD: To Marguerite

Stuns'ls

. . . whose light in the sea runs steady by the
  side of the ship.

CLARK RUSSELL: A Marriage at Sea

Reef-points

. . . an occasional light musketry of canvas as the swells launch her.

CLARK RUSSELL: *A Strange Elopement*

The fountain-like murmur of waters broken by the quiet progress of the ship.

CLARK RUSSELL: *A Marriage at Sea*

The Greek Army Sails from Troy

Glad to be off at last, we watched the fishes sporting in the water – and couldn't stop looking, so pleasant was the sight. But alas! near sunset the sea rose, thicker and thicker grew the darkness, and a black pall hid the sky, heavy with rain. Lightning flashed, heaven trembled with the thunder-stroke, torrents of hail and rain came suddenly pouring down, and every wind that blows burst its barrier. The whirlwind was upon us; the sea boiled.

PACUVIUS 200 B.C. (xxxii)

Nautical Terms

To take a liberty with technical language is a crime against the clearness, precision, and beauty of perfected speech.

JOSEPH CONRAD: from the *Mirror of the Sea*

A Silted Harbour

Do not bring up here, sailor; do not stow your sails because of me. The harbour you see is dry, I am but a tomb. Row on, then, to some other, happier, place; for thus Poseidon would wish it, and the hospitable gods.

Good luck to you, sea-wanderers! Voyagers, good luck and goodbye!

From the Greek Anthology

Another Grave by the Sea

Dead am I, who once was wrecked upon this coast; yet not even in death can I forget the unsleeping shore where, on the reefs, still vexed by the angry sea, I dragged myself from the water only to find a foreign grave. Ghost though I am, I must for ever hear the unceasing thunder of the hateful surge; no sleep is mine, no rest from misery. Others find peace in the tomb – but not I.

From the Greek Anthology

Calm Beaches

(i)   . . . as when heav'd anew
Old ocean rolls a lengthened wave to the shore,
Down whose green back the short-liv'd foam, all hoar,
Bursts gradual, with a wayward indolence.

JOHN KEATS: Endymion

(ii)   'Twas a quiet eve,
The rocks were silent, the wide sea did weave
An untumultuous fringe of silver foam
Along the flat, brown sand.

JOHN KEATS: Letter to Reynolds

Land-Longing

Surely, surely slumber is more sweet than toil, the shore
Than labour in the deep mid-ocean, wind and wave and
    oar;
Oh rest ye, brother mariners, we will not wander more.

ALFRED LORD TENNYSON: The Lotus Eaters

Rest

Ease after toil, port after stormie seas,
Peace after war, death after life, doth greatly please.

EDMUND SPENSER: The Faerie Queene

Sailor's Superstition

Sir, your queen must overboard. The sea works high, the wind
is loud, and will not lie till the ship be cleared of the dead.
    – That's your superstition.
    Pardon us, sir; with us at sea it hath been still observed, and
we are strong in custom. Therefore briefly yield her; for she
must overboard straight.

WILLIAM SHAKESPEARE: Pericles

For she lies deep, the *Inisfail* – ay, deep she lies an' drowned,
Farther'n ever a wave'll stir, deeper 'n a lead can sound,
Fifty mile from Fastnet Light, an' homeward bound.

C. FOX-SMITH: Inisfoil

Millamant

Here she comes, i' faith, with her fan spread and her streamers
out, and a shoal of fools for tenders.

WILLIAM CONGREVE: *The Way of the World*

Dalilah

But who is this, what thing of Sea or Land?
Female of sex it seems,
That so bedeckt, ornate and gay,
Comes this way sailing
Like a stately ship
Of Tarsus, bound for th' Isles
Of Javan or Gadier
With all her bravery on, and tackle trim,
Sails fill'd, and streamers waving,
Courted by all the winds that hold them play,
An Amber scent of odorous perfume
Her harbinger, a damsel train behind.

JOHN MILTON: *Samson Agonistes*

Weather Rhymes

(i)   When the rain comes before the wind,
Topsail sheets and halyards mind;
When the wind comes before the rain,
Soon you may make sail again.

(ii) Sudden rise when glass is low
Does foretell a stronger blow.

(iii)   Mackerel sky and mares' tails
                Make tall ships carry small sails.

(iv)   Long foretold, long last;
                Short notice, soon past.

Traditional

Channel Passage

How holy people look when they are sea-sick! There was a patient Parsee near me who seemed purified once and for ever from all taint of the flesh. Buddha was a low, worldly minded, music-hall comic singer in comparison. He sat like this for a long time until. . . . and he made a noise like cows coming home to be milked on an April evening.

SAMUEL BUTLER: The Note Books

Sea-sickness, or, indeed, any other sickness is the inarticulate expression of the pain we feel on seeing a proselyte escape us just as we were on the point of converting it.

Ibid.

The Yachtsmen

There is a world of difference between being outward bound by choice and homeward bound of necessity.

R. T. McMULLEN: Down Channel

Rough Waters

There's not a sea the passenger e'er pukes in
Turns up more dangerous breakers than the Euxine.

LORD BYRON: Don Juan

The Gibraltar Garrison gives a Dinner Party

I was very much pleased at this, as the officers had a general
invitation to dine with the mess, and all who could obtain
leave being requested to come, I was enabled to join the party.
The first lieutenant had excused himself on the plea of there
being so much to attend to on board, but most of the gun-
room officers and some of the midshipmen obtained leave.

The dinner was very good, and we were all very merry, but
after the dessert had been brought in, I slipped away with a
young ensign, who took me all over the galleries, and explained
everything to me, which was a much better way of employing
my time than doing as the others did, which the reader will
acknowledge. I was at the sally-port before gun-fire – the boat
was there, but no officers made their appearance. The gun
fired, the drawbridge was hauled up, and I was afraid that I
should be blamed; but the boat was not ordered to shove off,
as it was waiting for commissioned officers. About an hour
afterwards, when it was quite dark, the sentry pointed his arms
and challenged a person advancing with, 'Who comes there?'
'Naval officer, drunk on a wheelbarrow,' was the reply, in a
loud, singing voice. Upon which the sentry recovered his
arms, singing in return, 'Pass, naval officer, drunk on a wheel-
barrow – and all's well!' and then appeared a soldier in his
fatigue dress, wheeling down the third lieutenant in a wheel-
barrow, so tipsy that he could not stand or speak. Then the
sentry challenged again, and the answer was, 'Another naval
officer, drunk on a wheelbarrow,' upon which the sentry

replied as before, 'Pass, another naval officer, drunk on a wheel-barrow – and all's well!' This was my friend O'Brien, almost as bad as the third lieutenant, and so they continued for ten minutes, challenging and passing, until they wheeled down the remainder of the party, with the exception of the second lieutenant, who walked arm in arm with the officer who brought down the order for lowering the drawbridge. I was much shocked, for I considered it very disgraceful; but I afterwards was told, which certainly admitted of some excuse, that the mess were notorious for never permitting any of their guests to leave the table sober.

CAPTAIN MARRYAT: *Peter Simple*

A Sailor's Life

A ship is worse than a jail. There is, in a jail, better air, better company, better conveniency of every kind; and a ship has the additional disadvantage of being in danger. When men come to like a sea-life, they are not fit to live on land.

DR JOHNSON: from Boswell's *Life of Johnson*

Dear, Dear . . .

I was watching the morning star burning like a sacred furnace on the edges of the black hills when Satan sent that wind and tried to drown three men. But we reefed in time – there were three of us, one for the helm and two to reef; and when dawn broke, and the blessed colours of the east renewed the day, strange! – one end of the boom had three reefs down, and the other only two!

HILAIRE BELLOC: *The Cruise of the Nona*

355

Que diable allait-il faire dans cette galère?

MOLIÈRE: *Scapin*

How pleasant it is, when a gale of wind is blowing, to stand
on the shore and watch the other fellow, out there, in trouble.

LUCRETIUS: *de Rerum Natura* (xxxiii)

A Scurvy Tune

The master, the swabber, the boatswain and I,
   The gunner and his mate
Loved Mall, Meg and Marian and Margery,
   But none of us cared for Kate.
   For she had a tongue with a tang,
   Would cry to a sailor, *Go hang!*
She loved not the savour of tar nor of pitch,
Yet a tailor might scratch her where 'er she did itch:
   Then to sea, boys, and let her go hang!

WILLIAM SHAKESPEARE: *The Tempest*

The bowsprit got mixed with the rudder sometimes.

LEWIS CARROLL: *Hunting of the Snark*

Sam Swipes

Sam Swipes, he was a seaman true,
   As bold and brave a tar
As e'er was dressed in navy blue
On board a man-of-war.

One fault he had – on sea or land
  He was a thirsty dog;
For Sammy never could withstand
  A glass or so of grog.

He always liked to be at sea;
  For e'en on shore, the rover,
If not as drunk as he could be,
  Was always half seas over.

The gunner, who was apt to scoff,
  With jokes most aptly timed,
Said Sam might any day go off,
  'Cause he was always primed.

Sam didn't want a feeling heart,
  Though never seen to cry;
Yet tears were always on the start –
  The drop was in his eye.

At fighting Sam was never shy,
  A most undoubted merit;
His courage never failed, and why?
  He was so full of spirit.

In action he had lost an eye,
  But that gave him no trouble;
Quoth Sam: 'I have no cause to sigh:
  I'm always seeing double.'

A shot from an unlucky gun
  Put Sam on timber pegs;
It didn't signify to one
  Who ne'er could keep his legs.

One night he filled a pail with grog,
  Determined he would suck it;

He drained it dry, the thirsty dog!
  Hiccupped, and kicked the bucket.

CAPTAIN MARRYAT: *Poor Jack*

Bon Voyage

The omens are not good to-day,
  For smelly Maevius sails.
I hope that every wind that blows
  Will beat him as with flails.

Pray heaven a southern buster come,
  Or from black East a squall
Scatter him shattered on the sea,
  Gear, broken oars and all.

A norther, too, might do his bit
  With oak-uprooting force,
Nor star, when grim Orion sets,
  Be seen, to show his course.

I trust the sea may beastlier be
  Than drowned the Greeks from Troy.
When Pallas turned from the burnt town
  Bad Ajax to annoy.

O Maevius, how your tars will sweat
  When rain and wind together beat,
And, bellowing, burst you on the great
  And fierce Ionian wave!
And you, oh you, how green and blue,
When you will beg, with loud boo-hoo,
  Deaf Jove your life to save!

Let but the sea-crows eat your flesh
On some curved beach – a dainty dish –
    And my last hope's achieved.
I'll offer to the God of storms
Responsible for these alarms
A randy goat and a tender lamb,
To show him that I grateful am
    For benefits received.

HORACE: *Epode X* (xxxiv)

Envoi

What greater pleasure than to be safe ashore again
Drowsily listening to the patter of rain on the roof?

SOPHOCLES (fragment)

359

Notes

i. Wordsworth was a sound Latin scholar. His interest in Latin poetry was revived when he began to help his son John to study the language for entrance to the University. He translated three books of the *Aeneid*, and another result of his return to the classics was the unfortunate poem *Laodamia*, written a few years previously.

ii. *Nova Espero* is a twenty-foot boat. She was built by Stanley and Colin Smith in Nova Scotia and sailed across the Atlantic to England. A year or two later Stanley Smith and Charles Violet crossed in her to America again. My extract is taken from the book which describes this second voyage.

I remember only two other instances in which writers have described the rolling-over, or near rolling-over, of their craft: one by Uffa Fox and the other by Captain Voss – not in *Tilicum* but in *Sea Queen*. Conor O Brien tells of a wave which might have done it, had *Saoirse* been directly in its path. Deep sea yachting is indeed a remarkable form of amusement.

iii. Adepts in Browning's poetry will remember that this description of a bather has a lot of work to do in the poem, *Fifine at the Fair*, where it occurs. It is an image of the life of the spirit, worked out in the course of the next 10,000 lines or so, and glancing back at the 5,000 which precede it. *Tantae molis erat* . . .

iv. It has been pointed out that Browning in these well known lines has been less accurate than befits a poet over the points of the compass.

v. Swinburne was himself a powerful swimmer. In later life he told the story of how, when he was a schoolboy, he climbed the

200-ft. sheer face of Culver Cliff in the Isle of Wight. 'To nerve myself for the effort,' he wrote, 'I took a dip in the sea.' It was during the Christmas holidays.

vi. I suppose Keats meant by this the phenomenon which I have once in my life been lucky enough to observe. I was on Chale beach one sunny morning in winter, when there was a heavy swell coming in. There were fugitive rainbows in the spray thrown up by the waves as they broke on the shingle.

vii. The deep distress of which Wordsworth speaks in these verses was the death of his younger brother John, who went down off Weymouth in the *Earl of Abergavenny*, when she was lost with many of her passengers and crew. John Wordsworth was her master.

viii. Samphire is a herb which used to be picked from the face of chalk cliffs and used as a relish in salads. The trade, much too dreadful for modern times, has long since ceased.

ix. The reader, if he is unfamiliar with the essay in which this passage occurs, will like to know that Mr Jonah, the nib-driver, found to his astonishment and delight that the coastguard who took charge of his boat had read all his works and was proud to meet their author.

x. *Orion* was a cutter-rigged yacht of 16½ tons (she was later converted to a yawl). It is a commonplace nowadays for yachts much smaller than this to ride out gales of equal severity. What is remarkable here is *Orion*'s ability to keep running – and at the astonishing speed of 9 knots (at one period McMullen says it was 9½). This seems to suggest that little progress has been made in fundamental design since *Orion* was built, in 1865. Let us admit, however, that the gear and sails of these splendid old yachts were heavy, and made hard work for their crews.

McMullen died at sea, in mid-Channel, sailing alone in the little lugger *Perseus*, on a calm June night in 1891.

xi. Claude Worth, the distinguished oculist, was amongst the earliest of British yachtsmen to teach, by his own experience and by his published logs, the now accepted fact that a small yacht, well-found and properly handled, is not less safe (though much more uncomfortable) in bad weather *in open water* than a big one.

Sirius, mentioned in this passage, was one of McMullen's yachts. He had published logs of her cruises.

xii. That excellent mountebank, George Borrow, was certainly no seaman. He was better at describing gypsies and horses than the sea. Nevertheless, this account of his escape from shipwreck is interesting if only for the providential shift of wind. Borrow, when this adventure befell him, was on his way to Spain to sell Bibles to Spanish peasants who couldn't read.

xiii. Shakespeare, as always, is accurate in his technical terms. To 'lay a-hold' (or 'a-hull') means to lay the vessel to. 'Set her two courses' – the next manoeuvre, lying-to having failed – is an order to set the lower square sail (course) on both main and foremast in an attempt to claw off the lee shore.

xiv. Nansen's *Fram* was designed and built by the well known Scottish designer Colin Archer. Archer lived much of his life in Norway, and will be remembered by British yachtsmen for the many fine cruising yachts which came from his drawing-board.

xv. In command of the *Judith* on this occasion was Francis Drake, then 26 years old and not yet risen to fame. The propriety of his conduct in abandoning Hawkins has long been a matter of controversy.

xvi. The feat of turning a forest into a sea-going vessel was also performed by Captain Joshua Slocum, who, after the loss of his barque *Aquidneck* on the coast of South America in the 80's of last century, built, with the help of his son Victor and some natives, the 35-ft. boat *Liberdade*, and sailed her home to Washington D.C.

xvii. The gulf in which Cowper, the cheerful poet of *John Gilpin*, always felt himself to be drowning was the conviction that he was hated by God and damned to everlasting perdition.

xviii. The expedition ended in irretrievable disaster, from which Athens never wholly recovered.

xix. 'By water he sent them home . . . ' i.e. he threw his prisoners overboard.

xx. 'There on Cytorus her leaves whispered in the wind.' Shelley borrowed this beautiful fancy for his poem *To Jane, with a Guitar*.

xxi. I have always liked these verses in spite of the fact that to snatch one's rudder seems a manoeuvre more appropriate to a Snark hunter than to a grave Tyrian trader.

xxii. A few days after this famous action fourteen of the Spanish ships and *Revenge* herself with 200 Spaniards aboard her were driven ashore by a gale on to the island of St Michael.

It puzzles me to understand how the master-gunner could have blown the ship up, if, as Raleigh says (and as Tennyson says, following him), the powder was all spent to the last barrel.

xxiii. *Endeavour* was subsequently got into a river (named by Cook Endeavour River) further up the Australian coast, where she was put ashore and repaired. Four of her bottom planks had been cut through by the coral – 'as smoothly as if it had been done by a chisel.' One large hole was found to be partially stopped up by a piece of rock which had broken off and become jammed in it. Repairs were completed in just over a month.

Of this incident Cook himself wrote: 'In this truly terrible situation not one man ceased to do his utmost, and that with as much calmness as if no danger had been near.'

xxiv. The use of the heavy stone to give these vessels steerage way will remind some readers of the old Thames barges, which used to employ a similar method to get clear of a crowded anchorage in a calm. The bargemen, of course, used an anchor for the purpose, keeping it just touching the bottom. They called the manoeuvre 'dredging'.

364

xxv. This revolting account of the conditions in a man-of-war in the 18th century is in no way exaggerated. Smollet knew what he was talking about, having himself as a young man obtained a surgeon's commission in the Navy and served in the West Indies under Admiral Vernon.

I have myself talked with an old lady who, as a child, talked with a naval officer who served as a midshipman at Trafalgar. This officer described how he had frequently heard 'corpses', about to be sewn up and put overboard, protest that they were not dead. 'Oh yes, you are,' was the answer. 'The surgeon says so.'

xxvi. The Hydaspes is the river Jelum in Northern India. A few months later Alexander took a fleet down the estuary of the Indus and a short way out into the Indian Ocean. Caught by rough weather in the estuary, the vessels sheltered in a creek, where, to the surprise of the men who were familiar only with the tideless Mediterranean, they were left high and dry by the ebb. Probably Alexander was surprised too, though his respectful biographer does not admit it.

xxvii. Some may care to remember that Dante in his *Divine Comedy* takes Ulysses to the end of his last voyage – to the Great Brown Mountain which heralded his death. After crossing the equator, 'Five times (says the ghost of Ulysses in Hell) had the light under the moon been kindled and quenched since we had entered upon that hard passage, when a Mountain, dark in the distance, appeared to us, higher, I thought, than any I had seen. Our joy at the sight was quickly turned to grief, for from that new land there came a whirlwind, which striking the bows of the ship spun her three times round with all the waters, and at the fourth time lifting the poop thrust down the prow, until the sea closed above our heads.'

Dante apparently invented this story, as nothing like it is to be found in classical legend.

xxviii. I have used the words 'so beautiful' (not, in fact, a bad translation) in the first line of this rendering for love of Coleridge, who used them to describe the dead sailors in his *Ancient Mariner*.

De Quincey, when still very young and shy, once paid a visit to Lamb in his office at the East India House, and, to make conversation, reverently quoted this passage from Coleridge's poem. He was answered by a snort. 'B-beautiful?' stuttered Lamb. 'B-beautiful indeed! Two hundred Wapping vagabonds, all covered with tar . . . '

xxix. This passage from the anonymous 15th-century poem *Libelle of Englysshe Policie* was quoted by Quiller-Couch in one of his printed lectures. Q. added: 'This may not be good poetry, but it has the right ring. Of the two chief glories of our birth and state, Poetry and the pride of Sea-faring, the men of the age we have been considering maintained the second, at any rate, and passionately.'

xxx. 'Oft.' One would have thought that once was enough. But sailors like telling tall stories – witness Gonzalo in the *Tempest* and the tales he had been fed with about mountaineers dewlapped like bulls, whose throats had hanging at 'em wallets of flesh, etc.

xxxi. I have put this passage into the section called Strange Adventures; but perhaps, when one comes to think of it, it was a perfectly ordinary adventure after all. When a vessel (and a not over-handy one) has to get through some horrible narrow gut, where there is a boiling tide, strong eddies, and overfalls, it would be a rash helmsman who put her safe passage down solely to his own skill. The ship hopelessly out of control, the poor fellow might well ask himself how the deuce he missed the rocks *that* time. But he did miss them, thank God – or, in this instance, thank the Nereids.

xxxii. I have included this passage for the sake of the absurd picture of the Greek soldiery, brutalised by ten years of hard campaigning, leaning over the rail to watch the fishes. Only a Latin poet could have thought of this.

xxxiii. Evidently the Romans had no National Lifeboat Institution. Cads.

xxxiv. Presumably this nasty little poem made Horace's friends laugh, whatever it did to Maevius. It was Horace, too, who in a better known poem than this jeered at a woman whom age had robbed of her beauty for still wishing to appear beautiful. How difficult it is to read ancient literature without prejudice!

Acknowledgements

The Editor wishes to express his thanks to the authors and publishers whose permission has been obtained to quote from the works listed below. If any acknowledgements due to other authors and publishers have been inadvertently omitted, he offers his apologies.

To Miss V. Sackville-West and the Hogarth Press for the poem *Sailing Ships*; to Messrs Christy and Moore for the extract from *The Keeper of the Gate*, by the late Captain John Iron; to the Controller of H.M. Stationery Office for the extract from *The Irish Coast Pilot*; to the Executors of Francis Brett Young and Messrs Collins for the poem *Seascape*; to Mr Lawrence Durrell and Messrs Faber for an extract from *Reflections on a Marine Venus*; to the Literary Executors to Lady Milner and Messrs Hodder & Stoughton for an extract from Lord Edward Cecil's *Leisure of an Egyptian Official*; to the Trustees of the Hardy Estate and Messrs Macmillan for Thomas Hardy's poem *The Night of Trafalgar*, from *The Dynasts*; to the Oxford University Press for extracts from *The Journals and Papers of Gerard Manley Hopkins*, ed. Humphry House and Graham Storey, and from *The Poems of Gerard Manley Hopkins*, ed. by Robert Bridges and W. H. Gardner; to Messrs A. & C. Black for an extract from *A Middy's Recollections* by Rear-Admiral V. A. Montague; to Miss Rachel Carson and Staples Press for an extract from *Under the Sea Wind*, and from *The Sea Around Us*; to Mr Hugh Noyes and Messrs William Blackwood & Sons for the late Alfred Noyes' poem *Forty Singing Seamen*; to Mr Robert Frost, Messrs Henry Holt & Co. Inc., and Messrs Jonathan Cape for the poem *Once by the*

369

Pacific; to Mr Alan Villiers and Messrs Hodder & Stoughton for an extract from *Posted Missing*; to the Society of Authors and Dr John Masefield, O.M., for the poem *The Ship*, extracts from *Dauber*, *The River*, *Sard Harker* and *The Bird of Dawning*; to Mr Basil Lubbock and Messrs Brown, Son & Ferguson for an extract from *China Clippers*; to Mr Frank Baines and Messrs Eyre & Spottiswoode for an extract from *In Deep*; to Mr T. S. Eliot and Messrs Faber & Faber for an extract from the poem *The Dry Salvages* from *Four Quartets*; to Mr Eric Linklater and Messrs Macmillan for an extract from *The Art of Adventure*; to the Executors of J. E. Flecker and to Messrs Secker & Warburg for the poem *The Old Ships*; to the Society of Authors, as the literary representative of the estate of the late H. M. Tomlinson, for extracts from *London River* and *Gifts of Fortune*, and also to the publishers of these books, Messrs Heinemann and Messrs Cassell; to Penguin Books for permission to use extracts from the Editor's translations of Herodotus and Arrian; to Mr T. C. Worth and Messrs J. D. Potter for an extract from the late Dr Claud Worth's *Yacht Cruising*; to Messrs Robert Hale for extracts from the Editor's *The Channel Shore*; to the Society of Authors and the Literary Trustees of Walter de la Mare for the latter's two poems *Never More Sailor* and *The Wreck*; to Mr Arthur Ransome and Messrs Jonathan Cape for an extract from *Racundra's First Cruise*; to Mr Stanley Smith and Messrs Robert Ross for an extract from *The Wind Calls the Tune*; to the Trustees of the estate of the late Hilaire Belloc for extracts from *The Cruise of the Nona* and *Short Talks with the Dead*; to the Literary Executors of the late Joseph Conrad and Messrs J. M. Dent & Sons for extracts from *The Mirror of the Sea* and *Lord Jim*; to Messrs Rupert Hart-Davis for an extract from Conor O Brien's *Across Three Oceans*; to Mr W. A. Robinson and Messrs Jonathan Cape for an extract from *Deep Water and Shoal*; to Messrs Macmillan and the author for an extract from *Adventures of an Obscure Victorian* by W. G. Riddell; to Dr Alain Bombard and Messrs Andre Deutsch for an extract from *The Bombard Story*; to Thomas Reed

Publications Ltd for an extract from *Reed's Seamanship*;
to Messrs Constable for extracts from F. Nansen's *Farthest
North*; to Mr H. G. Dixey for extracts from his privately
printed poems *A Passage in Square Rig* and *The Way of a
Ship according to Apollonius Rhodius*; to M. Marin-Marie and
Messrs Peter Davies for an extract from *Wind Aloft Wind Alow*;
to Messrs Selwyn & Blount for John Freeman's poem *The
Moonbathers*; to Erskine Childers and Messrs Sidgwick &
Jackson Ltd for an extract from *The Riddle of the Sands*; to
R. C. K. Ensor and Messrs Sidgwick & Jackson Ltd for an
extract from *Catherine*; to the Executors of Rupert Brooke and
Messrs Sidgwick & Jackson Ltd for *A Channel Passage* and an
extract from *The Fish*.

Index of Authors

375